D1737253

TELEVOTE

TELEVOTE

Expanding Citizen Participation in the Quantum Age

CHRISTA DARYL SLATON

PRAEGER

New York
Westport, Connecticut
London

Library of Congress Cataloging-in-Publication Data

Slaton, Christa Daryl.
 Televote : expanding citizen participation in the quantum age /
Christa Daryl Slaton.
  p. cm.
 Includes bibliographical references and index.
 ISBN 0–275–93836–0 (alk. paper)
 1. Political participation—United States. 2. Television in
politics—United States. I. Title.
JK1764.S545 1992
323′.042—dc20   91–16687

British Library Cataloguing in Publication Data is available.

Library of Congress Catalog Card Number: 91–16687
ISBN: 0–275–93836–0

First published in 1992

Praeger Publishers, One Madison Avenue, New York, NY 10010
An imprint of Greenwood Publishing Group, Inc.

Printed in the United States of America

The paper used in this book complies with the
Permanent Paper Standard issued by the National
Information Standards Organization (Z39.48–1984).

10 9 8 7 6 5 4 3 2 1

To Ted Becker,
a Jeffersonian democrat of the Quantum Age
who has touched my mind, heart, and soul.

Contents

Figures and Tables

Preface

This book is the product of many years of thought and research. During the course of experimentation and evaluation, I have benefited from the intellectual and moral support of many diverse individuals, who all have influenced my work. First, and foremost, is Ted Becker, my partner in the Televote design and research. His sincere commitment to the application of his democratic theories has inspired and stimulated me. My work also has been greatly influenced by Jim Dator, who not only encouraged my innovations and creativity, but rewarded them and established a model for them. My gratitude also is extended to Ira Rohter and Betty Strom, who showed me the importance and value of balancing the heart and the mind by being there for me when illness delayed my studies and by helping me learn valued lessons through my hardships. Special thanks also go to Richard Chadwick for his invaluable assistance throughout my research and to Christopher Jones, Barbara Mauldin, and Trish Bell for their tremendous support and help through the final stages. And last, but certainly not least, I thank the Lowders and the Boans for all their love, support, and encouragement given to me over the years.

Introduction

While I wrote this book, police states around the world were imploding and people's movements were exploding with demands for "democracy." Student protesters in Tiananmen Square in Beijing, who erected a statue of the "Goddess of Democracy" in spring 1989, were asked what they wanted. They said they were not sure. The Soviet Union of Mikhail Gorbachev constructed new forms of representation and elections in a communist state, having no idea if or how they would evolve. Movements in the name of democracy have toppled despotic regimes in the Philippines and Argentina in recent years, and shaken them to their foundations in Burma and throughout Eastern Europe. So, "democracy" is on the offensive throughout the world even though what it means and how it works is different from place to place. What we do know now is that something loosely lumped under the rubric of democracy seems to be making great forward strides around the globe. Once again, as often in the past, the concept and symbolism of democracy is the wave of the future.

Meanwhile, the United States of America, the country in which the modern democratic nation-state was invented, the paragon of democratic virtue that other nations are trying so hard to emulate, is having its own troubles with democracy. In recent memory, scandals involving corruption, lawlessness, unaccountability, and incompetence have made a president resign, sent numerous officials to prison, scarred innumerable public reputations, and deepened widespread citizen apathy and antipathy toward the government "of the people, by the people and for the people." All these incidents, plus many other critical social, ecological, and economic problems, have intensified the traditional and perennial debate in the United States over its form of democracy and its future in this nation.

That is part of what this book is about. It is about what democracy has meant, means, and may yet mean in America. It is about discussions, arguments, and harangues over the nature of democracy—long before the U.S. Constitution was even thought about, much less ratified. It is about the debate at the Constitutional Convention and immediately after it. It is about the spirited controversy that still wages today in the United States among philosophers, academics, politicians, activists, technologists, lawyers, and, of course, the American citizenry.

This book is about that debate, but it is also about the heritage that includes actual changes and transitions that have occurred in American democracy over time. Yet it is more than that because its goal is to help influence the future of that debate about American democracy as well as to serve as a guide to possible future forms of American democracy, new shapes whose contours are already visible.

The major reason why this volume can add a healthy measure to the discussion and assist in fabricating future forms of American democracy is that it is not based strictly on other people's thoughts, work, and deeds, although there is some analysis and synthesis of that herein. Wholly new information is presented, too. The essence of this study is a series of 12 action experiments on a novel mix of modern communications techniques and techniques, conducted by several teams of theorist-researchers (often including myself) between 1978 and 1985, experiments designed to investigate and promote a new, evolutionary type of American democracy, one that emphasizes and increases the role of the citizen in all phases of governance.

The name of this nascent democratic communications system is *Televote*. The heart and soul of this study will be what the Televote projects revealed, particularly the Hawaii model of Televote—what we simply called *Hawaii Televote*. Nevertheless, the significance of the Televote experiences is how they help inform and enrich the ongoing debate about American democracy and how they help nurture the future of democracy in America.

The central focus of this book, then, is the Televote odyssey—a chronicle of the adventures of an innovative political communications device created to serve a mediational role between citizens and their representatives and to increase citizen awareness, knowledge on issues, lateral citizen interaction, and direct public participation in governance. The dozen Televote experiments located in California, Hawaii, and New Zealand generated new insights into the political capabilities and public interests of citizens and offer new guides on how to include a more representative, knowledge-able, enthusiastic citizenry in political agenda setting, planning, policy making, and even systems change.

To better grasp Televote's utility in promoting better representation in government, as well as more and better direct democracy, it will be helpful to understand some theoretical, historical, philosophical, technological, and technical changes over the course of American history that together create a superstructure strongly supportive of democratic innovation and invention—a firm foundation eminently capable of reinforcing a quantum leap in democratic futures and an evolutionary step in American democracy.

The first part of this book, then, will detail the superstructure already in place for an institutionalization of Televote and for increased citizen participation in various forms of democracy—whether past, present, or future.

Chapter 1 is about some key theoretical—or metatheoretical—developments. It will not rehash the tired, ages-old arguments in the *Federalist Papers* (as well as contemporary American political and political science discourse) about the public-as-mob. Instead, it will take a fresh look at new thinking in physical theory (quantum) and how that may help substantiate the political theory of participatory democracy (quantum politics). So, one major feature of a new superstructure for a new democratic political theory and politics is the shift in a worldview dominated by an exclusive reliance on Newtonian physics to one enriched by quantum theory. My first chapter will examine the significance of this major twentieth-century development in scientific thinking and knowledge in terms of its potential impact on and relevance for social theories and political design, particularly regarding democratic theory.

Chapter 2 sets forth another important segment of the superstructure for a future democratic system. This aspect has less to do with thought than it does with action. It deals with the realization of democratic values and aspirations through human struggle and strife. These two chapters are a brief historical investigation of the ebb and flow of American democracy, a study that zeroes in on the roles that citizens have played over time—from those of the Iroquois nation to those of the United States of America, circa the dawning of the Third Millennium. They comprise a select history of the bitter (and sometimes brutal) conflicts waged to resolve such questions as: Who should be allowed to be voting citizens? What rights should citizens have against government? What other political powers should citizens have? What new forms of citizen participation and/or protection must be added to the system to strengthen American democracy?

To my way of thinking, the next important part of a strong superstructure for a new stage or structure of American democracy needed to be philosophical. In my reading over the years, it occurred to me that the American political philosophical controversy has been devoted chiefly to argumentation over what *kind* or *degree* of democracy is best. One is hard pressed to find many modern American political philosophers debating the merits of dictatorship, anarchy, plutocracy, or gerontocracy over democracy.

Instead, the mainstream dispute—at least today—appears to center over the respective merits and demerits of what Americans like to call indirect democracy (or republican democracy) and direct democracy (or participatory democracy). It occurred to me that what was needed was a new typology of American democracy, one that could help bridge the theoretical, political, and philosophical disagreements about democracy of the past and present to the democratic potential of the future. Chapter 3, then, is my view of what that new classification system of modern democracy would include, each category allowing for different forms and levels of citizen involvement in government: (1) the Limited Representative System; (2) the Expanded Representative System; (3) the Participatory Representative System; (4) the Representative Participatory System; and (5) the Full Participation System. The preference of this thesis is for the democratic polity that provides the greatest participatory role for citizens within a partially representative state—the Representative Participatory System.

Chapter 4 discusses the last component of the Televote superstructure, the technological and technical support for Televote's role in promoting participatory democracy in the present and near-future world. Modern participatory democratic thought (discussed in Chapter 3), current communications technology and techniques, and an extensive education system are the necessary conditions for creating a well-informed, active, and interactive citizenry on a massive scale. Several major experiments designed to promote and expand citizen participation will be discussed as prelude to the Televote experiments. With information from these citizen participation projects, we approach the twenty-first century with new knowledge and capabilities that offer radically new possibilities for effective means to involve citizens directly in all phases of governance, even in nations comprised of hundreds of millions of people.

Having presented the superstructure for Televote's development, this thesis will then focus primarily on Hawaii Televote, a political tool that combines the quantum principles of randomness, interactivity, and uncertainty in a way that educates the public, stimulates lateral discussion and interaction, and promotes a more participatory state in a representative system. Each Hawaii model Televote experiment asked different questions and supplied new information about the roles citizens can and are willing to play in a modern democratic polity. That is what Chapter 5 is all about.

Finally, it is important to reemphasize that quantum theory opens up possibilities inherent in reality that democratic theorists have usually ignored (the importance of randomness, interdependence, and uncertainty in life). The history of citizen participation in America demonstrates the perpetual combat over the desire for more and more effective inclusion in the American political system. Televote and other participatory democratic projects, the operational consequence of the developing theory and philosophy of participatory democracy, are the means by which to tap a responsive cord of unflagging citizen interest, enthusiasm, and insight into important decision making in the Expanded Representative System and the impending Participatory Representative System, as well as in the possible, if not probable, Representative Participatory System of the future.

The only question left, at this point, is not what is left to be proved about the efficacy of Televote (and Electronic Town Meetings), but how can its efficaciousness and independence be maximized, and its structure best institutionalized, to insure its sustainability. Chapter 6 addresses some of the recent critics of Televote and handles some of the possible avenues toward institutionalization already in the works.

Of course, it is too early to come up with any final answers. But it is not too late to stimulate some serious thought about how to best resolve these problems for posterity.

1

Quantum Theory and Political Theory

A merican democracy, the subject of countless studies, articles, and books, has been analyzed and evaluated from a wide range of perspectives. Nevertheless, this chapter will attempt a novel approach; that is, to examine the role of citizen participation within American democracy from an emerging social theory based on a shift from a science subtly, but strongly, influenced by Newtonian physics to a science enriched by quantum physics.

THE RELATIONSHIP BETWEEN PHYSICS AND POLITICAL THEORY

While the natural sciences have discovered theories that supersede many of the theories and knowledge based on the Newtonian physics of the Enlightenment, most social science theorists continue to cling to concepts that fit neatly into a Newtonian worldview even when those concepts fail to explain many social phenomena. Studying politics and social phenomena within a quantum theoretical framework can produce radically different theories and hypotheses than those derived within a Newtonian theoretical framework. Indeed, as this study will demonstrate, the study of "democracy" and "citizen participation" is enhanced by quantum principles, which provide a firmer intellectual foundation for various forms of "democracy" than the Newtonian worldview that has been prevalent for the last two centuries.

The Newtonian and natural scientific influence on the social sciences, in general, and political science, in particular, has been profound. It provides a comprehensive worldview, replete with laws of nature that include the basic nature of humans, how humans relate to their environment, and how and what kinds of sociopolitical structures humans create.

The Newtonian world is a mechanical world, a predictable world.[1] It is a world that is studied by breaking it down to its smallest parts. It is a world that is understood through rational inquiry based on objectivity, certainty, and chain reasoning. Newtonian physics forms the theoretical basis for liberal democracy, which has been the premier theoretical perspective of American political theory. It guided the American Founders in the eighteenth century and has guided the actions of politicians and the research of political scientists up to this moment.

Although Newtonian theory had long been accepted as an "infallible world outlook,"[2] it is now being challenged, tested, and reevaluated by quantum physicists and theorists. Thus, some long-held Newtonian laws are being discarded or revised to fit within the new quantum cosmology. This cosmological shift provides a fresh approach to the study of democracy and offers a challenge to liberal democracy since it rejects the view of the world as a machine with parts that can be disassembled and studied piecemeal. Instead, the universe is seen as "one indivisible, dynamic whole whose parts are essentially interrelated and can be understood only as patterns of a cosmic process."[3]

This chapter will explore several relationships between Newtonian and quantum physics and American political thought and behavior. First, it will examine closely the impact Newtonian theory has had on science, in general, and then on American political science, in particular. Second, quantum physics will be examined, and its impact (or lack thereof) on political science will be explored. Third, it will discuss the theoretical foundation for liberal democracy and the theoretical foundation for participatory democracy.

The way in which quantum physics will be applied throughout this thesis is as a metaphor that can offer insights, hypotheses, and alternative explanations for political phenomena that have been studied since ancient Greece. While I am intrigued by the work of those who apply quantum theory more literally, as a social science theorist (not a physicist) I feel more comfortable using this new information as an instrument to help me approach the study of participatory democracy without the constraints of a science seeking predictability and determinism. It seems entirely plausible to me, if not probable, that if the natural sciences can no longer rest on the security of ultimate truths and objective reality, then social scientists ought to at least consider the possibility that the same applies in their world.

While it is true that (a) quantum mechanics looks at the subatomic world, (b) what applies at that level may not apply at the macro level, and (c) there are pitfalls in seeing no difference between the physical and the social world or between inanimate and animate objects, I believe that quantum mechanics sheds some valuable light for social scientists. It is like the discovery of a new kind of intellectual flashlight that lets us think into crevices heretofore inaccessible to thought. In addition, I hope to demonstrate its value to participatory democrats, who advocate greater citizen participation and inclusion of all segments of society in political decision making.

NEWTONIAN PHYSICS AND NEWTONIAN POLITICS: LIBERAL DEMOCRACY

Martin Landau discusses the universal application of Newtonian physics to both natural scientific and social scientific study. According to Landau not only did Newtonian theory provide the basis for scientific research, but "to the 18th Century the Newtonian system constituted a cosmological formula so powerful that 'Newton became not so much the name of a man as of an infallible world outlook.' "[4]

It is not surprising that Newton's comprehensive, comprehensible, and predictable system—one developed through his own observations, as well as his and his predecessors' research, and designed to explain the whole natural world—would provide the basis for social scientific inquiry. After all, such a brilliant and original explanation of the universe provided understanding that seemed entirely logical to those interested in predicting human behavior.

Major Newtonian Principles

First of all, Newton saw the world as a mechanical world—a closed system whose basic entities are discrete particles that move in orbit.[5] The components of Newton's system have distinct properties that act in space and time according to fixed laws. The movement of bodies in the system is determined by movement of other bodies. All behavior in the system is lawful. There are no alternatives. Therefore, careful observation and study can lead to a totally predictable structure. This allows one to simply build on prior knowledge in an attempt to reach a full understanding of the universe. The Newtonian world, then, is based on certainty, order, structure, status, and determinism.

Landau describes society and politics as perceived and interpreted by Newtonian theory:[6]

1. Social processes are seen as determined processes, directed into given paths by the action of impersonal external forces.
2. The motion (behavior) of bodies (human) is preset and controlled according to the laws of nature.
3. Natural man, whose properties include natural rights, was directed by natural forces to form societies.
4. A society is no more than a sum of its discrete parts, its elemental bodies.
5. Social and political processes result from the action of the separate parts on one another.
6. The perfect working of a state, as of any machine, depends only on the perfection of adjustment of the pushes and pulls of its constituent elements.

The American Founders accepted this image of the world as a machine and humans as material beings. Benjamin Barber makes a strong case for how liberal democracy is rooted in Newtonian theory and then argues that the fatal flaw of applying Newtonian physics to political theory is that it begins with a pre-theoretical given of a worldview.[7] This unquestioning of the starting point led to the major axiom of liberalism—humans are material beings in all they are and all they do. (Therefore, humans are governed by laws that correspond to the laws of physical mechanics.) Barber states that this non-questioning of the starting point leads liberalism to resist systems that have activity, uncertainty, spontaneity, complexity, ambiguity, and process as major components. Liberalism (Newtonian politics, according to Barber) is wrought with "pretentions to objectivity and philosophical certainty that have proved inimical to practical reason and to participatory political activity."[8]

If one starts with a major premise of liberalism, derived from Newtonian theory, that humans are material beings, then the corollaries derived from such an unproven premise are all suspect. The corollaries of Newtonian theory have been derived from an objective, rational, and logical process of obtaining additional knowledge and certainty by building on that which is already known. Barber metaphorically describes the process as building links in a chain.[9]

It is the unproven axiom—materialism—that has provided the foundation for some questionable corollaries, which form the bedrock for the

Newtonian politics of the liberal democratic system. These corollaries have a profound impact in the development of political theories and systems. They define the acceptable parameters for study and design. They lead to the labeling of challenges to "givens" of the materialist axiom and its corollaries as nonscientific, irrational, or impractical. Acceptance of the corollaries as "truth" has stymied political science and theory. Unanswered questions continue to be asked in the same way by most without a recognition that the framework in which they are asked is flawed, limited, and inadequate for obtaining answers.

Corollaries

In order to address the inadequacies of Newtonian politics, it is necessary to examine the corollaries which Barber states are derived from the materialism axiom, which forms the basis for liberal democratic theory.[10]

Atomism (Individualism). Humans are viewed as separate, self-contained, unitary particles or atoms. Humans act as isolated individuals in a world made up of a multitude of "physical ones." This is the philosophical essence of such as Thomas Hobbes and Ayn Rand.[11] The result of this atomism, in the minds of many observers, is "alienation" and the death of community.[12] As Robert Nozick puts it, the single most important fact of human existence is "the fact of our separate existences."[13] It is the ultimate egoism.

Indivisibility (Hedonistic Psychology). Humans are unitary wholes acting in consonance with unitary motives. The inner condition of humans is tranquil and unfragmented. There is no internal dissonance. Instead the motivations that drive humans are precise, rational, and predictable— Everyman and Everywoman strive directly to maximize their own personal needs and to satisfy their own personal desires. Barber maintains that liberal democrats agree with Herbert Spencer's belief that "everything that is true of the higher animals at large is of course true of man."[14] As a result, "complex human motives can be restated as simple motives and then, in the final reduction, as a physical mechanics of the passions."[15] Political theories that attempt to predict human behavior on the basis of rational decision making, such as Anthony Down's *An Economic Theory of Democracy* and John Rawls' *A Theory of Justice*, are derived from this corollary.[16]

Commensurability (Equality). Humans are commensurable with one another. Each is governed by the same laws of behavior and is thus interchangeable. These laws are the laws of nature. There is no truly unique individual operating according to alternative laws of behavior. All humans are ruled first by their passions (self-gratification). Reason is second for all, and finally comes will. Therefore each individual thinks and acts according to the same, predictable laws of behavior, making each interchangeable with any other and equal to one another.

For Barber, this corollary becomes justification for the competitive world of liberal democracy. Assuming that individuals are equal assumes that the struggle for self-gratification is based on fair and equal competition. To the liberal democrat, maximization of personal needs and desires only comes through the maximization of liberty. Equality is the given. Liberty is the struggle. Attainment of safety and pleasure for the individual is the goal.[17]

Mutual Exclusivity (Power and Conflict). Humans cannot occupy the same space at the same time. This leads to conflict among humans, which becomes a primary mode of human interaction. One is, more often than not, either aggressively trying to obtain space occupied by another or defending one's space against an intruder. In American liberal democracy this becomes the struggle for the attainment and protection of private property.

This corollary is at the heart of James Madison's most famous "Federalist Paper No. 10," in which he maintains "the most common and durable source of factions has been the various and unequal distribution of property."[18] It, therefore, became an important goal of the Founders, clearly influenced by John Locke's view that property ownership is power,[19] to protect private property, particularly from those who had none and sought to take from the "rightful" owners. As C. B. Macpherson writes, the concepts of liberal freedom and ownership of property cannot be separated. For the liberal democrat, "the human essence is freedom from dependence on the wills of others and freedom is a function of possession."[20]

Sensationalism (Utilitarianism and Interest Theory). Humans feel, think, and imagine in response to physical causes (sense impressions or sensations). Therefore, all human behavior and thought is derived from physical sensations. As a result, theorists can develop scientifically derived explanations for all political behavior. Study is reserved for the world that we observe. This provides the philosophical basis for "interest politics." Each individual person acts on the basis of pursuing her or his self-interest in this isolated, individualistic dog-eat-dog world.

In the liberal democratic tradition, Madison argues in "Federalist Paper No. 51" that men seek their own private interests. Therefore, "ambition must be made to counteract ambition. The interest of the man must be connected with the constitutional rights of the place. It may be a reflection of human nature that such devices should be necessary to control the abuses of government."[21] He argues that the political system should promote competition among its self-interested citizenry in order to force compromise that will benefit society as a whole. A modern-day Madisonian, Charles Schultz, has argued that by aggregating private interests, government is able to attain the public interest.[22]

These corollaries, Barber maintains, underlie the American liberal democratic political system. They are evident in the Founders' view of man as rational (indivisibility), competitive (mutual exclusivity), and individualistic (atomism). They also provide the justification for a system designed to maximize the opportunity for "virtuous" men to control government. After all, it was through objective knowledge that the right paths would be seen and chosen. And finally, these corollaries have been widely accepted by political scientists regardless of their approach or specialization.

Challenging Newtonian Politics: Alternative Thinking

The challenge to these corollaries, however, comes from several quarters. In speaking of the transition from Newtonian physics to quantum physics, Henry Margenau states: "The dazzling successes of a universal application of mechanical reasoning had blinded men's awareness to all alternative modes of understanding."[23] In like fashion, there are political scientists who do not necessarily agree on alternative theories, but who recognize that Newtonian-influenced political science is limited and that it is time to explore new theories that enrich or challenge the objective, rational, materialist world of Newtonian theory. These include Glendon Schubert, Ben Barber, Martin Landau, James Dator, and others who are breaking the grip of the unquestioned Newtonian paradigm, exposing its flaws, and seeking alternatives.

For Landau, the object is to recognize the metaphorical nature and value of natural science utilized as a basis for models in political science, but to maintain a critical perspective in the creation and utilization of models. Models are extremely useful to help us create political science theories, develop hypotheses, and design research. However, once we take metaphors literally and begin to uncritically accept the paradigms we have designed (which Landau believes occurred with the use of the classical physics paradigm in American constitutional design and study), we start to blindly accept one way of thinking and reject all alternatives.

As noted previously, Barber is most concerned with the pre-theoretical component of classical physics (or any paradigm). The adherents of Newtonian physics have gone astray by starting with a premise (humans are material beings) that is accepted as truth by all rational beings. Since the premise is never questioned, the logical, deductive nature of Newtonian physics rejects any theory or hypothesis that is incompatible with the starting premise.

To emphasize his critique of the classical physics paradigm and its flawed axiom, Barber states that an alternative and plausible axiom is: "Humans are spiritual or psychic beings."[24] It is important to point out that Barber would not accept the absoluteness of this statement any more than he accepts as truth that humans are material beings. However, he points out that this starting point can lead us to radically different corollaries from those discussed earlier. For example:[25]

> *Alternative Corollary 1*: divisibility. Human beings are contradictory, diversified, and ambivalent. Persons may have conflicts within themselves. They are best defined by their environment and relations.

> *Alternative Corollary 2*: incommensurability. Individual desires, intentions, and talents are unequal. There is no objective, or predictable, reality.

> *Alternative Corollary 3*: mutualism. We can share common space with other beings without surrendering our distinctive abilities and freedoms.

> *Alternative Corollary 4*: intentionalism. Behavior is not merely determined by external stimuli, but is created out of common discourse and action. There is interconnectedness and interaction.

While Barber maintains the truth is not known in politics, he believes these corollaries offer a better explanation for political behavior than the Newtonian axiom and corollaries. He admonishes us to abandon the Newtonian view that there is objective reality to be discovered that will completely legitimize and justify liberal democracy.

Schubert is far more critical than either Barber or Landau of the current, prevailing paradigms in political science. As a science, he states, "political science is best characterized as a preclassical or antiquarian discipline."[26] In addition, Schubert wishes to move political science beyond the metaphorical stage that Landau finds useful in order to develop an integrated political science that recognizes the essential interconnectedness of the natural and social sciences.

Describing some of the limitations of Newtonian physics, Schubert argues, "Among the principles of classical or antiquarian physics that political science continues to take for granted are those of irreversible causality, action by contact, and absolute time. All of these are incompatible with experimental observations that led to Einstein's special relativity theory."[27]

Schubert challenges social scientists to at least "seriously consider the possibility that models of political behavior will be better informed by an awareness of what physical theory includes (and political theory doesn't) that would bring our theory closer to the facts of political life."[28] Yet he cautions social scientists who are attempting to utilize quantum principles to keep in mind that "the laws of physics apply to humans, but the laws of human behavior do not necessarily apply to physical interactions."[29]

Schubert predicts that the paradigm of modern or quantum physics will become more familiar to political scientists and will gradually become a part of their training, thinking, and explication.[30] A political scientist and futurist who has been influenced by Schubert, James Dator, argues that our Newtonian (and also Aristotelian) worldview has determined the technology we use and the social institutions we create.[31] For Dator, the revolution in physics through quantum theory is a clear signal that as a political scientist he needs "to understand quantum in order to see how or if it can be made an ontological basis for the design of new political institutions and/or systems (or whatever they may subsequently be more appropriately designated)."[32]

Dator, who is at the forefront in the application of quantum theory in political design, states:

> normally political institutions and behavior (and their rationale; and that of the dominant institutions and behaviors in society) are based upon a worldview which is substantially understood and believed in by members of that society. Technology prevalent in the society is based upon that worldview, and used to construct the institutions of the society. This connection generally existed in all societies, from the earliest tribal and hunting and gathering groups, through the earliest civilizations, up to the late 19th century.[33]

He argues that there has been a "prolonged gap" in this connection because contemporary social technologies and political institutions have not caught up with quantum theory and remain primarily stuck in Newtonian theory. He believes that the American representative and legal systems have never worked as designed and advertised. According to Dator, any political system or analysis of political systems focusing on rationality as the basis for decision making will inevitably come up short. Newtonian thought overlooks the subjective, the "irrational," the emotional. There is no room for such in choosing representatives, in legislating, and in interpreting the positive law. The Newtonian world ignores the subjective in its search for the "truth," a complete explanation of the system, and the capacity to predict the future precisely.

QUANTUM PHYSICS AND QUANTUM POLITICS: PARTICIPATORY DEMOCRACY

At this point it is useful to examine quantum physics and how it differs from Newtonian physics in order to grasp the differences between these two theories and worldviews and how they provide the foundation for radically different political theories.

Major Principles of Quantum Physics

Physicist Fritjof Capra in his book *The Turning Point* provides a very clear nonmathematical explanation of quantum theory and how it came to be.[34] He explains that as physicists in the twentieth century began atomic experiments, they found that the laws (Newtonian) they were following produced paradoxes. It eventually became clear to them that "their basic concepts, their language, and their whole way of thinking were inadequate to describe atomic phenomena."[35] This led physicists from all over the world, such as Werner Heisenberg, Paul Dirac, Max Planck, Albert Einstein, Louis De Broglie, Niels Bohr, Erwin Schrodinger, and Wolfgang Pauli, to unite in developing the mathematical formulas and conceptual framework of modern-day quantum theory. Four of the major quantum principles developed will be discussed since they offer such radically different interpretations and explanations of the world than does Newtonian theory.

Uncertainty: Objects Defined by Their Environments and Their Relationship to Others. One of the first principles established under quantum theory was the uncertainty principle developed by Werner Heisenberg.[36] When scientists began their atomic experiments, they found that electrons, which they believed were particles, often took on the traits of waves. That defied the classical definition of electron. The scientists discovered that Newtonian notions like particle, wave, position, and velocity were interrelated and could not be defined precisely at the same time, as had been assumed. The more precisely one dimension is fixed by the physicist's observation, the more another becomes uncertain. The exact relation between them is defined by the uncertainty principle. This means that in the example of the electron (or any atomic or subatomic "object") the electron has no inherent properties separate from its environmental context.

Probability. The acceptance of the "uncertainty principle" led scientists to question the very foundation of the mechanistic worldview—the concept of the reality of matter. As Capra explains:

> At the subatomic level, matter does not exist with certainty at definite times and in definite ways, but rather shows "tendencies to exist," and atomic events do not occur with certainty at definite times and in definite ways, but rather show "tendencies to occur." In the formulation of quantum mechanics, these tendencies are expressed as probabilities. . . . We can never predict an atomic event with certainty; we can only predict the likelihood of its happening.[37]

Seventeenth- and eighteenth-century Newtonian physics was based on absolutist notions, laws that were immutable and inexorable; twentieth-century quantum physics is not.

Interconnection and Interaction. These two discoveries showed that particles have no meaning as isolated entities, but can be understood only as interconnections, or correlations, between various processes of observation and measurement. In quantum theory you never end up with "things"; you always deal with interconnections, interactions, and processes. Capra says that "this is how modern physics reveals the basic oneness of the universe."[38] We can no longer divide the world up into independently existing smallest units. Things can no longer be defined without considering their relations to others.

This new information implied a new notion of causality. Classical science was constructed by the Cartesian method of dissecting the world into parts that were directed by causal laws. In addition, the universe was understood in terms of a machine. But to twentieth-century atomic physics, such a deterministic picture is inadequate. The principles of quantum theory demonstrated that the world could no longer be analyzed as existing isolated elements. The notion of separate parts "is an idealization with only approximate validity; these parts are not connected by causal laws in the classical sense."[39]

The result is that in quantum theory we cannot predict when and how a phenomenon is going to happen. This does not mean that events happen in an arbitrary fashion—only that they are not brought about by proximate, direct causes. In addition, we must understand that quantum theory indicates that the behavior of the parts no longer determines the behavior of the whole. Contrariwise, the behavior of the whole determines the behavior of the parts.

No Objective Reality. There is a major lesson derived from the discoveries of quantum mechanics. Quantum physics not only invalidated the classical ideal of an objective description of nature, it also challenged the myth of a value-free science. The patterns or processes that scientists see in nature are intimately connected with the ideas, preconceptions, and values of the scientist (in other words, things that have no meaning by themselves). As mentioned earlier, things are defined in relation to other things. If one electron behaves as either a particle or a wave, depending on how we experimentally measure it, the electron does not have objective properties independent of our mind. We can no longer pretend that our observations are totally objective because we are to a great extent determining our findings by deciding what we choose to see.

Capra sums up the themes of quantum theory as such:

> The concept of the universe as an interconnected web of relations is one of the two major themes that recur throughout modern physics. The other theme is the realization that the cosmic web is intrinsically dynamic. The dynamic aspect of matter arises in quantum theory as a consequence of the wave nature of subatomic particles, and is even more central in relativity theory, which has shown us that the being of matter cannot be separated from its activity. The properties of its basic patterns, the subatomic particles, can be understood only in a dynamic context, in terms of movement, interaction, and transformation.[40]

How does one take the principles of quantum theory that contradict or challenge Newtonian theory and apply them to a political theory that has been significantly influenced by Newtonian concepts?

On the Importance of Metaphors and Worldviews

Following in the footsteps of other social scientists, one can develop metaphors to structure inquiry and to provide an interpretive system. In doing so, it is important to heed Landau's warning not to take the metaphor too literally. Quantum metaphors can be useful in helping design hypotheses to test what is unknown to us. Yet at all times it is necessary to keep the true nature of the metaphor in mind in order to avoid the presumption of fact that has yet to be proven.

There is more, however, to the application of quantum theory to political theory than the mere use of metaphors. Quantum theory offers a worldview, a view of the universe that can be applied to political science. While Schubert and Capra both point out that one must be careful not to treat animate and inanimate objects as though there were no difference, both are applying quantum physics in the study and analysis of social phenomena. There is no fault in using physical theory to develop a systems view that helps one understand the similarities and interconnections of the natural and social world. The failing of Newtonian politics is not that the two worlds were combined under one theory, but that Newtonian theory is too absolute, too limiting, and too simplistic. It provided, however, a very good starting point for scientific study that begins to integrate the two worlds. Quantum theory initiates the next step in creating a more sophisticated, more complex, and more modern political theory.

To begin, Dator, who advocates a quantum theory worldview, states that one of the basic assumptions of quantum theory is:

> Things are not what they seem. If we restrict our understanding of the world to only that narrow band which our human senses perceive, we will have only a shallow and misleading notion of the structures and processes of the world. The assumptions, theories, and methods of positivistic science are simply too restrictive and limiting.[41]

Principles of Quantum Politics

From that perspective, the impact of quantum theory on political science is profound. How can there be any discipline, any definitions, any causal explanations, any predictions in politics if one cannot determine absolutely from observation the realities of the situation? The following principles based on the four quantum principles discussed earlier will provide the guide to exploring some of the political implications of quantum political theory.

Uncertainty: Objects Defined by Their Environments and Their Relationships to Others. Liberal democratic political theory in America (guided by Newtonian theory) began with the assumption that man had a predictable nature. He was rational and as such could be predictable. Theories abound in American politics that attempt to predict and explain man's behavior on the rational grounds that man would always pursue his own self-interests.[42]

When modern physicists began to see that the subatomic world acted differently than Newton's laws predicted, they had to change their way of thinking. That is where quantum politics comes in.

A better explanation of human nature is that we are complex, contradictory creatures that cannot be classified or identified out of our environments. We are at cross-purposes, self-promoting and self-destructive, good and bad—in short: uncertain. People are fiscal conservatives and liberal on foreign affairs. People can be cooperative and self-effacing—even while having strong egos. Individuals can be classified as more or less democratic in relation to others in the same environment. That definition changes as the environment and/or the relations change. A quantum politics would be based on the unpredictable nature of humans and would take into account many more recent findings about the human subconscious than does Newtonian politics.

Probability. Cause-effect determinism and rational decision making are not at the root of all human interaction, or even primary in human affairs. Instead, in quantum theory, as Dator states, "probability, randomness, uncertainty, and complementarity are 'normal.' "[43] The role of political science, then, is to theorize and experiment with new political structures and processes based on the principles of uncertainty and probability.

Once political scientists move away from seeking absolutes, patterns of probability can be studied and used as the basis for research and analysis. This methodology, although at first glance it appears more ambiguous, would actually provide a better explanation for political phenomena than cause-effect determinism. The baffling exceptions to the rule, the apparent inconsistencies, and the random deviances could be accounted for through probability formulas, much like those used in public opinion polling. Political scientists would certainly have to be cautious not to explain too cavalierly the unexpected occurring, but a scientific utilization of probability theory could prove immensely useful in political analysis.

Interconnections and Interaction. The political system—indeed, the universal system—cannot be divided into discrete units for analysis, a la Newtonian politics. Instead political analysis focuses on the effects of interactions and process. In the case of "democracy," it cannot be adequately defined in terms of its branches of government, means for election, tenure of office, and checks and balances. As Majid Tehranian points out, democracy, above all, is a dynamic, moving process.[44] In addition, the whole of the democratic system determines its parts; the parts do not determine the whole. That explains why tinkering with the U.S. system and altering various parts is not going to change the overall character of the system and make it truly democratic. It also explains how political institutions, political leaders, and even political scientists are the creations of the political system and are supported by the system.

It may be argued that of course the present Newtonian mechanistic system places an emphasis on interaction among the three branches of government and that it has a "process" orientation. After all, the Senate approves treaties made by the president; the president can veto legislation passed by the Congress; the Supreme Court determines the constitutionality of laws, and so forth. The point is that the major emphasis of the Founders, a principle strongly adhered to even today, was separation of powers—to use the branches of government as checks and balances—to isolate power and function so that no one part became all-powerful. Yet the reality of application of the separation of powers doctrine proves that the ideal cannot be implemented. Indeed, controversies that have existed for quite some time focus on the overlapping of powers. Is the Supreme Court really legislating when it declares laws of Congress unconstitutional? Can Congress force the president to implement laws or to turn over presidential papers? Can the president send armed troops into a country when Congress has not declared war? A quantum approach to assigning powers to branches of government would recognize the essential need for interconnectedness and interaction among the branches and would provide for that in determining the powers of each branch. It is conceivable that a system designed focusing on interconnection and interaction rather than separation could provide a greater check against the abuse of power.

In addition, quantum politics challenges the Newtonian influenced liberal democracy concept of individualism, with men and women pursuing their own self-interests, seeking maximization of personal power, and striving for privatization rather than community. This individualism results in the development of interest groups that are created to pursue special interests of members of the group. All too often the interest groups, whether they are unions, conservation groups, social welfare groups or whatever, become individualized themselves—with the leadership losing touch with the membership. The leaders—not the members—begin defining the interests of the group, which is done in a way that is very unconnected to the overall membership.

Quantum politics sees us all connected in the system and all affected by the decisions of that system. Rather than designing institutions that encourage us to live in private worlds pursuing narrow self-interests, quantum politics would provide mechanisms and institutions that encourage interaction and broaden perspectives in how we are all connected and affected by decisions made within the system. Quantum politics attempts to maximize participation, interaction, and a recognition that we are inalterably connected in the system. To lose track of the whole is to work against one's self-interest anyway.

No Objective Reality. The important lesson for the political scientist in quantum theory is that there is no objective real world apart from one's consciousness or as Dator states, "different observer, different

world."[45] Our observations are limited to our perceptions and consciousness.

This is consistent with psychological research in the twentieth century
that demonstrates that "selective perception"—that different people see
and/or describe phenomena differently—is a normal phenomenon.[46] It is
essential to keep in mind that our observations, no matter how precise, are
determined by our own concepts, thoughts, and values that vary with each
individual and under varying circumstances.

Political scientists operating in the late twentieth century should be
willing to evaluate the degree to which long-held beliefs and theories are
compatible or incompatible with the scientific knowledge derived over the
last century. They need to question whether political institutions and
procedures designed 200 years ago with a solid foundation in Newtonian
thought are effective within the context of the quantum world.

American political science has at least implicitly accepted Newtonian
theories as a valid basis for indigenous American political theory, in
other words, the prevailing liberal democratic model. To be consistent
and up-to-date, it should develop political theories that have the potential to further an understanding of the world by constructing new
theories based on modern knowledge. Quantum theory may prove in
time to have as many limitations and errors as Newtonian theory. Still
it offers fresh insights and plausible explanations where Newtonian
theory falters. Indeed, with current knowledge, it is clear that it has
much to offer in developing a heuristic framework for a new political
theory.

Explication of Strong, Participatory Democracy

Barber takes a step in this direction by moving beyond Newtonian
politics. After liberal democracy, he proposes a political alternative presently viewed as radical and unworkable by most American political scientists
and political leaders. This alternative—participatory democracy (or to use
Barber's term, "strong democracy")—is described by Barber as "dialecti-
cal, sustaining itself while in motion, looking for conviction in the process
as an unfolding logic rather than its genesis."[47]

Sidney Verba and Norman Nie also emphasize the essential nature of
citizen participation in democratic theory: "Participation, when and if
effective, has a particularly crucial relationship to all other social and
political goals. It represents a process by which goals are set and means are
chosen in relation to all sorts of social issues. Indeed, this is why it is crucial
to democratic theory."[48] Peter Bachrach adds that if there is not a revitaliza-

tion of a broad democratic participation, then political decision making is going to have less and less democratic control.[49]

Quantum Elements in an Emerging Participatory Theory

To date, political scientists who describe or favor forms of participatory democracy rarely mention quantum theory in their theoretical explorations. Yet their hypotheses, axioms, and corollaries fit well into the quantum theoretical framework and may well help develop a more systematic, emerging theory of participatory democracy.

Restating the quantum principles discussed earlier (Uncertainty: Objects Defined by Their Environments and Their Relationship to Others; Probability; Interconnection and Interaction; and No Objective Reality), one recognizes that participatory democratic theory has these principles at its core. As a matter of fact, definitions and descriptions of participatory democracy have these principles essentially interwoven so that the principles cannot be neatly separated and examined independent of each other.

For example, Carole Pateman implicitly emphasizes the quantum nature of democratic theory when she states: "A democratic theory . . . is a theory of interrelationships between individuals, their characteristics and forms of social and political institutions, between concepts and social life, between concepts themselves, and between political theory and political practice."[50] Her criticism that liberal theory "tries to separate these things"[51] goes to the heart of the critique of Newtonian theory. In discussing the necessity of more emphasis on participation in democratic theory, Bachrach also implicitly addresses quantum principles by discussing the essential interconnectedness of ends and means in a democracy. As he observes, "the interaction of means and ends—of process and policy—stimulates and encourages the self-development of a free people."[52]

Participatory democracy, activity, interaction, transformation, uncertainty, consciousness, and perception—all principles of quantum—come together in Peter Manicas' statement: "Democracy is a process, a process of permanent revolution in which the forging of the self-determined individual goes hand in hand with the transformation of hierarchical institutions into democratic and self-managed institutions. As so conceived, the democratic community is not merely an abstract but a mode of action."[53]

Elements of quantum theory appear throughout descriptions of the democratic process. For example, Barber's metaphor for political reasoning is "weaving" as opposed to the Newtonian metaphor of connecting links in a chain.[54] The corollaries discussed earlier—divisibility, incommensurability, intentionalism, and mutualism—that he derives from perceiving humans as psychic or spiritual beings, rather than material, are compatible with quantum theory and participatory democratic theory.

Barber does not attempt to replace the Newtonian absolute of materialism with another of spirituality. He believes these corollaries offer a more accurate appraisal of political behavior than do the Newtonian axiom and corollaries. Moreover, they provide an alternative view readily reconciled with the scientific revolution created by quantum physics.

Not believing in absolutes, cause-effect determinism, and the "truth," Barber abandons liberal democracy (Newtonian politics) in favor of "strong" or participatory democracy. The dominant virtue in strong democracy is also a key component of quantum theory—activity. Things are defined and developed through interaction and reciprocity with others. In terms of participatory democracy, this involves dialogue—receiving and giving. This process of interaction leads to transformation with others, a process that helps to redefine who we are.

It is important to reemphasize that advocates of participatory democracy see democracy as a process—an ongoing process.[55] Manicas calls democracy a process that cannot be separated from its goal.[56] John Dewey goes even further by stating that society is a process designed to maximize personal growth through interaction with others, which evolves into the creation of the public good. In his words:

> Society is the process of associating in such ways that experiences, ideas, emotions, values are transmitted and made common. . . . Only in association with fellows does [the individual] become a conscious centre of experience. Organization, which is what traditional theory has generally meant by the term Society or State, is . . . subordinate because it becomes static, rigid, institutionalized whenever it is not employed to facilitate and enrich the contacts of human beings with one another.[57]

Participatory democracy requires an interaction and interconnection that recognizes that there is no objective reality for wise and virtuous representatives to discover and promulgate for the remainder of the citizenry. Every person, as a subjective and objective individual, has her/his own perceptions of reality and of what are correct paths to follow—based on their own values, backgrounds, and shifting circumstances. Barber maintains that the greatest good would be served if the American ("thin" democratic) political system would discard the Newtonian (Platonic and Burkean) ideas that virtuous men know best and adopt a strong democratic system that generates maximum support and development for and responsiveness to all citizens of the system.

In other words, strong democracy's central virtues are participation, citizenship, and political activity. Participatory democracy "may be the political answer to the question of moral uncertainty—the form of interaction for people who cannot agree on absolutes."[58] Or, as Schuman says, "Maybe we should consider more carefully the 'unreal world.' "[59]

Dator's political designs based on quantum account for the subjective— the "unreal world"—with the acknowledgment that there is no single reality, that we are limited or enriched by our perceptions, and that there are no absolutes. The political institutions he proposes all display the hallmark of participatory democracy.

He states that a "quantum approach to representation might be simply to use random sampling."[60] The concept is hardly new. The Greeks used a lottery system during the "Golden Age" of Pericles in Athens.[61] In modern times, political analysts like Ted Becker have long advocated participatory democracy and the "random house legislature." More recently Ernest Callenbach and Michael Phillips in A Citizen Legislature also have discussed the merits of such a proposal.[62] However, none, from the Greeks to the modern analysts, have discussed the formal connection to quantum theory. Taking representative samples from a citizen universe would maximize participation in a diverse, highly populated society by increasing the chances of various groups of citizens being able to participate in key decision making. Becker believes it is the best way to ensure the presence of more women, minorities, and younger citizens in Congress.[63] The chances would be even more increased by limiting the terms of office and rotating people in and out on a regular basis. Of course, "representation," even of the random type, limits the absolute number of people who can have direct power in policy making—other than by participating in the public debate. A quantum system that maximizes citizen participation would involve direct democracy—for example, town meetings and citizen initiatives.

TELEVOTE: QUANTUM THEORY IN THE STUDY OF CITIZEN PARTICIPATION

Dator offers other political designs based on quantum theory, but his vision of a random legislature is a quantum-type design that offers a means of increasing citizen participation. This book will examine various forms of citizen participation in American democracy. It will discuss how theories and research of citizen participation are approached differently if one is guided by a belief in objectivity and predictability (Newtonian) or guided by a belief in randomness and no objective reality (quantum). It also will explore the future of citizen participation and public input in decision making in America. This study is guided by the question: "If we are faced with radically new scientific theories and technologies, what does that mean for American democracy?"

Televote, a method of public opinion polling designed to be implemented in a participatory democratic society at the threshold of the quantum age, is a polling method that is emerging in a space between the fading Newtonian predominance and the increasing quantum thought. As a result, it is a transitional tool that incorporates both Newtonian and quantum principles. Not only is it designed to measure public opinion, but unlike all conventional, Newtonian-era public opinion polling, it also stimulates citizen interaction and participation in the democratic process.

Like all scientific polling done today, Televote utilizes random sampling based on probability (quantum). Its unique features are: (1) It provides information to respondents—undisputed facts and pro and con arguments (Newtonian); (2) it encourages respondents to discuss the facts, opinions, and issues with others—interaction (quantum); (3) it allows time for deliberation before respondents reply (Newtonian); and (4) it is designed to be used simultaneously with Electronic Town Meetings on the same subject (quantum).

Although Televote may well be a transitional tool from one worldview to another, it nevertheless has successfully operated in a predominantly Newtonian world. The current American political system is virtually the same as that the Founders created with their mechanistic worldview. Although Televote seeks to transmit views of the public and their representatives through two-way interaction of knowledge and views, it is limited by a political system that frequently holds public opinion in low regard because it believes that the citizenry will never be as sufficiently informed or enlightened as their representatives. Televote seeks to alter that perspective but faces roadblocks from entrenched powers that derive benefits from the current worldview.

In evaluating Televote's role in quantum politics, a very important aspect of quantum theory must not be overlooked. Televote is merely a component of the political system within which it functions. Its role is defined by the system—it does not define the system.

Thus, it is only within the quantum worldview and a political system consistent with that whereby Televote can reach its maximum potential for helping increase public knowledge and discussion of issues, and directly linking that into decision-making processes that create public policy and law.

If indeed a form of participatory democracy were to become widespread or even predominant, Televote would be only one part in a complex, dynamic, interactive environment. In the media world, it could be an aspect of electronic town meetings, begun prior to town meetings to create public awareness, discussion, and interaction, and then completed after the multiple-way communication aspect of the town meetings in order to yield a scientific sample of informed and duly deliberated public opinion on the topic. In the legislative world, it could (a) help develop initiatives through a consensus-building process; or (b) help set legislative agendas or persuade legislators to construct alternatives to be voted on in a referendum (indirect initiative). It may even be that Televote will be overtaken by the visual media rather than relying so heavily on the print media. In conclusion, its nature (function) would be determined by the extent of the democratic environment in which it exists.

CONCLUSION

Quantum theory and politics do not replace all that is connected to Newtonian theory and politics. There are occasions when cause-effect determinism exists, predictions are appropriate, order exists, and deductive reasoning prevails. Quantum politics does not aim to purge these concepts from the political sphere. As Tehranian points out:

New scientific metaphors do not replace, and new theories do not refute, the old ones but somehow remake them; even scientific revolutions preserve some continuity with the old order of things. This is as true of theoretical speculations about society as it is of the social system itself. No social system can be born by a fiat; the so-called revolutionary developments in society are not more than recreations of the past.[64]

Quantum politics may be a re-creation of Jeffersonian politics,[65] but its quantum theoretical base enriches political understanding and uncovers limitations of Newtonian thought. It provides a seriously needed, new worldview that is based on twentieth-century knowledge, not held hostage by slavish devotion to eighteenth-century theoretical thought.

As we learn from quantum physics, we are limited in our understanding by the way in which we define things. When we define an object as a particle, we are stymied in our understanding when it demonstrates the characteristics of a wave. We have to expand our concept. Quantum theory helps us look at democracy as more than a mechanical system of distinct components with neatly divided functions. Quantum theory forces us to view democracy as a process—an interactive process that evolves and transforms the system and the citizens that create the system.

Rather than seeking absolutes, quantum theory finds patterns that assist in understanding and future planning. Abandoning the belief in absolutes does not necessarily create chaos and confusion. Instead, it challenges us to seek more alternatives—alternatives that may provide answers where exclusive deductive thought would never take us. Quantum theory allows us to consider the merits of intuitive thought and to expand the realm of participatory possibilities for citizens in a democracy.

The challenges for social scientists who wish to utilize quantum theory in research are many. As Landau warns, one must be forever cautious against developing a rigidity in the use of models based on the physical sciences. We cannot assume we have found the truth and proceed to explain all social phenomena based on mathematical formulas provided us by quantum physics. Schubert understands the difficulties before us in his insistence that social theories must be more complex than physical theories, since humans are more complex than inanimate objects, and the laws that apply to human interactions do not necessarily apply to physical interactions.

All social scientists utilizing quantum theory today are novices. There are many questions being asked and debated over the extent to which quantum physics can be useful in political theory. While there is widespread agreement among many of them regarding the limitations of Newtonian theory, they are only beginning to crawl into the quantum world. One must learn to crawl, however, before one can walk or run.

The challenges and insecurities that lie ahead for the quantum political theorists are matched by the conviction that social science theory must address the radical changes in physical theory in the last century.

The following chapters will develop several themes presented in this first chapter. Chapter 2 will investigate historical developments in citizen participation in the United States.

NOTES

1. Martin Landau, "On the Use of Metaphor in Political Analysis," *Social Research* 28 (1961): 331–353. Landau states that Oppenheimer argues that Newton's work was limited to the phenomena of motions. In addition, Newton rejected all notions of a priori certainty and believed all propositions and hypotheses were to be empirical,

set "firmly on the rule of observation." Nevertheless, the cosmology of the last two centuries has been categorized by natural and social scientists as Newtonian albeit it distorts Newton's own worldview (p. 346).

2. Ibid., p. 338.

3. Fritjof Capra, *The Turning Point: Science, Society, and the Rising Culture* (New York: Simon & Schuster, 1982), p. 78.

4. Landau, p. 338.

5. Ibid., p. 337.

6. Ibid., pp. 338–339.

7. Benjamin Barber, *Strong Democracy: Participatory Politics for a New Age* (Berkeley: University of California Press, 1984), pp. 26–27.

8. Ibid., p. 29.

9. Ibid., p. 32.

10. Ibid., pp. 33–35.

11. Thomas Hobbes, *The Leviathan* (Middlesex, England: Penguin Books, 1968); and Ayn Rand, *The Fountainhead* (New York: New American Library, 1943).

12. For example, see: David Schuman, *Preface to Politics* (Lexington, Mass.: D. C. Heath, 1986), Chapters 6 and 7. According to Schuman, alienation is the result of our liberalism. There is no community, only individuals living "together apart." To be left alone, according to the liberal democrat, is to be free. Robert Nisbet, *Community and Power* (New York: Oxford University Press, 1962). Nisbet discusses the difference between community and the liberal individualism to which we adhere in America. Philip E. Slater, *The Pursuit of Loneliness* (Boston: Beacon Press, 1971). Philip Slater points out the irony that Americans are encouraged to individually seek their own ends, but the society defines what is worthy of pursuit. Therefore, Americans, as individuals, compete for the same ends in a society that pushes them into conforming to the norm, thereby giving up the individualism they claim to hold so dear.

13. Robert Nozick, *Anarchy, State, and Utopia* (New York: Basic Books, 1974), p. 33.

14. Barber, p. 72.

15. Ibid.

16. Anthony Downs, *An Economic Theory of Democracy* (New York: Harper & Row, 1957); and John Rawls, *A Theory of Justice* (Cambridge, Mass.: Harvard University Press, 1971).

17. Barber, p. 78.

18. James Madison, "Federalist Paper No. 10" in Alexander Hamilton, James Madison, and John Jay, *The Federalist Papers* (New York: New American Library, 1961), p. 78.

19. John Locke, *Second Treatise of Civil Government* (Cambridge: Cambridge University Press, 1967).

20. C. B. Macpherson, *The Political Theory of Possessive Individualism* (New York: Oxford University Press, 1964), p. 3.

21. James Madison, "Federalist Paper No. 51" in Alexander Hamilton, James Madison, and John Jay, *The Federalist Papers* (New York: New American Library, 1961), p. 322. Jeremy Bentham and John Stuart Mill also sought to address the issue of maximizing the public good while protecting individual liberty in a world ruled

by men seeking to promote their own self-interests. See John Stuart Mill and Jeremy Bentham, *Utilitarianism and Other Essays*, edited by Alan Ryan (New York: Penguin Books, 1987).

22. Charles Schultz, *The Use of Private Interest* (Washington, D.C.: American Enterprise Institute, 1977).

23. Henry Margenau, *The Nature of Physical Reality: A Philosophy of Modern Physics* (New York: McGraw-Hill, 1950), p. 308.

24. Barber, p. 42.

25. Ibid.

26. Glendon Schubert, "The Evolution of Political Science Paradigms of Physics, Biology, and Politics," *Politics and the Life Sciences* 1.2 (1983): 98.

27. Ibid., p. 101.

28. Ibid.

29. Ibid.

30. Consistent with Schubert's prediction is a panel presentation at the August 1987 American Political Science Association Convention focusing on the bicentennial of the U.S. Constitution entitled "Quantum Theory and Constitution Building."

31. James A. Dator, "Quantum Theory and Political Design," paper presented at the G. Duttweiller Institut Conference, January 1984, p. 2.

32. Ibid., p. 3.

33. Ibid., p. 2.

34. Capra, pp. 75–97.

35. Ibid., p. 76.

36. Ibid., pp. 78–79.

37. Ibid., p. 80.

38. Ibid.

39. Ibid., p. 85.

40. Ibid., p. 87.

41. Dator, p. 4.

42. For examples, see: Sigmund Freud, *Civilization and Its Discontents* (London: Hogarth Press, 1930); Adam Smith, *The Wealth of Nations* (New York: P. F. Collins & Sons, 1959) and *Theory of Moral Sentiments* (Indianapolis: Liberty Classics, 1976); Hugo Black, *A Constitutional Faith* (New York: Alfred A. Knopf, 1968); and David Hume, *Philosophical Works*, edited by Thomas H. Green and Thomas H. Grose, 1882, reprint (London: Scientia Verlag Aalen, 1964). See also Henry S. Kariel, *Beyond Liberalism, Where Relations Grow* (San Francisco: Chandler and Sharp, 1977). Kariel states that "Hobbes, Locke, Smith, and Madison believed that man was also rational and could logically determine his best interests. In addition, they favored a society "in which everyone would be committed to the rational pursuit of self-interest" (Kariel, p. 5).

43. Dator, p. 4.

44. Majid Tehranian, "Electronic Democracy: Information Technologies and Democratic Prospects," UNESCO Report, Honolulu, 1985, p. 52.

45. Dator, p. 6.

46. See, for example, Janas F. Saltis, *Seeing, Knowing and Believing* (Reading, Mass.: Addison-Wesley, 1966); Marshall H. Segall, Donald T. Campbell, and Melville J.

Herkovits, *Influence of Culture on Visual Perception* (Indianapolis: Bobbs-Merrill, 1966); and R. L. Gregory, *Eye and Brain: The Psychology of Seeing* (New York: McGraw-Hill, 1973).

47. Barber, p. 44.

48. Sidney Verba and Norman H. Nie, *Participation in America: Political Democracy and Social Equality* (New York: Harper & Row, 1972), p. 4.

49. Peter Bachrach, *The Theory of Democratic Elitism: A Critique* (Lanham, Md.: University Press of America, 1980).

50. Carole Pateman, *The Problem of Political Obligation: A Critique of Liberal Theory* (Berkeley: University of California Press, 1985), pp. 175–176.

51. Ibid.

52. Bachrach, p. 6.

53. Peter Manicas, *The Death of the State* (New York: G. P. Putnam's Sons, 1976), pp. 256–257.

54. Barber, p. 32.

55. Majid Tehranian points out that "democracy" is more a process than an end in itself. He warns us that "it is often lost the moment we assume we have achieved it" ("Electronic Democracy," p. 52).

56. Manicas, p. 256.

57. John Dewey, *Reconstruction in Philosophy* (Boston: Beacon Press, 1948), pp. 187–213.

58. Barber, p. 65.

59. Schuman, p. 40.

60. Dator, p. 8.

61. Theodore L. Becker, *American Government: Past, Present, Future* (Boston: Allyn & Bacon, 1976), pp. 468–469.

62. Becker, pp. 467–469; Alvin Toffler, *The Third Wave* (London: William Collins Sons, 1980), pp. 434–435; and Ernest Callenbach and Michael Phillips, *A Citizen Legislature* (Berkeley, Calif.: Banyan Tree Books, 1985).

63. Becker, pp. 467–469.

64. Tehranian, "Development Theory and Communications Policy: The Changing Paradigms," *Progress in Communication Sciences* 1 (1979): 141.

65. See an excellent presentation of Jeffersonian politics in Richard K. Matthews, *The Radical Politics of Thomas Jefferson* (Lawrence: University Press of Kansas, 1986).

2

Tracing the Paths of Expanding Citizen Participation in America

Citizen participation in America has evolved over time. Its pattern has not been linear—on a straight trajectory toward greater and greater participation. Neither has it been cyclical, which implies a continuing return to a previous starting point.

Instead the pattern has the following characteristics. First, there are waves—pulses—that surge and recede. Second, the intensity of each wave or pulse varies. Third, the direction of the path is sometimes erratic. We can trace its path, but not be certain of how far it will travel or where it will extend its reach. Fourth, each wave reaches a high point somewhere and then ebbs. However, the ebb at its lowest never recedes beyond the high point of the previous wave. Thus, the cumulative effect is a decidedly advancing motion with constantly expanding openings for future movement.

Thus, this chapter will consist of a brief, select history of citizen participation in the United States, one that illustrates this wave-pulse pattern by surveying various eras which sought to expand and broaden participation. It also will provide an analysis of the theoretical and practical relationship between leaders and citizens and a systematic evaluation of the extent to which political structures limited or encouraged citizen participation. As the arguments are reexamined in the modern context, the new scientific discoveries of quantum research will be added to propel the debate into the next century.

THE PRE-EUROPEANIZATION PERIOD: THE ROOTS OF
AMERICAN POLITICAL THINKING ON CITIZEN
PARTICIPATION

In American Eurocentrist thought, most writings on the roots of American political theory focus on the influence of such European philosophers as Locke, Rousseau, Montesquieu, and Hume. Forrest Mc-Donald does broach the topic of non-European political thinking in early times by referring to John Locke's political theories wherein he mentions Indian life as a model of a society existing in a state of nature, in other words, living in a society with no organized political system or government.[1] On the other hand, this very brief tidbit about Indians, coupled with his acknowledgment that Thomas Jefferson concluded "that the primitive stages [of the Indians] produced happier and more virtuous men,"[2] actually trivializes the substantial knowledge gained from the political ideology and governmental practices of the American Indian and its profound and deep influence on American political thought and the building of political institutions. It has only been in recent years that scholars have begun to acknowledge the influence of the native American Indian, particularly the Iroquois tribes, on American thinking and political design—especially regarding the important role of citizen participation and public opinion in governance.[3]

Bruce Johansen discusses the Iroquois influence in *Forgotten Founders*. The Iroquoian governmental system was probably founded in the fifteenth century when five previously warring nations united under a constitution called "The Great Law of Peace." Three centuries later, an additional nation joined the alliance to expand the confederacy to the League of Six Nations. As Johansen points out, the Iroquoian constitution

> rested on assumptions foreign to the monarchs of Europe: it regarded leaders as servants of the people, rather than their masters, and made provisions for the leaders' impeachment for errant behavior. The Iroquois' law and customs upheld freedom of expression in political and religious matters, and it forbade the unauthorized entry of homes. It provided for political participation by women and the relatively equitable distribution of wealth.[4]

Representatives or chiefs sent to the lawmaking body, the Council, were chosen in two forms: (a) those nominated by women of extended, titled families (the hereditary chiefs) and (b) those elected outside of the hereditary family structure on the basis of personal leadership qualities (the pine tree chiefs). Policy discussion and decision making were divided into two phases (the equivalent of two houses), which acted as a check and balance against hasty decision making. After two of the tribes discussed and agreed on the matter before a third tribe, the third tribe took the decision to the other two tribes to accept or reject. All decisions in the confederacy had to be unanimously agreed to by all Council members.

There were mechanisms for removing chiefs who did not truly represent their people or who abused their power by enriching themselves. As noted above, Iroquois chiefs were viewed as servants of the people, unlike the European kings and queens of the time, and were "generally poorer than the common people, for they affect to give away and distribute all the Presents or Plunder they get in their Treaties or War, so as to leave nothing for themselves. If they should be once suspected of selfishness, they would grow mean in the opinion of their Country-men, and would consequently lose their authority."[5]

According to Felix Cohen:

> Universal suffrage for women as for men, the pattern of states within a state we call federalism, the habit of treating chiefs as servants of the people instead of their masters, . . . [and the] insistence that the community must respect the diversity of men and the diversity of their dreams—all these things were part of the American way of life before Columbus landed.[6]

Ruth Underhill states that many believe the Iroquois government, which was the "most integrated and orderly north of Mexico," gave ideas to writers of the U.S. Constitution and to "Franklin, Jefferson, and Washington [who] were quite familiar with the [Iroquois] League."[7]

Johansen discusses several areas in which Benjamin Franklin, Thomas Jefferson, and Thomas Paine refer to Indian society as a model that offers lessons for Americans. Franklin served as a British diplomat to the Iroquois nation. The British purpose was to establish an Anglo-Indian alliance against the Spanish and the French. However, the Iroquois required that the colonists recognize they were in a foreign nation and had to learn the native rituals in order to discuss diplomatic initiatives. To be a successful diplomat, then, Franklin and the other British emissaries had to learn and understand Indian culture. They were exposed to concepts of freedom, property ownership, liberty, democracy, and a form of confederacy that had no parallel in the kingdoms of Europe. Johansen states: "These observations would help mold the political life of the colonies, and much of the world, in the years to come."[8]

As an example, in 1744, nearly a decade before Franklin began his diplomatic service to the Indian nations, an Iroquois chief, Canassatego, urged the American colonies to form an alliance, a confederacy as the Iroquois had done three centuries earlier. He argued that an American colonial confederation would make it easier for the Indians in their dealings with the colonists and would strengthen the colonies as long as they required all action taken to be approved unanimously by colonial representatives to the confederacy.

But it was not until after the Stamp Act and other oppressive British measures that the colonists accepted a Franklin proposal, revised from one he made in 1754 that was beholden to Canassatego, and adopted the Articles of Confederation. On August 25, 1775, commissioners from the newly united colonies met with the Iroquois chiefs at Philadelphia and smoked a peace pipe. The commissioners told the Iroquois that they had finally taken the wise advice given to them by Canassatego 30 years earlier and had formed a federal union. In their speech they praised the Iroquois: "The Six Nations are a wise people, Let us hearken to them, and take their counsel, and teach our children to follow it."[9]

It was not merely the political structure of the Iroquois that intrigued Franklin. As Johansen emphasizes, Franklin drew on the whole of his experiences in developing his political theories. While Franklin was well educated in European and Greek philosophy, the American Indian's theory and practice "affected Franklin's observations on the need for appreciation of diverse cultures and religions, public opinion as the basis for a polity, the nature of liberty and happiness, and the social role of property."[10]

For Jefferson, who was a student and admirer of Indian culture, there were two major aspects of Indian society from which Americans could learn. First, there was a lack of poverty among the Indians and virtual equality among all segments in the society. Second, there was a reliance the Indian chiefs placed upon the public opinion among their people. "[T]o Jefferson, public opinion among the Indians was an important reason for their lack of oppressive government, as well as the egalitarian distribution of property on which Franklin had earlier remarked."[11]

Jefferson believed that excess or uncontrolled power in the hands of leaders led to corruption and that the best means to prevent it was to retain ultimate power in the hands of an educated people. In his famous letter to Edward Carrington after Shays' Rebellion, Jefferson reaffirms his faith in the masses and indicates his belief that

[in Indian societies] public opinion is in the place of law, & restrains morals as powerfully as laws ever did anywhere. Among [European governments], under pretence of governing they have divided their nations into two classes, wolves & sheep. . . . Cherish therefore the spirit of our people and keep alive their attention.[12]

The democratic nature of Indian society's influence on American politics also became evident a few years later when the debate took place over the current U.S. Constitution. "Agrippa," an Antifederalist from Massachusetts, used Indian society as an example of a natural and democratic system based on the principle that all powers are derived from the people: "With [the Indian tribes in America] the whole authority of government is vested in the whole tribe. Individuals depend upon their reputation of valour and wisdom to give them influence. Their government is genuinely democratical. This was probably the first kind of government among mankind."[13]

To most British subjects, such ideas on equality, liberty, and pursuit of happiness with which many colonists became imbued were heretical. Whether inspired by Indians, European philosophers, or the ancient Greeks, American colonists developed demands for input into governing structures. "The United States founders may have read about Greece, or the Roman Republic, the cantons of the Alps, or the reputed democracy of the tribal Celts, but in the Iroquois and other Indian confederacies they saw, with their own eyes, the self-evidence of what they regarded to be irrefutable truths."[14]

THE CONFEDERATION PERIOD: EARLY AMERICAN DEMOCRACY

The years between the Declaration of Independence (1776) and the ratification of the U.S. Constitution (1789) were ones of violent revolution, temporarily unifying all classes of society, followed by a clever, peaceful political revolution, establishing a quasi-American aristocracy that successfully deflected and then pushed back the forward thrusts of increasing democracy and citizen participation. During the period that Americans lived under the Articles of Confederation, however, the powerful surge in democratic ideals and institutions established a firm hold on American soil that continues to contribute to the erosion of beachheads captured by opponents of democracy.

There were a number of institutions that flourished in the American Confederation Period—some involving the greater democratization of the representative system, some being direct democratic forms of governance.

Virtual versus Actual Representation

American colonists came to think quite differently about political representation than the British. As Gordon Wood points out, English political theory of the time was almost entirely based on the theory of "virtual representation."[15] This meant that elected representatives to the English House of Commons represented all the people—not particular districts, regions, or classes. All citizens—no matter where they lived—were Englishmen and were represented by those in the House of Commons. "None are actually, all are *virtually* represented; for every Member of Parliament sits in the House, not as a Representative of his own Constituents, but as one of the august Assembly by which all the Commons of Great Britain are represented."[16]

So it was truly perplexing to the English when the colonists became so inflamed by the Stamp Act in 1765 and other measures the British took to force the colonies to help pay the Crown's war debts. The colonists screamed "No taxation without representation." They began to unite in challenging the Crown and took actions as citizens, such as the dumping of the tea in Boston Harbor in 1774 to protest British economic imperialism.

The audacity of the colonists shocked the British, who could not understand the colonists' demands for consultation and participation in decision making. The British believed that they already had a representative system of government, a system that represented the interests of all British subjects, including the colonists.[17] Why, they asked, did the colonists demand more rights in government than British citizens who lived in Great Britain enjoyed?

The American colonists thought quite differently about representation, so much so that they were willing to oppose the British government violently if their views and concerns continued to be ignored. In fact, "no political conception was more important to Americans in the entire Revolutionary era than representation."[18] The American idea of representation has been termed "actual representation." John Adams stated his idea of a representative assembly as follows: "in miniature an exact portrait of the people at large. It should think, feel, reason, and act like them."[19]

The colonists did not accept the idea that "virtual representation" was true representation. Instead, they advocated and waged war for "actual representation" committed to "equal electoral districts, the particularity of consent through broadened suffrage, residence requirements for both the elected and the electors, the strict accountability of representatives to the local electorate, indeed, the closest possible ties between members and their particular constituents."[20]

"Instruction of Representatives"

Once the states began to establish their own governments, free of British rule, the issue of the type and role of representatives began to divide Americans. One of the areas of increasing disagreement was over the degree to which the people should "instruct" their delegates to the legislature. A nation formed after armed rebellion of a citizenry that demanded more input, more decision-making powers of the citizens, and more responsiveness of government officials was not likely, however, to readily accept aristocratic rule and the quashing of the democratic, participatory zeal aroused and nourished during the bloody, violent Revolutionary Period.

Actually, from the first years of the Massachusetts settlement, the colonists had drafted clear instructions on what they wanted their representatives to do. In other words, citizens issued written mandates of their wishes to their representatives to ensure that their local interests were heard. Elected representatives in Orange County, North Carolina, were instructed by their constituents to "speak our Sense in every case where we shall expressly declare it, or when you can by any other means discover it."[21] Wood points out that while even the most radical citizens expressed some doubts about requiring legislators to obey every word in the instructions, "in the eyes of most patriots the instructing of representatives had become an undoubted right. And several of the states explicitly provided for the right in their constitutions."[22] During this time, many Americans believed their representatives to be "mere agents or tools of the people who could give binding directions whenever they please to give them."[23]

At this point, American "aristocrats" became extremely uncomfortable with the growing democratic fervor of the masses. It worried them that citizens from all walks of life across the nation considered themselves competent to make governmental decisions and rebelled at the arrogance of representatives who did not adhere to their will.

It was this lack of "proper" respect for elected officials—and the practice of some citizens to disobey or nullify laws that were passed without adhering to instructions—that distressed and repulsed some more "conservative" Americans. They feared the demise of "true" republicanism, which granted only elective power to the citizenry and delegated deliberative power to the elected.

In addition, events leading up to the Revolutionary War demonstrated that even many normally law-abiding and morally upright citizens were ready to disobey laws they considered unfair. This "unsteadiness of the people" finally led Benjamin Franklin to write that "We have been guarding against an evil that old States are most liable to *excess of power* in the rulers, but our present danger seems to be *defect of obedience* in the subjects."[24]

Direct Democratic Organizations: Town Meetings and Grand Juries

Town meetings, begun in the New England colonies in the seventeenth century, have become one of the most notable direct democratic features of American politics. While participation in town meetings often was restricted to adult males, property holders, and church members, the attendees participated equally and usually sought unanimity in their decisions rather than a mere majority.[25] Jane J. Mansbridge describes the extensive activities of town meetings in Dedham, Massachusetts:

> The town meeting created principles to regulate taxation and land distribution; it bought land for town use and forbade the use of it forever to those who could not pay their share within a month; it decided the number of pines each family could cut from the swamp and which families could cover their houses with clapboard. The men who went to that town meeting hammered out the abstract principles under which they would live and regulated the most minute details of their lives; the decisions they made then affected the lives of their children and grandchildren.[26]

The grand jury system began in the American colonies in Massachusetts in 1635. It had developed the reputation in England as being the only buffer between the state and the individual. Colonial grand juries performed several functions: indicting for criminal offenses; making presentments, which consisted of the grand jurors themselves initiating an investigation and offering any evidence they found; proposing legislation; and acting as a watchdog over government officials, departments, and agencies. In some colonies, such as New York, which had no representative assembly, the grand jury "actually assumed direct ordinance making powers."[27]

Although the procedure for selection of grand jurors varied, there was usually a requirement that the juror own property and an exclusion of all women and slaves from participating. Despite the fact that the selection process for grand jurors could be manipulated by members of the established government, during the pre-Revolutionary and Revolutionary Periods, the grand jury developed into an institution with substantial independence and power—often opposing judges.

After the creation of the national government, the state grand juries took over the functions of the earlier grand juries. In his book *The People's Panel*, Richard D. Younger describes the importance of the state grand jury and some of the significant responsibilities assumed by citizens serving on them:

> While the federal grand jury, intimately involved as it was in the political and constitutional battles of the 1790's had yet to prove itself, the local grand jury remained an accepted and essential part of American government. . . . Juries in each of the counties throughout the new nation continued to hear the complaints and protests of any and all persons, to supervise law enforcement activities of the sheriff and constables, and to keep a watchful eye on all other public officials . . . recommended laws for the consideration of the state legislature, and publicly rebuked those public officials guilty of laxity or corruption. . . . For many this service on the grand inquest constituted the only active part, save perhaps for voting, they would ever take in their government.[28]

Constitutional Conventions

During the American Confederation Period, the American political mind also dreamed up the idea of a "constitutional convention," another citizens' institution that could supersede and/or dictate to legislatures. In the emerging American style, constitutions could totally change the structure of governance and were drafted by delegates who were completely independent of and apart from elected legislatures.

Once agreed to by the people, constitutional changes controlled what legislators could or could not do. Of course, constitutional conventions were extraordinary occasions and opened the door for rapid, rather than slow, change. Citizens in post-Revolutionary America understood the importance of constitutional conventions and organized a number of them on a regular basis to reduce aristocratic control of their state governments. Perhaps the most threatening constitution of the time—to the more conservative element in American society—was the Pennsylvania Constitution of 1776. It (1) formalized governmental accountability to citizens; (2) expanded their access to government leaders and records; and (3) expanded citizen participation. Wood describes the result as "the most radical constitution of the Revolutionary Era, which everyone—supporters and critics alike—regarded as a monumental experiment in politics."[29]

A number of drastic innovations were fashioned. First, the two-house legislature was abolished. In its stead was the new, one-house (unicameral) legislative body. Also, to help keep the representatives in check and to remind them constantly that they were there to serve all the people, a broad series of "sunshine-type" laws were installed.

For example, the doors of the assembly were always to be open, its votes were to be published weekly; the press was free to examine its proceedings or those of any part of the government. Every bill passed by the assembly had to be printed for the consideration of the people at large before it could become law in the next legislative sessions.[30]

Because the radical pro-democrats were skeptical of an aristocratic class taking over the assembly, the constitution not only required annual elections, but also included a four-year limit on the term of office of any legislator. Consistent with this democratic sentiment, the constitution also provided for the broadest rights of suffrage of the time.[31]

The newly displaced political groups in Pennsylvania joined together in opposition to the new constitution in order to obstruct its implementation and to undermine this "radical," new government in any way possible. These "anticonstitutionalists" or "the Gentry" (as the pro-democrats called them) argued that "too many ignorant persons . . . were meddling in business that was over their heads . . . undertaking things beyond their reach, and unsettling the social order by advising people to avoid electing gentlemen of the learned."[32]

The anticonstitutionalists ultimately prevailed in their fight against the new government of Pennsylvania. But in the process, they added to the deep division in political and social thinking that was developing in the new American Confederation and helped establish the lines for the ultimate political confrontation between the Federalists and Antifederalists.

The Articles of Confederation

The Articles of Confederation established a decentralized political entity that produced varying forms and degrees of democracy in the United States. Under the Articles, each state was equally represented in the national government. At the same time the state governments were superior to the central government whose powers were limited by those specifically granted by the states. The effect of 13 independent governments uniting in a league to deal only with matters that mutually concerned them—very much like the Iroquois League of Nations—was to allow the maximum diversity and uniqueness of each state to develop.

The decentralized nature of the Confederation, however, produced government and representatives that were more closely a reflection of the values and interests of the people of each state. Power closer to the people also allowed the people to keep closer tabs on those vested with the power to govern, thereby increasing the potential for accountability.

Opposition to the Articles of Confederation came from many quarters, but certainly included those who were alarmed by the democratic penetrations all over the nation. Many yearned for an ebbing of the democratic tide in order to firmly establish a republic ruled by men of wealth, education, and refinement. It is against this backdrop that the U.S. Constitution was drafted covertly in Philadelphia in the summer of 1787.

THE CONSTITUTIONAL PERIOD: REESTABLISHING ELITISM IN AMERICA

The Founders of the U.S. Constitution were men "well above the average in wealth and education."[33] They drafted the Constitution behind closed doors and operated in secret without any public input and without keeping an official record of the proceedings. This was done despite the fact that their legal mandate was limited to amending the existing Articles of Confederation. However, the Founders, advocates of a strong central government who adopted the misnomer Federalists, went significantly beyond their role and created a radically new form of government.

Like those who saw the distortion of republican "virtue" overtaken by the overzealous democratic spirit of the 1780s, the Federalists sought to restore a social and political hierarchical system that would be based on "merit" (wealth + formal education + experience in public affairs + social refinement). Wood states that "the Federalists were filled with an enlightened zeal for energy and efficiency of government set against the turbulence and follies of democracy as expressed by the lower houses of the state legislature, the democratic parts of (state) constitutions."[34]

Federalist Alexander Hamilton put forth strong arguments for the necessity of "a fine union [that] will be the utmost moment to the peace and liberty of the States as a barrier against domestic faction and insurrection."[35] As he saw it, the American Confederation was insufficient to preserve the Union. The situation had "reached the last stages of national humiliation."[36] He saw the Confederation paralyzed and degraded because huge debts were owed to foreigners for their aid during the Revolutionary War; foreign powers held valuable territories in America; Spain excluded the American Confederation from freely navigating the Mississippi; the nation had no credit; and so on. These circumstances, he believed, were caused or intensified because there were no national troops, national treasury, nor government to enforce treaties, pay off debts, or unite states in common cause.

James E. Ferguson argues that an assessment of the American Confederation Period does not provide incontrovertible proof of Hamilton's view of a crisis.[37] In his opinion, the Confederation and the states had done a great deal to stabilize the economy and handle the war debt. Contrary to Hamilton's description of the times, Jensen argues the Confederate Period was marked by extraordinary economic growth. Ferguson points out also that the states were willing to assume the war debt and had absorbed at least one-third of the debt through tax credits, sale of land, outright payments, and so forth. The Confederation Congress, however, composed largely of nationalists, not only clung to the debt, but enlarged it.[38]

Even though merchants and creditors made money during this period, they desired a centralized system to regulate trade, impose national tariffs, and loosen the grip each individual state had over economic policies. Moreover, from the Federalists' point of view, democratic and egalitarian principles accepted by the masses of the time were placing "Demerit on a Footing with Virtue."[39] They felt that many of the problems in the states were due to the "large number of obscure, ignorant, and unruly men occupying the state legislatures."[40] The solution to restore the stability of the government and thereby perpetuate liberty, all agreed, was to replace the loose-knit, locally oriented Confederation with a strong, central government composed of men of "merit."

What was more, the instruction of representatives was totally unacceptable to Federalist thinking and particularly, according to James Madison, when people feel passionately about an issue.[41] Such inventions as citizens committees and citizens conventions—formed to investigate governmental matters and to press political demands—were to be abolished, since from the Federalist perspective, they weakened government and, therefore, the nation. Indeed citizens needed to be reminded that government was deserving of "reverence."[42] Madison also was opposed to such democratic institutions because citizens will "lose their awe of government."[43]

Though most did not share the crisis analysis made by the plutocratic minority voices, there was a near-consensus that some changes needed to be made to the Articles of Confederation in order to ensure their strength both from within as well as outside the Confederation. Thus all the states, except Rhode Island, sent delegates to the Philadelphia Convention to revise the Articles. It became immediately obvious, though, that the delegates were actually a well-organized minority with a shared vision because they "promptly discarded their Congressional mandate and promptly proceeded to the discussion of an entirely *new* constitution,"[44] one "antithetical to liberty which most Americans associated with self rule."[45] As Peter Manicas points out, and most writers on the subject agree, if a Gallup poll had been taken at the time, it would have indicated majority opposition to the new constitution.[46]

ENTER: THE ANTIFEDERALISTS

The relatively undemocratic nature of the new U.S. Constitution did not escape the attention of those who opposed its ratification—the Antifederalists. They were keenly suspicious of the Federalists, who were willing to place so much faith in the "virtue" and "honor" of the "experienced," "educated," monied oligarchy. Had not the Federalists learned that "the Spirit of '76 was not trust in rulers"?[47]

Anti-Elitist Elites

It should be pointed out that the Antifederalists themselves were often men of means and, according to some, were "as socially and intellectually formidable as any Federalist."[48] On the other hand, many Antifederalists were offended by a snobbery and conceit that oozed from the Federalists, whose attitudes and behaviors the Antifederalists found totally inconsistent with the spirit of the American Revolution and with the root values of the new nation itself.

Thus, it is not surprising to find a major, consistent thread throughout Antifederalist writing to be total opposition to the new governmental aristocracy that would be created under the new Constitution. Their primary, stated position against the new, powerful central government was their belief that it would prevent representatives from responding to the multiple interests of the citizenry-at-large and would, instead, respond more quickly and most favorably to the narrow interests of the few (the Gentry).

The Antifederalists, by and large, represented the status quo, in other words, the pro-democratic, active public participation tenor of the time. Their belief was in the common person—but it was not based on the infallibility of the public. It was, instead, deeply nurtured in their distrust of the aristocratic ruling class. "They were inclined to think, with Patrick Henry, that harm is more often done by the tyranny of the rulers than by the licentiousness of the people."[49]

Philadelphiensis, one of the few Antifederalists who preferred direct democracy over representative government,[50] called the framers of the Constitution the "basest conspirators that ever disgraced a country."[51] His belief was that the leading Federalists had connived and deceived the people while all the time they schemed to establish a government that "would be a compound monarchy and aristocracy" without a "tincture of democracy."[52]

Particularly offensive to Philadelphiensis and many of the other Antifederalists was the secretive manner in which the new constitution had been drawn up. He said that the proceedings of the convention, which took place in the "dark conclave" in Philadelphia, were a betrayal of "unsuspecting freemen of America."[53] He believed the covert activities of the convention delegates and the pressures they exerted to rush ratification of the constitution only added weight to his arguments that the Federalists had abandoned the democratic ideals of the new nation.

The Undemocratic Constitution

While the Antifederalists attacked the aristocratic backgrounds and antidemocratic ideology of the Federalists, as well as the undemocratic means of designing the Constitution, they also defined the various ways in which the new "constitution was not sufficiently democratic." For instance, the first House of Representatives would consist of only 65 members.[54] George Clinton was indignant: "The number of senators and representatives proposed for this vast continent does not equal those of the [State of New York]."[55] How could the "middle or lower orders" in society ever be a part of such a body—with so few seats? They were certain that under such a system, "nine times out of ten, men of the elevated classes in the community only can be chosen."[56]

This Antifederalist position was entirely consistent with the prevailing democratic sentiment that supported "actual" representation and instruction of representatives. As Melancton Smith noted, "representatives should be a true picture of the people; possess the knowledge of their circumstances and their wants; sympathize in all their distresses; and be disposed to seek their true interests."[57]

Not only were the Antifederalists aware that different classes existed and needed to be represented, but they recognized that citizens from the larger states would have a tendency to trample on the interests of those in smaller states. It was their view that no large, central government could fully and equally represent the people "from all parts of the union" having "different opinions, customs, and views" and "differences peculiar to Eastern, Middle, and Southern states."[58] Any system that sought to "refine and enlarge the public views" by limiting the number of views and interests that would be represented in the legislative body—as the Federalists proposed—was totally changing the nature of government in the new nation.

The new government, therefore, provided for very little citizen participation in contrast to the expansion of democratic structures developed in the American Confederation Period. For example, the only federal officials elected directly by the people were members of the new House of Representatives, and their terms of office were made to be the shortest of all officeholders. Conversely, as the selection process became further removed from the direct control of the American citizens, the term of office became longer.

The Antifederalists argued that even the single political office—the House of Representatives—for which the citizens voted did not allow much citizen participation. The fact that each representative would represent districts with populations of at least 30,000 people meant that most citizens would not know their representatives and would not be able to elect one of their own—one of the "middling class" (often farmers of modest means).

It was also astonishing to the Antifederalists that the proposed Constitution, which provided for such extensive elitist government, failed to provide an expressed Bill of Rights for individual citizens against potential arbitrary and ruthless central governmental actions. They argued if ever a Bill of Rights were needed, it was needed under this new government, which replaced state and local governmental supremacy. Its new powers to tax, to establish an army, and to declare wars made them all the more concerned that precious political and civil freedoms of individual citizens would be curtailed, if not lost.

Hamilton's defense of not including a Bill of Rights in the new constitution made the Antifederalists even more skeptical. His position was that a written, expressed Bill of Rights was unnecessary under a form of government "founded upon the power of the people and executed by their immediate representatives and servants."[59]

Moreover, according to Hamilton, such a Bill of Rights as demanded by the Antifederalists would be "dangerous." Why? Because it "would contain various exceptions to powers which are not granted; and, on this very account, would afford a colorable pretext to claim more than were granted."[60]

The Antifederalists saw these lines of argumentation as being an insidious and contorted play on thoughts. After all, this new document contained many extremely broad generalities that could throw the door wide open for governmental abuse. For example, the "necessary and proper clause," which allowed Congress to make any law in accordance with its powers to regulate commerce, declare war, support an army, and so forth, could lead to prohibiting freedom of the press or assembly and trample on many personal rights of individual citizens. The Antifederalists also pointed to the "supremacy clause" of Article VI, fearing that it could undermine already existing protections of individuals which they enjoyed under their state constitutions, particularly if the two documents came into conflict.[61] Vagueness and ambiguity did not work in favor of the people—and it was not something to be ignored or embraced.

John DeWitt maintained that history taught that if people did not clearly define their rights and privileges, there were always individuals with "that insatiable thirst for unconditional control over our fellow creatures"[62] who will take the opportunity to distort the meaning of powers granted them to grab as much power as they could. The Bill of Rights finally passed as a compromise between the Federalists and Antifederalists in 1791. It was the guaranteeing of personal freedoms, which was won by the more democratic Antifederalists, that assured an environment in which democracy could grow in the indefinite future.

Indeed, subsequent periods of democratic growth in the United States carried on the legacy of the Antifederalists. As Gordon Wood points out, "Whatever else may be said about the Antifederalists, their populism cannot be impugned. They were the true champions of the extreme kind of democratic and egalitarian politics expressed in the Revolutionary Era."[63]

Although the Constitutional Period was an ideological resistance to the expanding democratic movements of the Revolutionary and American Confederation Periods, it has been followed by movements that established new avenues for the growth of democracy in America.

THE JACKSONIAN PERIOD: THE ERA OF THE "COMMON MAN"

The Jacksonian Period ushered in a new surge of the irrepressible democratic energy. Like the similar-minded Antifederalists who preceded them by half a century, the Jacksonian Democrats were a diverse group who held no single ideology. Where the Antifederalists failed to unite against a government created by a minority, the Jacksonian Democrats were unified in their opposition to the government of privilege they believed to exist in America. While solidly united in what they opposed (not what they advocated or in their reasons for opposition), the Jacksonians helped broaden democratic thinking and citizen participation in America at the national level.

Broadening the Presidential Pool

The flow began to turn toward more democracy and egalitarianism immediately prior to and during Andrew Jackson's term of office. The mere election of Jackson as president was a significant deviation from the narrowing of political opportunity and the growth of American oligarchy, which the Founders would have called the "meritocracy." As Joseph L. Blau points out, every president after George Washington until Jackson was selected from the ranks of the Presidential Cabinet,[64] a pedigreed insiders club.

Jackson became the first president who was elected from outside the inner presidential circle to receive support from all sections of the country. He was a Tennessean, a frontiersman, who served as a rallying force for ideas from all sections of the country and he was not tied to the traditional factions that had molded and run the country for the previous half century.

Another deviation from tradition in the election of Jackson as president was the fact that he was not as well-educated, or from one of the "best" families, as had been the previous presidents, and not a practitioner of the social graces and customs of the Northeast and Southeast. While his predecessors, for the most part, had a distrust, fear, or even scorn of the masses, Jackson embraced an identification with the "common man." He came to symbolize for the first time for the American people the possibility that any citizen (a restrictive term at the time, since blacks and women and many non–property holders were not classified as such) could become president.[65]

The New "Spoils" System: Bringing the Common Man into Other Governmental Positions

Another important democratizing feature of the Jackson presidency was the implementation of the "spoils system." Jackson's theory was that there was no particular education or experience necessary for government service, but that "any citizen was competent to the performance of any duty within government."[66] To his critics, Jackson was simply awarding government jobs to his friends and handing out political payoffs. In truth, all presidents had a "spoils" mentality. In this case, though, the patronage system also represented a strong ideological deviation from Jackson's predecessors that was a product of his times. It was a period in American history in which there were greater demands for universal suffrage, abolition of imprisonment for debt, and representation of the working class in government.

Jackson also viewed the spoils system as a necessary "rotation in office" and a guarantee against bureaucratic tyranny. He rejected the Whig arguments expounding bureaucratic expertise derived from years of experience. Instead, he argued that not only could all men serve the public, but it was essential to good public service that men not remain permanently in government jobs because the longer they stayed in office the more apt they were "to acquire a habit of looking with indifference upon the public interests and of tolerating conduct from which an unpracticed man would revolt."[67] As Frank Otto Gatell and John M. McFauk point out, the Whig tirades against Jackson's spoils system and its replacing expertise with inexperience did not dampen his egalitarian spirit. After all, he had not forgotten that "the Adams forces had called him a nonexpert in government, unfit to govern."[68]

Of course, not all men from aristocratic backgrounds or prestigious occupations were dismissed from appointed government positions in favor of uneducated and inexperienced common people. As a matter of fact, Jackson's attempt to democratize the elite fell far short of his goal, since he frequently relied on criteria used by his predecessors—education, family reputation, previous positions of political leadership, eminence—to provide a practical guide for determining talent and honesty. Jackson's spoils legacy was actually a continuation of a trend begun by Thomas Jefferson, which was to place a greater significance on education than aristocratic background in appointing government officials. This also indirectly led to the expansion of the educational system creating "free tax-supported schools for all Americans, and thus [making] it possible for the newly enfranchised masses to pick up the training so essential for the performance of high political roles."[69]

The Social, Economic, and Political Divisions in the Jackson Era

The class struggle that was fought during the Jacksonian Period was actually between two levels of the middle class: upper and lower middle class. The upper middle class, composed of industrial and commercial capitalists and financiers, benefited from the Hamiltonian program of subsidy, protection, and monopoly that had become the governmental economic policy. The Jacksonians referred to it as the politics of "privilege." The program for this group called for a high protective tariff, the building of roads and canals at government expense, and a strong central government.

On the other side was the lower middle class, composed of landowners, farmers, artisans, and mechanics, who were taxed for roads and canals built by the government and for subsidies that protected industries that they believed benefited only the industrial and commercial interests. They were joined by states rights advocates, who feared such concentration of power in the federal government, and those who preferred pure democracy. Their interests became represented by the Jacksonian Democrats, who called for lowered tariffs, removal of special privileges for corporations, local control over local improvements, maintenance of states rights, universal suffrage, and expanded participation of the lower middle classes in government. Blau points out that the Jacksonians were good politicians, more alert to trouble brewing than the Whigs, and aware that "laborers could not forever be excluded from representation in a country whose revolution had been inaugurated with the slogan 'No taxation without representation.' "[70]

The Jacksonians, and notably James Fenimore Cooper (who came from an aristocratic, landowning family), criticized the Whig "stake in society" principle that had widespread support throughout the short American constitutional history. This principle rested on the theory that only property owners should have the right to vote because only they had an interest or "stake" in government. The Whig doctrine exemplified the hostility toward the masses that Tocqueville found among wealthy Americans.[71]

In describing political life in America after Jackson's "democratic party got the upper hand [and] took exclusive possession of the conduct of affairs," Tocqueville argues the wealthy tried to hide their wealth from the masses who had so much control in government and whom they had to relate to as equals in public matters. However, "beneath this artificial enthusiasm and these obsequious attentions to the preponderating power, it is easy to perceive that the rich have a hearty dislike of the democratic institutions of their country. The people form a power which they at once fear and despise."[72] The Whigs, therefore, repeatedly argued, as had the Federalists before them, that self-government and popular suffrage were not natural rights, but privileges—privileges that should be exercised only by those possessed of property and intelligence.

The Jacksonian Democrats had a different view of prosperity and how to achieve it. Many of the Jacksonian Democrats (although not all) were truly interested "in political democracy, in social justice, and in the maintenance of a general condition of liberty and equality. . . . They were more alive than were the Whigs to the potential menace of privilege that existed in specially chartered corporations."[73] Their move toward more democracy was to attack privilege and to take up the causes of the People's Party, the Workingmen's Party, and other political movements that gained momentum in reaction to the increasing powers and abuses of the industrial and commercial capitalists.

Jacksonian Democracy: The Reestablishment of
Antifederalist Thought and Action

Lee Benson calls the Jacksonian Period "the Transformation of American Society from the Aristocratic Liberal Republic of the Late-Eighteenth Century to the Populistic Egalitarian Democracy of the Mid-Nineteenth Century."[74] Benson's ideas about a transformation or transition may be overstated, but there can be no doubt that the Jacksonian Period was indicative of a change from the predominant ideology that had been established in U.S. government by the Federalists at the beginning of the Constitutional Period. Antifederalist thought had not died. It had lain dormant and reemerged as a newly respected and major political perspective. The populistic and egalitarian views of the Jacksonians are frequently compared to Jefferson's political theories and views expressed by Tom Paine, Jeremy Bentham, and more radical eighteenth-century democrats.[75] Their ethical views had their roots in the English Enlightenment of the "moral sense" school in England and Scotland in the eighteenth century.[76]

Thus, Jacksonian Democracy did not spring up overnight. It was not designed by Jackson. It was a product of the political tensions between elitist and democratic thought that have always been present in American politics. There are periods in which different sides prevail, but neither is ever completely successful or totally quashed.

While most noted for its revival in the belief in the common man, the Jacksonian Period saw substantial changes in the political equality of American citizens. For example, in many areas, suffrage was extended to propertyless white males and the "stake in society" theory became an albatross around the necks of its advocates who were defeated in election after election across the United States.

The political liberalism of the Jacksonians embraced a populism that fought not only to increase citizen participation through expanding voting eligibility, but also sought to give American voters more powers than they had under Federalist-inspired government through (a) popular election of more government officials and (b) the popular nomination of candidates by delegated party conventions "fresh from the people."[77] For example, in New York, not only was there expanded suffrage, but for the first time (in 1826) the president and justices of the peace were popularly elected by the people and nominations were no longer secured in private caucuses, but were chosen by popularly elected delegates who attended political conventions.[78] More direct accountability to the people was built into these reforms. While a far cry from citizen-initiated conventions called to establish public policy or the instruction of representatives of the Revolutionary and American Confederation Periods, these reforms began to overcome the resistance of increased aristocratic control over American government and to regenerate the flow of the democratic wave that had been dammed up for two score years.

New calls for public education were made by Democrats (as well as by their opponents). Concerns for the rights of the "common man" received new attention. A more active, aware, educated, and informed citizenry was created. Strengthening the foothold of democratic thought in U.S. politics built a firm foundation for the later surges.

The Civil War victory of the Union produced the next major change in extending the voting franchise. The Fourteenth Amendment, a product of Reconstruction in 1868, allowed blacks to vote in all states for the very first time. It was a dramatic and drastic increase in the potential for citizen participation. Except for a brief period, however, in which blacks held offices and participated in politics—while many whites were denied these rights as punishment for trying to disband the Union—the real political effects of this constitutional change did not take place until a century later. It was left to the Progressive Era to become the next period to produce the greatest permanent changes in citizen participation in the United States.

THE PROGRESSIVE ERA: REESTABLISHING DEMOCRACY IN AMERICAN GOVERNMENT

The Progressive Era is one of the most controversial periods in American history. Historians, political scientists, and commentators hold radically different views of the period. Was it primarily a democratic movement? Was it activated and driven by economic concerns? Did it seek to expand participation or reestablish displaced powers? Was it primarily liberal or conservative? Did it succeed or fail in its goals?

As David M. Kennedy and numerous other scholars have pointed out, many thousands of individuals called themselves Progressives during the first quarter of the twentieth century.[79] Can any one interpretation of who they were, what motivated them, what they sought to achieve, and what they accomplished speak for the Progressives as a whole? What is clear, though, is that there was a reawakening of the democratic spirit and fervor in the Progressive Era. In their book *The Case Against the Constitution*, John F. Manley and Kenneth M. Dolbeare point out that many historians and political scientists believe that democracy was established for the first time in the Progressive Era since the expansion of citizen participation possibilities ran counter to the Constitution as originally designed—that is, to "*permit political participation* but *prevent democracy* in the United States."[80]

While the Jacksonian Period ushered in a new respect for the "common man," it was a period that focused on elites and/or holders of power. It is not noted for its emphasis on more citizen participation in government—except as it related to expanding the voting franchise. It is more renowned for its emphasis on providing the opportunity for one to achieve power in the United States (even the highest office in the nation) regardless of background, status, education, or wealth and for providing the necessary philosophical foundation for future democratic changes. In the Progressive Era, however, the American democratic wave pulsed in a totally new direction—and it was an extremely intense, strong, and new course of democratic energy.

The Progressive Movement: Elitist Reforms to Maintain the Status Quo Ante?

The Progressive Era, which focused much of its attention on limiting the ever-expanding powers of the corporations and the corporate elites in the United States, also generated the next level of democratic change in America by increasing the means by which citizens exercised power in the United States. The growth of the Progressive Movement in the United States paralleled an era where tremendous corporate expansion was accompanied by an increasing popular awareness that government was getting further and further away from the control of the people.

It is true that many Progressive leaders were men of wealth—sometimes great wealth—and many of them sought to regain their own special status in society.[81] But the period itself is celebrated for the dedication of other leaders and many rank-and-file Progressives: "intelligent, decent people who were giving their best to the [movement] without self-interest, and solely in the hope of forging a weapon with which they could fight for the things they believed in."[82] Many Progressives shared the views of Progressive newspaper editor William Allen White, who argued that "as the state grew more powerful, it had to become a more democratic institution, more accessible to the people and more responsive to the popular will."[83] White's guiding ideology was the belief that the "remedy for the ills of democracy was more democracy."[84]

There are several insightful interpretations of the Progressive Era that uncover the undemocratic and elitist motives behind many of the changes that occurred.[85] For example, it is viewed as a response to the challenges of the Socialist Movement and the growing unrest of the working class, immigrants, and powerless in America, who were described by Louis Brandeis as living under conditions "worse than that of the Negro under slavery."[86] Amos Pinchot, a very wealthy Progressive, pointed out that the working conditions of labor (the long hours, the low salaries, the blacklisting of those with unpopular views, in other words, union organizers and socialists) were inhumane and destructive. He noted that at least under slavery, "only owners of little foresight and of exceptionally brutal nature treated their property so as to destroy its value."[87] In the United States, the large corporations seemed to have no regard for the human condition of the workers. They could easily be replaced with eager new immigrants when they lost their usefulness.

Some argue, therefore, that the democratic changes that took place during the Progressive Era were clearly guided by the elites who wished to reform the U.S. economic system so as to maintain it. This actually resulted in less equality and opportunity than a more radical change in the economic and political system would have produced. Writings of Progressive politicians at the time lend credence to this view. Theodore Roosevelt—a paragon of patrician privilege—made careful distinctions between Socialists and Progressives. To him the Socialists promoted class consciousness, which would certainly upset the social order, while the Progressives promoted social consciousness, which would not take away the powers of businesses but would, instead, make them more responsive to society's needs.[88] Roosevelt took the Progressive view—rooted in Jeffersonian thought—that assumed the "innate decency of man" and also applied it to the nature of business. His conservative, reform approach to business found him and other Progressive leaders often in partnership with business, to the detriment of more fundamental democratic change in America. Nevertheless, as the Reverend Jesse Jackson is fond of saying, "the people are usually ahead of the leaders." It may be through politicians that Americans ultimately have to effect change, but at times politicians find themselves forced to respond to the strong demands of the people. The Progressive politicians were much more conservative and far less innovative than many of the activists in the movement.[89] Yet the attitudes and political climate that prevailed at the time made it clear that the politicians had to respond, not merely rhetorically, but in concrete ways.

The Progressive's Democratic Legacy

Many of the economic reforms of the Progressive Period are well known—the federal income tax amendment, the modern national banking system, regulatory agencies to exercise some measure of control over transportation and manufacturing, and so on. Acknowledging the changes in tax laws and business regulation, however, Progressive William Allen

White adds, "the important thing, the permanent thing, manifest in our growth as a people is the growth of democratic institutions—the broadening and deepening of the power of the people."[90] These democratic changes ranged from democratizing elitist institutions to expanding the voting franchise to allowing citizens to make laws directly.

Democratizing Elitist Institutions

Tied to the economic reforms was the belief that "money and aristocracy" had to be removed from controlling politicians and power had to be given to the people.[91] A number of reforms that democratized heavily elitist political institutions can be attributed to the Progressives. First, in limiting corporate power over and money in the political system, the Progressives led the successful move to establish the first mandatory record keeping of campaign contributions (1907). Next they achieved a prohibition on corporate contributions to political campaigns for federal office. Then, in 1925, Congress passed the Corrupt Practices Act, which limited the amount of money that could be spent on congressional campaigns. These alterations in campaign financing not only affected individual candidates, who had to devise campaign strategies to appeal more to the people, but began to change the relationship between political parties and the people.

Prior to the restrictions on corporations, S. J. Duncan-Clark, a particularly eloquent and insightful Progressive Party leader, argued that corporations had established a particularly insidious plutocracy in America, one that controlled both the Democratic and Republican parties. The political parties had been used as a pretense of democracy—allowing the people a voice while the "moneyed few" controlled the leaders and therefore the party platforms and practices. Duncan-Clark described how cleverly the corporations controlled party politics in the name of democracy.[92]

So, changing who controlled the political parties was considered an important priority of the Progressives. Thus, Progressives began to implement changes in the actual operation of the parties. For example, they believed it essential to the integrity of democracy that voting within party organizations be done by secret ballot. It was believed that public voting was vulnerable to manipulation by those bent on corrupting the democratic process through threat, intimidation, and bribery. Secret ballot was the best means to maximize free choice made by conscience.

After the secret ballot was instituted in party elections, the Progressives moved to make the parties more open and democratic. In many of the states, the direct primary was instituted. Party candidates were no longer selected by a tiny elite of party leaders in conventions, but were nominated directly from the people.[93] Minnesota became the first state to employ the direct primary, which allows for the state to finance and to determine the method for selection of party nominees for public office rather than leaving the decision to individual parties in the states.

The Progressives challenged the theory that the party convention system is necessary because there "is superior wisdom in delegated assemblies." Instead, they argued that the party convention system itself "has become the convenient tool of bosses, machines and special interests."[94] Their success, however, in establishing direct primaries was sporadic, with many states retaining the party convention system or instituting indirect or closed primaries. Thus, it was a Progressive reform that remained exclusively in the hands of the individual states which has produced varying degrees of success in expanding the ability of all citizens to participate in the process of nominating candidates for office.

A more dramatic and comprehensive Progressive-led move to democratize institutionalized elitism in the American system occurred at the constitutional level with an amendment to the U.S. Constitution that required compliance by all of the states. The Seventeenth Amendment, adopted in 1913, gave all U.S. citizens the right to elect U.S. senators directly. Prior to this change, senators were elected indirectly by being selected by the state legislatures. Amendment Seventeen was the first and last amendment that expanded the number of federal officials elected by the people.

Expanding Suffrage

The greatest expansion of citizen voting participation opportunities in American history came with the passage of the Nineteenth Amendment in 1920 giving women the right to vote. The Progressive Movement and Party were among the leading crusaders for women's rights. Even before women received suffrage in all the states, Duncan-Clark pointed out, women were included as both auditors and speakers in "all conventions, conferences and gatherings of those interested in the Progressive programme. . . . She has been into the party councils, and has been given a position of leadership in no degree less prominent than that of men. Moreover a significant fact is that her presence and the promise of her larger participation in the duties of citizenship and of government have been greeted with greater enthusiasm than any other phase of the Movement."[95] The Progressive Party professed quite strongly that it refused to recognize sex distinction in the rights of citizenship.[96]

Innovative Direct Democracy

Progressives, however, did not limit their vision of a greater American democracy to trying only to make elitist institutions less elitist, or to get more citizens to participate in a quasi-democratic, republican system. In a historic move away from a reliance upon representative democracy toward a system with more direct democracy, the Progressives were successful in establishing reforms in several states that allowed citizens to directly make laws through initiative, approve or disapprove legislative action through referendum, and directly recall elected officials for not responding to the will of the people.

Even in the heyday of democratic activity in the American Confederation Period, where citizens in some states held their own conventions, instructed representatives, and investigated government leaders, the rights and opportunities of so many American citizens had never been as broad. Although indirect initiative was established in South Dakota as early as 1898, it was considered inadequate by most Progressives since the proposed law had to go to the state legislature first for action. If the legislature did not pass the law or enact it, it was required to refer the initiative to the people to vote on in the next general election. However, there were no means by which to compel the legislature to observe this constitutional requirement if they chose not to place the initiative on the ballot.

The first successful direct initiative process was established in Oregon in 1902. One Progressive called Oregon's initiative and referendum laws "the very foundation of progress in the state."[97] Not only does Oregon's initiative process apply to statutory legislation, but it also can be used to make amendments to the state constitution. Progressives praised Oregon's initiative law for the responsible way in which it involved the citizenry. Its procedures included a way to inform the public that became a model copied by other states, including South Dakota.

A major aspect of this system was the voters' pamphlet. It contained information on all initiative issues compiled by the secretary of state. Included in the pamphlet as well were arguments for and against the measure that were paid for and inserted by private citizens and organizations. Duncan-Clark stated: "This 'voter's text book' is the chief reason why the initiative and referendum have proved in Oregon to be so useful an expression of intelligent citizenship."[98]

Benjamin Parke DeWitt, the first historian of the Progressive Movement, saw "Progressivism as a successful episode in the continuing development of American democracy. In the tradition of democratic reform that stretched from Jefferson through Jackson, the abolitionists, and the Populists, Progressivism, to DeWitt, represented the latest in a series of triumphs of the less privileged over the powerful."[99]

Describing the change that took place in the Progressive Era and its impact on democracy in the United States, White states: "Democracy is arming itself with the full power of the ballot. It is vastly more important that it shall have weapons and equipment for the fight than that it shall have a programme."[100] In actuality, for many Progressives the process became the program—the means as important as the ends. "The broadening and deepening of the power of the people as shown by the adoption of the secret ballot, the purification of the party system, the spread of the direct primary, and the popular acceptance of the initiative and referendum and the recall"[101] contributed to a society—in the eyes of most active American citizens—that would result in more equality, fairness, and justice for all.

THE 1960S AND BEYOND: BURSTS OF CITIZEN PARTICIPATION

The 1960s spawned perhaps the greatest and most varied increase in citizen participation in U.S. history. Alienated, oppressed, underrepresented, ignored groups in society including blacks, women, and youth rose to challenge the status quo and to demand effective participation in the political system of the United States. It was a time when Americans began to examine the extent to which the laws and practices of the land lived up to the ideals expressed in the Declaration of Independence and the Bill of Rights; a time when citizens sought not only more democracy, but more equality and more justice; a time when numerous citizens actively embraced civil disobedience and confronted political leaders; a time when excluded groups came to understand that rights in America were not granted by enlightened leaders, but gained through struggle; a time when freedom was lost by some in order to obtain greater freedom for all.

The Black Civil Rights Movement

A major component of the expansion of citizen participation in the United States during the 1960s was the black Civil Rights Movement that demanded adherence to the political and legal principles established, but long ignored, in the Fourteenth Amendment of the Constitution.

Laws Alone Do Not Freedom Make. While the Thirteenth, Fourteenth, and Fifteenth Amendments had abolished slavery, granted black citizens equal protection under state as well as federal laws, and prohibited the denial of voting privileges due to one's race, black people had made very little headway in obtaining equal political opportunity in American society. Their second-class citizenship was perpetuated decades after the abolition of slavery through Jim Crow laws that segregated the black and white races in virtually all areas of public life and through stiff voting requirements, such as the poll tax and literacy tests.

Although black Americans had struggled for parity even as slaves, it took a civil war in America to terminate the legal right of white Americans to treat them as private property. Then, even though Congress passed the Civil Rights Act of 1875 to provide specifics for Fourteenth Amendment guarantees, and to forbid discrimination in public accommodations on the basis of race, the U.S. Supreme Court in 1883 ruled such civil rights legislation to be unconstitutional. Justice Bradley argued that the Fourteenth Amendment only addressed deprivation of rights by states and did not encompass private acts of discrimination. He added ironically that black Americans could no longer be the "special favorite of the law" but must take on the "rank of mere citizen."[102] This decision, plus the 1896 *Plessy* decision (which established the doctrine that as long as facilities and/or accommodations were equal, segregating blacks was compatible with the Constitution), contributed to the denial of equal rights and opportunities for black people in the United States for nearly a century after such rights were constitutionally granted.

Although there were many illustrations of a continuing black struggle for equality prior to the 1960s, the Civil Rights Movement did not become a cohesive force until the 1950s. Rosa Parks, a black seamstress, often is credited for bringing the black protest movement to national attention in 1955 when she refused to give her seat to a white man and move to the back of a bus. Actually a lesser-known black woman, Linda Carol Brown, had earlier been a party to a federal suit—*Brown v. Board of Education* (1954)—that led to the Supreme Court's formal reversal of the "separate but equal" doctrine established in *Plessy* and its declaration that separate educational facilities were inherently unequal and therefore unconstitutional.

Modern political science literature is replete with evidence that although the U.S. Supreme Court can declare a decision, it cannot enforce it.[103] Except for a few notable incidents—Dwight Eisenhower sending troops to Little Rock, Arkansas, in 1957 to enforce the *Brown* decision; John Kennedy sending federal marshals to Oxford, Mississippi, in 1962 to allow a black student's entrance into the state university; and the nationalization of the Alabama National Guard in 1963 to prohibit Governor George Wallace from blocking integration in Alabama—the Supreme Court decision remained unenforced for over a decade in the South until federal legislation was passed to deny funding to any state that ignored the civil rights acts of the Congress.

Emphasis on Nontraditional Forms of Participation. Blacks did not sit idly by accepting unjust laws once Rosa Parks initiated the nonviolent act of civil disobedience to openly defy the segregation of buses in Montgomery, Alabama. The bus boycotts in Alabama spread and expanded into other forms of citizen defiance such as "freedom riders" ignoring the segregation regulations on buses all over the South; sit-ins at lunch counters; and demonstrations in protest of various types of segregation in cities across the South. Various political groups, impatient with the slow progress made in Congress and the courts, formed to advance civil rights and to fight injustice—the Southern Christian Leadership Conference (SCLC) headed by Dr. Martin Luther King, Jr.; the Congress of Racial Equality (CORE) led by James Farmer; and the Student Non-Violent Coordinating Committee (SNCC) led by John Lewis and later by Stokely Carmichael and H. Rap Brown.[104]

The work of these groups was in nonviolent forms of citizen participation, in other words, protest, that often led to deliberate violation of laws (civil disobedience) that discriminated against and repressed and humiliated black Americans. Martin Luther King, Jr., who was arrested in Birmingham in 1963 for parading without a permit, echoed themes rich in U.S. history beginning with American Revolutionaries fighting oppressive British laws when he responded to critics who asked, "How can you advocate breaking some laws and obeying others?" He stated: "One has a moral responsibility to disobey unjust laws. . . . An unjust law is a code inflicted upon a minority which that minority had no part in enacting or creating because they did not have the unhampered right to vote."[105]

In August 1963, nearly a decade after the Brown decision, black leaders organized a "March on Washington" to protest the lack of federal support of civil rights. Over two hundred thousand people—both black and white—participated in the march that was highlighted by King's "I Have a Dream" speech, which spoke of his vision of blacks in America being "free at last." Pres. John F. Kennedy sought civil rights legislation that same year that would provide more federal support for black equality, but Congress showed no willingness to act on the extensive Kennedy package.

Less than a year after Kennedy's assassination, however, Pres. Lyndon B. Johnson was able to get the legislation through Congress and to sign the Civil Rights Act into law in 1964. The law prohibited racial or religious discrimination in public accommodations; discrimination by unions and employers on the basis of race, color, sex, or religion; and, most importantly for political participation, the use of different standards for blacks and whites who attempted to register to vote. Commissions were created to ensure the law was enforced and authorization was given to the government to cut off federal funds for institutions and organizations that violated its provisions.[106]

In 1965, Congress dramatically aided the black struggle for the right to participate in American politics by passing the Voting Rights Act. Federal examiners were appointed to stop discrimination in voter registration in the South. Voter registration drives were enacted and became extremely successful among blacks.

Charles Hamilton, a noted black political scientist at Columbia University, analyzed data from a 1973 Voter Education Project and concluded that black participation in voting had more than doubled since the Voting Rights Act.[107] Hamilton also noted that the increased number of black voters in Southern states "elected many of their own race to public offices at all levels of government—congressional, state, county, and municipal."[108] Presently there are many black mayors throughout the country, including some of the nation's largest cities, such as Atlanta, Los Angeles, New York, Cleveland, Detroit, and so forth.

While studies indicate that the civil rights legislation led to increased voter registration among blacks and a significant increase in the number of black elected officials,[109] political scientists such as Benjamin Ginsberg and Edward S. Greenberg point out that mere participation in *electoral* politics is not sufficient to provide greater opportunity for blacks or more economic equality for them. Indeed, Ginsberg provides data to demonstrate that as black registration increased and more black leaders were elected, the number of civil rights demonstrations, the number of pieces of legislation particularly favorable to blacks, and the ratio of black income to white income decreased.[110] Other data indicates that compared to 1969 when the black unemployment rate at 7 percent was double the white unemployment rate, in 1985 the black unemployment rate at over 15 percent was nearly triple the white unemployment rate.[111] The conclusion that both Ginsberg and Greenberg derive from black participation data is that other forms of political activity, such as boycotts, marches, demonstrations, sit-ins, and civil disobedience can be—and certainly in the black struggle were—more effective than voting.[112]

Although the current participation data tends to support the view that the expansion of suffrage often paves the way for "political quiescence," it has become a necessary first step for citizens to build upon in expanding democratic participation within the system. The gains of the Civil Rights Movement were limited, as Greenberg points out, because the goals were limited—in other words, to expand civil rights and liberties. Black leaders such as King felt expanded suffrage had to be achieved before other conditions of blacks could be addressed.

The legitimacy that blacks have achieved within the system has provided the basis for the Reverend Jesse Jackson, a student of King's, to carry the struggles for equal opportunity beyond the very narrow focus of voting rights. He gained prominence through founding and developing PUSH, an organization devoted to encouraging education among urban blacks. His efforts have aided in the dramatic increase in the number of blacks obtaining a high school education—nearly triple the number who reached such levels in 1960.[113] In just two decades after the King assassination, Jackson, a black Democratic candidate for the American presidency forming a "rainbow" coalition of all races and stressing economic equality, outran five white opponents and came in second for the 1988 Democratic Party's nomination for president behind a Northeastern Greek-American liberal with financial backing more than four times greater than Jackson's. In addition, Jackson won or finished second in state primaries that were almost exclusively white. The connection between the blacks' ability to fully participate in the American system and their ability to win positions of power that represent black (and other) citizens in governmental decision making has been dramatic. Given the opportunity to participate, they have demonstrated their eagerness, commitment, and understanding of how to convert votes into political power. Moreover, the mid-1960s ushered in a new era of citizen participation with blacks as the spearhead of a civil rights movement that also impacted upon and inspired other ethnic minorities and women and clearly established the effectiveness of nontraditional forms of political participation in America.

The Women's Liberation Movement

Even as the Declaration of Independence in 1776 was being drafted declaring all men to be equal, Abigail Adams wrote to her husband to remind him and other American Revolutionaries that they should not forget the women. She wrote: "If particular care and attention is not paid to the Ladies, we are determined to foment a Rebellion, and will not hold ourselves bound by any laws in which we have no voice, or Representation."[114] Not only did John Adams ignore what his wife said, but so did the Constitution and the Bill of Rights—which did not recognize women as free and equal.

During the struggle for the abolition of slavery, women involved in the freedom movement began to draw attention to their own lack of equality and denial of citizenship. It dismayed many that the Fifteenth Amendment of 1870 granted the right to vote to black men and continued the denial of women's suffrage. A few years later, during the centennial celebration of the signing of the Declaration of Independence, Susan B. Anthony, one of the leading suffragists, pointed out that "the women of this nation, in 1876, have greater cause for discontent, rebellion, and revolution than the men in 1776."[115]

The first state to grant women voting privileges was Wyoming in 1890. It was not until 1920, though, that women ultimately got the right to vote at the national level. Most women came to realize, as black males had discovered a half century before, that the mere privilege of voting fell far short of granting equality or full citizenship in the United States. It took the Women's Liberation Movement of the 1960s and 1970s to pursue that equality in reality, the one that had been verbally granted in the Nineteenth Amendment. In the same manner that blacks had to win federal legislation to enhance and ensure a constitutionally granted equality, women needed other avenues, besides voting, to gain equal political—and economic—participation. As long as the female gender is discriminated against in hiring practices, wage scales, business and property privileges, and other areas of public and private life, the right to vote does little to enhance women's citizenship potential.

Under pressure from women activists, who organized protest demonstrations and political action groups, Pres. John F. Kennedy created a Commission on the Status of Women in 1961. The findings of the commission indicated that women were "second-class citizens" in America and led to the establishment of similar commissions at the state level and a national advisory council to advance the equality of American women. Legislation that followed included the Equal Pay Act of 1963 and the amendment of the 1964 Civil Rights Act to prohibit sex discrimination in private employment.

Two very important feminist political groups were formed during this period in order to mobilize women in the struggle for equality. In 1966, the National Organization for Women (NOW) was organized; its aim, to pressure political leaders to recognize and respond to the views and concerns of women. Not content to allow the political power to legislate, enforce, and interpret laws to remain in the hands of men, the National Women's Political Caucus was founded in 1972. Its objective was to elect more women to public office, to lobby political parties and the government for action on issues important to women, and to press for ratification of an Equal Rights Amendment to the United States Constitution assuring equality of women in all aspects of society.

Opportunities for citizen participation of women in U.S. politics have had to be won through collective struggle—as they have been for blacks, as well as for the original founders of the nation. The fact that the Equal Rights Amendment failed to gain sufficient support for passage is an indication that women still have a long way to go in American society. While there are growing numbers of women mayors and representatives, and an occasional elected female governor or senator, none has ever been seriously considered by the American public for the United States presidency. The only female vice-presidential candidate, Geraldine Ferraro, concluded that the intense scrutiny she and her family received when she ran for the second highest office in the land had a lot to do with the fact that she was a woman being subjected to higher standards than her male peers.

The gains for women trail those achieved by blacks. As an example, the 101st Congress (1988–1990) is illustrative of the American patriarchal political system. It was composed of 91 percent Caucasian males, 5 percent women, and 5 percent blacks. Considering that women comprise over half of the U.S. population and blacks around 12 percent, women are underrepresented by approximately 90 percent and blacks by over 50 percent. Meanwhile, males are overrepresented by 90 percent. Of course, women obtained voting privileges 50 years after black males. This could be a contributing factor to the slower progress in other areas. In addition, the number and size of the civil rights sit-ins, demonstrations, and boycotts overshadow the efforts of women. Also, the public and private violence that characterized some of the black Civil Rights Movement may have catalyzed changes more rapidly. The task for women also has been complicated by the need to unite more diverse and dispersed groups—crossing economic and racial lines in every corner of society.

Nevertheless, the tide has turned for women in the United States. In just two generations, polls show that the American public has gone from a 22 percent approval rating of women in business in 1937 to 89 percent in 1986. Also, in 1937 32 percent said they were willing to vote for a qualified woman for president, but in 1986 88 percent stated a willingness to vote for a qualified woman for president.[116] While women have actually not advanced much beyond tokenism in the higher echelons of government and business, the percentage of their entries into professional schools and male-dominated occupations continues to rise. Other political changes abound—such as the Hawaii Democratic Party's rules that require half the delegates to its political conventions to be female.

The Continuing Struggle for Equal Participation

The movement toward expanding rights and opportunities for women and blacks has been joined by other ethnic minorities and young people demanding their own input into and active participation in the political system. During the Vietnam war, young people protested vehemently that a significant portion of those dying in a battle waged by this country were not even allowed to vote—due to age restrictions—for the representatives who sent them off to war. Less than two years after the 18-year-olds received the right to vote by way of the Twenty-Sixth (and last) Amendment to the Constitution in 1971, the Vietnam war, which had lasted under four U.S. presidents, ended.

Fred Harris, a former U.S. Senator from Oklahoma, writes: "Equal rights and full political equality, promised in the Declaration of Independence, are still not realities, but unmistakable advances have been made in modern times. These advances have come largely because people have organized themselves to demand equal treatment . . . because that is what they deserve."[117]

The democratic spirit born in the American Revolution has thrived in the United States. Disenfranchised, excluded, or oppressed segments of society have taken turns keeping the spirit alive through continuing demands for participation—meaningful participation that includes more than mere voting rights. Each new manifestation of that spirit seems to bring renewed vigor to the democratic energy and provides more advanced positions for an even more inclusive and active democracy.

SUMMARY

From the American Confederation Period, U.S. citizens have demanded more than mere voting privileges. As various disenfranchised groups in society have received the right to vote, they also have come to realize or conclude that voting alone, or the participation in other forms of electoral politics (such as contributing to a campaign, working in a campaign, attending candidate forums, and so forth), is inadequate in a nation that has long claimed its international mission is to "Make the world safe for democracy."

It seems that in the history of citizen participation in the United States, each movement or period builds on the former and the result is that democratic trends rarely lose the totality of gains made, although the net gains may be small indeed. For example, once the voting franchise is extended, and once powers of citizens are increased under our Constitution, citizens do not yield those gains. They (or succeeding generations) want more, demand more, and move toward obtaining more. There are periods of more or less activity of citizens, more or less rebellion against injustice and inequality, more or less energy to struggle or hope for success, but there is rarely a retrenchment to remove the legally increased powers of citizens.

One is struck while tracing this phenomenon by the strong quantum characteristics of an often unpredictable pattern. As with the unpredictability of the stock market or the national economy, one finds it difficult, if not impossible, to find a precise cause-effect relationship as to when a burst of democratization will appear or what form it will take. A review of the past can help one develop probabilities of the next surge or to discover similar patterns, yet the randomness that crops up in our natural environment (volcanic eruptions, tornados, hurricanes) also occurs in our sociopolitical environment. It is with this understanding that I use the historical information to study citizen participation in the United States today and move to help design new forms of citizen participation that can continue the forward push toward a more democratic society.

Chapter 3 will examine how political scientists, theorists, and activists have defined, studied, and helped expand citizen participation in America. As one moves from a predominantly Newtonian-influenced worldview to one that incorporates principles defined in quantum physics, the way in which one studies, analyzes, and values citizen participation also changes. The emphasis focuses less on cause and effect than on interaction and interconnection. Thus, voting for representatives can no longer be the primary or exclusive focus of empirical study, either as the independent or dependent variable. Instead, the analysis should include a study of the various means by which citizens interact and the ways in which the environment (broadly defined) interfaces participation. The following chapters on citizen participation will place the emphasis on examining process and mechanisms designed to maximize the democratic process in a world of uncertainty.

NOTES

1. Forrest McDonald, *Novus Ordo Seclorum: The Intellectual Origins of the Constitution* (Lawrence: University of Kansas Press, 1985), p. 62.

2. Ibid., p. 158.

3. See Bruce E. Johansen, *Forgotten Founders: How the American Indian Helped Shape Democracy* (Boston: Harvard Common Press, 1982); Felix Cohen, "Americanizing the White Man," *American Scholar* 21:2 (1952); and Ruth M. Underhill, *Red Man's Continent: A History of the Indians in the United States* (Chicago: University of Chicago Press, 1953).

4. Johansen, p. xiv.

5. Ibid., p. 39. Description of the Iroquois political system is discussed in Chapters 2 and 3.

6. Cohen, p. 181.

7. Underhill, pp. 83–94.

8. Johansen, p. 32.

9. Ibid., pp. 75–76.

10. Ibid., p. 84.

11. Ibid., p. 103.

12. Thomas Jefferson, "Letter to Edward Carrington," 16 January 1787, in *Jefferson Writings* (New York: Literary Classics of the United States, 1984), pp. 879–881.

13. "Agrippa," address, Massachusetts Convention, 20 January 1788, in *The Antifederalists*, edited by Cecelia M. Kenyon (Indianapolis: Bobbs-Merrill, 1966), p. 148.

14. Johansen, p. 117.

15. See Gordon S. Wood on "Representation" in *The Creation of the American Republic, 1776–1787* (Chapel Hill: University of North Carolina Press, 1969), pp. 162–196.

16. Ibid., p. 174.

17. Ibid.

18. Ibid., p. 164.

19. Ibid., p. 165.

20. Ibid., p. 188.

21. Ibid., p. 190.

22. Ibid.

23. Ibid., p. 371.

24. Ibid., p. 432.

25. See Jane J. Mansbridge, *Beyond Adversary Democracy* (Chicago: University of Chicago Press, 1983), pp. 130–135.

26. Ibid., p. 131.

27. Leroy Clark, *The Grand Jury: The Use and Abuse of Political Power* (New York: Quadrangle/New York Times Book Co., 1975), p. 14.

28. Richard D. Younger, *The People's Panel: The Grand Jury in the United States, 1634–1941* (Providence, R.I.: Brown University Press, 1963), p. 52.

29. Wood, p. 225.

30. Ibid., pp. 231–232.

31. Ibid., p. 367.

32. Ibid., p. 234.

33. Kenyon, p. xcix.

34. Wood, p. 474.

35. Alexander Hamilton, "Federalist Paper No. 9," in Alexander Hamilton, James Madison, and John Jay, *The Federalist Papers* (New York: New American Library, 1961), pp. 71–76.

36. Alexander Hamilton, "Federalist Paper No. 15," in Hamilton, Madison, and Jay, pp. 105–112.

37. James E. Ferguson, "What Were the Sources of the Constitutional Convention," in *The Confederation and the Constitution*, edited by Gordon S. Wood (Lanham, Md.: University Press of America, 1979).

38. Ibid., pp. 7–11.

39. Wood, p. 494.

40. Ibid., p. 507.

41. Gary Wills, *Explaining America: The Federalists* (New York: Doubleday, 1981), p. 26.

42. Ibid.

43. Ibid., pp. 24–25.

44. Peter T. Manicas, *The Death of the State* (New York: G. P. Putnam's Sons, 1974), p. 187.

45. Ferguson, p. 4.

46. Manicas, p. 188.

47. Herbert J. Storing, *What the Anti-Federalists Were For* (Chicago: University of Chicago Press, 1981), p. 51.

48. Wood, pp. 484–485.

49. Storing, p. 40.

50. Ibid., p. 39.

51. Philadelphiensis, "Letter to *Independent Gazetter*," 21 February 1788, in *The Antifederalists*, p. 77.

52. Ibid., p. 72.

53. Ibid., p. 77.

54. Kenyon, p. li.

55. George Clinton, "Letter to the Citizens of the State of New York," 22 November 1787, in *The Antifederalists*, p. 312.

56. Richard Henry Lee, "Letter," 10 October 1787, in *The Antifederalists*, p. 216.

57. Storing, p. 17.

58. Lee, p. 218.

59. Hamilton, "Federalist Paper No. 84," in Hamilton, Madison, and Jay, p. 513.

60. Ibid.

61. Kenyon, pp. lxx–lxxi.

62. John DeWitt, "Letter to the Free Citizens of the Commonwealth of Massachusetts," 27 October 1787, in *The Antifederalists*, p. 99.

63. Wood, p. 516.

64. Joseph L. Blau, ed., *Social Theories of Jacksonian Democracy* (Indianapolis: Bobbs-Merrill, 1954), p. ix.

65. Ibid., p. x.

66. Ibid.

67. Andrew Jackson, "Jackson Defends the Spoils System," in *Jacksonian America 1815–1840*, edited by Frank Otto Gatell and John M. McFauk (Englewood Cliffs, N.J.: Prentice-Hall, 1970), p. 122.

68. Gatell and McFauk, p. 121.

69. Sidney H. Aronson, "Jackson's Political Appointments," in *New Perspectives on Jacksonian Parties and Politics*, edited by Edward Pressen (Boston: Allyn & Bacon, 1969), p. 239.

70. Blau, p. xiv.

71. Glyndon G. Van Deusen, "Major Party Thought and Theory," in *New Perspectives on Jacksonian Parties and Politics*, p. 143.

72. Alexis de Tocqueville, *Democracy in America*, vol. 1 (New York: Alfred A. Knopf, 1945), pp. 186–187.

73. Van Deusen, p. 154.

74. Lee Benson, *The Concept of Jacksonian Democracy* (Princeton, N.J.: Princeton University Press, 1961), p. vii.

75. Blau, p. xi.

76. Ibid.

77. Benson, p. 7.

78. Ibid.

79. For an excellent survey of historical interpretation of the Progressive Era, see David M. Kennedy, ed., *Progressivism: The Critical Issues* (Boston: Little, Brown, 1971).

80. John F. Manley and Kenneth M. Dolbeare, eds., *The Case Against the Constitution* (Armonk, N.Y.: M. E. Sharpe, 1987), p. x.

81. See, for example, Samuel P. Hays, *Conservation and the Gospel of Efficiency* (Chicago: University of Chicago Press, 1957); Robert H. Webe, *The Search for Order, 1877–1920* (New York: Hill and Wang, 1967); Gabriel Kolko, *The Triumph of Conservatism* (New York: Free Press, 1963); and Amos R. E. Pinchot, *History of the Progressive Party 1912–1916* (New York: New York University Press, 1958).

82. Pinchot, p. 179.

83. Kennedy, p. 19.

84. Ibid.

85. See, for example, Michael Parenti, *Democracy for the Few* (New York: St. Martin's Press, 1983); and Jerold S. Auerbach, *Unequal Justice* (London: Oxford University Press, 1976).

86. Pinchot, p. 168.

87. Ibid.

88. Theodore Roosevelt, "Introduction," in *The Progressive Movement*, edited by S. J. Duncan-Clark (Boston: Small, Maynard, 1972), p. xvi.

89. Pinchot, p. 171.

90. William Allen White, "Changes in Democratic Government," in *Progressivism*, p. 29.

91. Ibid., p. 25.

92. Duncan-Clark, pp. 39–40.

93. White, p. 25.

94. Duncan-Clark, pp. 56–57.

95. Ibid., p. 90.

96. Ibid., p. 42.

97. Ibid., p. 78.

98. Ibid., p. 79.

99. Kennedy, p. viii.

100. White, p. 29.

101. Ibid.

102. Alan F. Westin, "Ride-ins and Sit-ins of the 1870s," in *Freedom Now*, edited by Alan F. Westin (New York: Basic Books, 1964), pp. 71–72.

103. See J. W. Peltason, *Fifty-Eight Lonely Men* (New York: Harcourt, Brace & World, 1961); Neal A. Milner, *The Court and Local Law Enforcement: The Impact of Miranda* (Beverly Hills, Calif.: Sage, 1971); Theodore L. Becker, ed., *The Impact of Supreme Court Decisions* (New York: Oxford University Press, 1969); and Deborah J.

Barrow and Thomas G. Walker, *A Court Divided* (New Haven, Conn.: Yale University Press, 1988).

104. Fred R. Harris, *America's Democracy: The Ideal and the Reality* (Glenview, Ill.: Scott, Foresman, 1980), p. 109.

105. Martin Luther King, Jr., "Letter from Birmingham Jail," in *Freedom Now*, p. 15.

106. Harris, p. 110.

107. Charles V. Hamilton, *The Bench and the Ballot* (New York: Oxford University Press, 1973), p. vii.

108. Ibid.

109. Everett Carl Ladd, *The American Polity: The People and Their Government* (New York: W. W. Norton, 1987), pp. 143 and 591–592.

110. Benjamin Ginsberg, *The Consequences of Consent: Elections, Citizen Control and Popular Acquiescence* (Reading, Mass.: Addison-Wesley, 1982), pp. 106–109.

111. Ladd, p. 593.

112. See Ginsberg, p. 109; and Edward S. Greenberg, *The American Political System: A Radical Approach* (Cambridge, Mass.: Winthrop, 1977), pp. 428–438.

113. Ladd, p. 593.

114. Harris, p. 129.

115. Ibid., p. 130.

116. Ladd, p. 373.

117. Harris, p. 137.

3

Toward the Representative Participatory State: A Quantum Step in Ideology and Theory

A s we have seen in the history of democracy on the North American continent, there has been protracted ideological struggle, theoretical disagreement, and political hostility between those who favor minimizing the extent of citizen participation in government and those who favor maximizing it. As we have also noted, to some degree, whether they were aware of it or not, their views have been influenced by a deep set of beliefs about the way the universe works.

FROM LIMITED REPRESENTATION TO FULL PARTICIPATION: ANALYTIC MODELS

In the former camp are those who share the ideology of the "Founders" of the U.S. Constitution, who established a Limited Representative State, one that placed heavy restrictions on the nature of the roles citizens could play—limiting activities to indirect means of policy making such as voting for representatives, lobbying them, campaigning for them, and so forth.

Furthermore, as we noted in Chapter 1, there is a strong attraction toward Newtonian thinking among those who laud the Limited Representative State. Notions of mechanistic lawmaking lace their political thought. They think in terms of laws being made on the basis of fact through applied logic. They conjure up notions of legislators as wise men, experts in fields of knowledge who know the "objective" way to proceed toward the public good. They set up systems—such as bicameralism—

designed to insulate this "rational" process against the passions of the general public.

As we also have observed, since the ratification of the U.S. Constitution in 1789 there has been a general trend toward greater participation in the American polity by more citizens (the Bill of Rights, the Civil War amendments, women's suffrage, the Voting Rights Act). In addition, major improvements have been made in the quality of citizen participation in the representative system (direct election of U.S. senators; initiative, referendum, and recall at some state and local levels).

Even though these expansions of the Limited Representative State have cost much in blood, time, life, and energy, there are few who currently advocate repealing them. The mainstream of American political science accepts (and generally applauds) this past progress in the direction of a more participatory representative political system as being desirable and useful. The result is a present-day general acceptance of what might well be called the *Expanded Representative State* that exists in the United States today. And, as I argued in Chapter 1, the general underlying worldview of those who favor the maintenance of this type of state is also decidedly Newtonian in character and context.

This does not mean, however, that the ideological battles, theoretical infighting, and political warfare have ceased in the political or academic arenas. There are still wide discrepancies in the thought of the two camps. As we have just noted, there are those who believe that the present contours of the expanded, yet still limited, representative polity are fundamentally sound and that only some occasional fine-tuning of today's constitutional structure may still be necessary. An example of this is former President Reagan, who intends to spend the 1990s campaigning for constitutional amendments to eliminate the two-term limitation on presidents, compel Congress to balance the budget, and provide the president with a "line item veto." Moreover, most American political scientists (whether liberal or conservative or Democrat or Republican) fit into this category. They have developed theories and conducted extensive studies to defend the rectitude and propriety and prove the relative efficiency of the present expanded version of the Limited Representative State. Occasionally they, too, agree that a constitutional amendment or two might be warranted.

On the other side is a group of political theorists, researchers, and activists who generally believe that the quality of the vote in the Limited and Expanded Representative State is not as meaningful as it is purported to be, and that the other kinds of roles that citizens are allowed to play in such a system remain much too narrow, constrained, and unrewarding. Those in this group have different theoretical imperatives, often with ideological ties to the Antifederalists, and therefore a much different research and political agenda. They see a need for more fundamental changes in the system itself, ones that would make the state far more participatory and much more representative of the entire population.

Among the advocates of a more participatory democracy, albeit within a representative context, are those who place primary emphasis on more purposeful and more direct participation and those who place primary emphasis on true, exact representation. Those who favor an improved system of citizen participation that simply evolves out of the present Expanded Representative State can be called advocates of a Participatory Representative State. The advocates of a more drastic shift switch the adjectives and favor a Representative Participatory State.

Both of these states are based on thinking more consistent with quantum theory than the Limited and Expanded Representative States, which are more compatible with Newtonian theory. At this point, the quantum principles of uncertainty, probability, interconnection and interaction, and no objective reality become important considerations of participatory democrats. A few illustrations will help illuminate this point.

In the *Participatory Representative State* advocated by many contemporary participatory democrats, the relationship between citizens and their representatives must be stronger than it is in the Limited or Expanded Representative State of the United States. A greater proportion of citizens would be kept more and better informed and more directly involved in politics. More effective forms of participation would have to be encouraged and devised. Government officials would have to be held more strictly accountable for their behavior, which would compel them to be more responsive to the citizenry. In other words, citizen influence and/or control over representatives would be greatly strengthened in the Participatory Representative State. The emphasis, however, would remain in a system based on elected representatives as the major policy makers.

There are a number of factors that make increased citizen participation desirable from the point of view of most contemporary participatory democrats. In the first place, they believe that citizens know best their own needs—not representatives who are frequently far removed socially, economically, and geographically from those they represent. After all, quantum theory posits that there is no objective reality. Therefore, to apply that concept to a political theory, one might hypothesize that there is no "objective good" for representatives to discover that would provide absolute guides for the best society for all. These decisions ultimately rest on our values and varying perceptions, not objective reality. In addition, increased and improved participation also should lead to better representation of traditionally underrepresented groups in society.

Another argument of participatory democrats is that citizens generally become more self-actualized through increased participation. This increased enhancement of each participating citizen's life in turn contributes to a more advanced society through some sort of synergy, in other words, that the sum of the parts is somehow greater than the mere number of its components. Chapter 1's discussion of the quantum principle of interconnectedness and interaction pointed out that an analysis which focuses on individual action without consideration of the interconnected and interactive components related to that action causes one to lose sight of the total picture. In quantum thought, the whole cannot be separated from its parts for evaluative purposes. From a political analytical perspective utilizing this quantum principle, one sees the political system as defining and influencing political behavior, not individual citizen behavior doing much to influence or change the system. Participatory democratic theory is consistent with quantum in that it encourages, energizes, facilitates, and allows the greater political activity and interacting that is already a tendency of the human social animal to reach its fullest potential.

Important also from the perspective of the participatory democrat is the development of political community. Through increased interaction and a recognition of interdependency (the quantum principle of interconnection), citizens develop a nurturing behavior toward society and other citizens. Sharing in problem solving for society at large replaces isolated citizens simply pursuing self-interests with more cooperative, socially minded citizens who begin to place collective, public interests in a higher echelon of priorities.

Although participatory democrats who favor the Participatory Representative State stress the importance of increased opportunities for involvement, greater access to information, and better communication between citizens and representatives, they, too, often offer only tinkerings with the representative system to make it more responsive to citizens. Examples of this include calls for easing voter registration requirements, expansion of open hearings through sunshine laws, and more civic education on how to operate within the present system.

However, according to another group of participatory democrats, who are even closer to implicit expression of quantum principles in their political thought, entreaties for greater involvement in and stronger controls of representatives by a broader band of the entire citizenry are not enough. Their view is that one must also look at the possibility of inherent design problems in all elected representative systems—in other words, social and economic inequalities of opportunity and distribution that are fostered and reinforced by the elected representative system itself. What good is more opportunity for participation and control of the legislative process if that participation and control requires time, money, and resources that disadvantaged groups in society do not have and can never achieve because of the structural bias built into the system itself?

Thus, some more radical participatory democrats try to address the questions of structural inequalities in society by proposing fundamental changes in the governmental system itself. Their state, which may best be called the *Representative Participatory State*, goes beyond simple improvements in the representative state. In their view, what is needed are resources, incentives, and training for all segments of society in new methods of easy, effective, direct participation in political agenda setting, planning, problem solving, issue formulation, and in the processes of lawmaking and administration.

There is no past model for this state, which requires revolutionary changes in the liberal democratic model of government that we have termed the Expanded Representative State or even the Participatory Representative State. In such a polity, the overriding emphasis would be on citizen participation. Representation would still exist, but it would be determined in large part by random selection, which would leave room for some forms of election. Clearly, adding the concepts of randomness and probability to the structures of agenda setting and policy making is quite consistent with the quantum emphasis of randomness and probability factors in our physical universe.

A working model for the Representative Participatory State might integrate a number of proposals advocated by a diverse group of radical participatory democratic thinkers. First, all or most citizens should be educated and trained in civic responsibility and public service. Public service might be required of all, most, or randomly selected groups of citizens along the lines of military service or extended jury duty.

Rather than electing representatives, astronomical expense could be spared the taxpayer, yet representation made truly representative (of all segments of society including those based on gender, age, region, class, race, and so forth) by applying the quantum theory of randomness and selecting representatives by lot from the total citizen population. In addition to providing a means to truly attain representation of the entire citizenry, this model allows for responsible citizen behavior without requiring all citizens to become full-time actors for all policy making on a permanent basis. (See Figure 3.1 for basic parameters of each representative state model.)

Figure 3.1

Continuum of Citizen Participation in Representative States*

Limited Representative State	Expanded Representative State	Participatory Representative State	Representative Participatory State

Minimum Participation			Maximum Participation

As one moves through the continuum, each state reduces restrictions on citizen participation and increases the variety of roles for citizens to participate.

* The chart is not intended to be definitive, but to establish basic parameters that distinguish the various forms of representative states as defined in this thesis. Also there may be overlap between the various states.

Limited Representative State
(1) Voting for representatives is primary act of citizenship
(2) Restrictions on participation by adult citizens, such as:
    (a) Property qualifications
    (b) Sex
    (c) Race
    (d) Literacy tests
    (e) Poll taxes
(3) Representative role frequently defined as trustee role
(4) Political leaders selected primarily through indirect means or appointed

Expanded Representative State
(1) Voting for representatives is primary act of citizenship
(2) Fewer restrictions on participation by adult citizens
(3) Representative role also seen as delegate role
(4) More direct election of political leaders
(5) More democratization in political parties
(6) Sunshine laws
(7) Broadcasts of public officials' speeches, debates, etc.

Participatory Representative State
(1) Voting for representative an important act of citizenship
(2) Voting on issues through initiative and referendum accompanies voting for representatives
(3) Recall power keeps public officials more accountable to the public
(4) Direct election of political leaders
(5) Fewer barriers to political party participation--open primaries, presidential primaries, etc.
(6) Sunshine laws
(7) Use of two-way media communication between representatives and public

Representative Participatory State
(1) Citizen participation is primary act of citizenship
(2) Random selection of representatives from the total adult citizenry
(3) Randomly selected citizens increasing roles in the legal system as well as the legislative system
(4) Increased use of initiative and referendum
(5) Sunshine laws
(6) Mandatory rotation of office holders
(7) Increased use of communication media to promote interaction among and between representatives and the public
(8) Public education in the functions of government, civic role, and responsibilities

The rationale behind the model of the Representative Participatory State is that it is not practical or fair to require every citizen to keep informed and stay involved in all aspects of politics all the time. There are other personal, family, and economic activities and demands required of individuals in society. Regular rotation of all randomly selected legislators would help insure an accurate system of true representation of all interests in society without requiring all of these citizens to participate in policy making on a regular and/or daily basis. This is consistent with the ideology and practice of the German Green Party, which requires rotation for all leadership positions.

Another major aspect of a Representative Participatory State would be to require substantial direct legislative power for the entire citizenry at all levels of governance—that is, initiative and referendum at the national, state, and local levels. Someone advocating a system like this—with no elected representative aspects whatsoever—would be favoring what might be called the *Full Participation State.*

No type of complex national polity such as the Full Participation State has ever existed on this planet. Moreover, there appear to be no advocates for such a national system of government. There have been small, utopian communities to practice such an ideology in the United States and elsewhere, such as some early European and American communes and Israeli kibbutzim. But economies of scale and function would make such a system at a national, state, or provincial level a virtual impossibility.

A Representative Participatory State, however, would include a high degree of such direct democracy at all levels and for many, if not most, of the major issues confronting the citizenry. Many contemporary nation-states already have national referenda (England, Italy, Korea); state and local initiative (United States, Switzerland); and other methods of direct democratic decision making, like the lay jury system (United States, England) or the lay judge (England, Sweden). And the Representative Participatory State also would have elements of the elective representative system in it, more rather than less in its transformational phases.

As one moves from a firm and exclusive belief in certainty, predictability, rationality, and cause-and-effect determinism into a willingness to think as well in terms of uncertainty, probability, randomness, interdependency, there is less reason to rely completely on experts and assorted sages to deduce what is in the best public interest. Whereas a Newtonian view puts great stock in political expertise because of notions of the key role of "objectivity" and pure logic as major factors in establishing rational policies, the quantum view does not.

From a quantum perspective, there is evidence and reason to rely more on the political proactivity, reactivity, and interaction of the general public to attain that which is probably closest to the general public interest. Participatory democrats stress activity and interaction. Their view of politics and citizen participation is broader than that of the typical liberal democrat. Their expansive universe requires more attention to nontraditional forms of behavior, patterns, and interactions that can offer understanding if not absolute predictability. Their theories require attention beyond the individual decision maker and must include the effects and the results of the political community on the actor. There is often less certainty stated in the theories of the participatory democrats, who emphasize that the process cannot be separated from the end goal in political decision making, also a principle that seems closer to quantum physics than Newtonian.

This chapter will not attempt to prove one camp correct and the other incorrect either ideologically, theoretically, or empirically. Indeed, applying a mode of analysis with a quantum perspective, I hold that there is no objective reality that allows our observations to be totally neutral because our observations, which we use to test our theories, are limited to our own perceptions and consciousness. My analysis, however, attempts to emphasize Dator's statement—"different observer, different world"—throughout the presentation of the theories and research of citizen participation. Therefore the model of democratic states developed above is simply an analytic tool that will help further develop and analyze the following statements.

First, there is a readily detectable ideological bias in mainstream American political science that favors a predominantly representative system along the lines of what we have called the Expanded Representative State. Furthermore, there is also a strong sentiment against any further movement toward a more participatory polity, not even along the lines of the Participatory Representative State.

Second, there has been and is currently an active group of American political scientists and theorists who strongly favor the development and institution of a greater participatory polity in the United States, either along the lines of the Participatory Representative State or the Representative Participatory State. They have constructed a number of theoretical hypotheses and/or propositions, many of which are consistent with quantum theory.

Third, there have been some applied research and political action projects by those seeking to advance the cause of more participatory states. This research is innovative and future-oriented and has produced a large volume of work experimenting with new methods, technologies, and techniques to assist the public in its roles of communicating with its representatives, with itself, and in making informed and deliberated opinions and decisions on major and complex public conundrums and issues. Many of these experimental techniques and methods are also consistent with quantum theory.

MAINSTREAM AMERICAN POLITICAL SCIENCE AND THE IDEOLOGY OF THE EXPANDED REPRESENTATIVE STATE

It is neither original nor radical to say that political ideologies permeate the study, research, writing, and teaching of political science, in general or the American version thereof. Indeed, as recently as 1988, Stanford University's Gabriel Almond, an extremely well-known and highly respected former president of the American Political Science Association, writing in an official organ of that organization, calmly divided all of American political science into four warring political philosophical and methodological factions, what he calls "schools" and "sects." According to his way of thinking, they are the "hard right," "soft right," "hard left," and "soft left."[1] Words like "Marxist," "liberal," "liberal pluralist," "conservative," "neo-conservative," and "humanist moderate left" color his analysis, concepts with a decided political ideological loading.

While Almond's political analysis squares well with what most Americans and most political scientists believe to be the outer borders of the ideological factionalism in American political and political scientific life, it does not help much in our analysis. There appears to be a major ideological conflict in American politics and political science between those who favor system maintenance in U.S. government and those who desire and strive toward substantial to radical change in that system. As has been pointed out, both sides have strongly opposed ideological positions rooted deeply in a complex belief system that links the natures of the universe and of human behavior.

Regardless of their specific content, all ideologies have a conscious and subconscious impact on how people see and interpret the world in which they live. Ideologies blot out certain aspects of reality and sharpen others in the minds and eyes of their believers. Ideologies slant perceptions and shade interpretations. And researchers, theorists, and academicians are hardly immune from this relationship, no matter how aware of it they may be, how hard they try to overcome it, or how open they are about it.

Being aware of, attempting to overcome, and conceding one's ideological prejudice(s) may help temper its effects on theoretical, research, and interpretative agendas. This approach also will help the audience and/or consumer evaluate the analysis more effectively. On the other hand, being unaware, not attempting to overcome, and consciously or unconsciously ignoring such create a hidden agenda and make it hard for the audience and/or consumer to evaluate the analysis effectively.

Most mainstream American political scientists, whatever their Almondian school or sect, are grounded, to one degree or another, into the Federalist values and ideology built into the American constitutional system. This helps account for why they tend to rank voting for representatives or officials as the pinnacle of citizen participation in America— sometimes even ignoring other forms of citizen activity or mentioning them only as marginal activities. As a matter of fact, this even holds true among those American political scientists who emphasize "citizen participation" as their primary area of study.

A prominent example is Margaret Conway's *Political Participation in the United States* (1985). Despite what the title of the book might lead one to believe regarding the contents, her attention centers almost exclusively on voting for candidates for public office. Her only reference to other forms of citizen participation appears in a three-page discussion of a 1974 study of "unconventional" political action. The "unconventional" forms of behavior she cites include signing petitions, engaging in lawful demonstrations, and participating in boycotts.[2] At no time in the entire book does she mention initiative, referendum, or recall—where citizens themselves pass laws—occasional processes that occur (in conjunction with elected legislatures) even in the Expanded Representative State of contemporary America.

Even when she discusses ways to influence policy and law through citizen participation, no word is uttered about the initiative process, either indirect or direct, that is the essence of participatory democracy. Since there is every reason to believe that Professor Conway is aware of these important American processes, it seems reasonable to conclude that an ideological filter prevents her—knowingly or unwittingly—from including such in a treatise devoted wholly to "citizen participation in the United States."

Through her narrow treatment of political participation, which focuses almost exclusively on voting, Conway reveals an ideological bias in favor of the Limited Representative State and against participatory democracy. For instance, she cites National Election Studies survey data that indicates the following general trends in the United States since 1964: (1) increased perception of the present form of government as not responsive to citizens' views; (2) perception that government in general and Congress in particular are not attentive to citizens' preferences; (3) perception that the present two major political party system is not an effective mechanism to force government attentiveness to citizens' views; and (4) perception that parties are only interested in obtaining votes, not reflecting citizens' opinions.[3] She does not interpret this data, however, as an indication that there is growing dissatisfaction with the overall system.

When one combines this data with such facts as that only 53 percent of eligible American voters actually voted in the 1984 presidential election,[4] and only 50 percent in the 1988 election,[5] and that the United States ranks twentieth among the world's democracies in voter turnout,[6] one who is not ideologically inclined to support the Limited Representative State might mention that a majority or near-majority of Americans do not place the premium on voting for candidates that mainstream American political science does.

It is understandable, however, that political scientists place such emphasis on voting. As one study on political parties in the United States points out, "voting is the political activity in which the greatest proportion of the electorate participates."[7] Furthermore, voting for candidates is the quintessential act for a citizen in the representative state.

Moreover, since it is the representatives who actually have the major power of citizenship, in other words, establishing the legislative agenda and/or passing laws, it is understandable that people who buy into the ideology of the supremacy of the representative state think that the only other major acts of citizenship must be related either to the election of the representatives or the influencing of their legislative activity and, ultimately, their votes.

This helps explain why American political scientists are paying increasing attention to the activities of lobbyists, political action committees, and special interest groups. These groups operate in an arena with the representative vote as their major target, and resources such as money, time, skills, and energy are utilized to influence elected representatives mostly in the way they vote. The fundamental goal of these groups is to pressure representatives to respond to their interests or to replace them with others who will.

Whether one applies David Truman's "group theory," which holds that government acts as a referee among the various and sundry competing groups in this struggle for a majority of representatives' votes (plus agreement or non-hostile action by the executive and judicial branches),[8] or Robert Dahl's "polyarchy theory," which views citizens as being virtually represented by and in a multitude of well-organized groups that participate for them in the representative process,[9] the focus remains almost exclusively within the indirect democratic governmental frameworks of the Limited Representative State established by the Founders and the Expanded Representative State that exists at the present time.

Underlying all this description and analysis of the contemporary American governmental process is a generally accepted belief that its nature, and the content of the many problems that face government today, are too complicated and take too much time, energy, and expertise for the average, everyday citizen to understand or appreciate. Thus, their participation must be confined to voting for their representatives, helping them obtain office, or letting them know their opinions (by mail, telephone, office visits, etc.). But as Chapter 2 points out, these limited roles for U.S. citizens were established by design, and that ideological imprint has worked well, maintaining many adherents and true believers in American politics, political science, and the general population to the present day.

Indeed, these ideologically based notions of the limitations of ordinary citizens also permeate the research and interpretations of political scientists who choose to focus their work directly on citizen participation. For example, Lester Milbrath and M. L. Goel, in their book *Political Participation*, appear to be friendly to a more participatory polity when they support equal opportunity for all citizens to participate, but they contend that there will be varying degrees of citizen participation because the nature of the system requires role specialization—in other words, "only a few can lead while others must follow."[10]

Milbrath and Goel's view is that this role specialization, which some would consider antidemocratic, is desirable because it produces better ends. They warn that one should "not be trapped by the traditional exhortations of democratic theory. The only value that matters . . . for evaluating political systems is the quality of life of the people living in them."[11] Equality and citizen influence over government officials are not ends in themselves, but only means to a "happy society." If they do not produce the "happy society," then other means should be used.

Even though Milbrath and Goel advocate the removal of barriers to participation and oppose the system favoring participation of certain groups over others, they also reject the notion that society is better off with more participation. Indeed, they argue that for the system to be truly democratic, it must allow citizens to be uninvolved. In the debate between pluralists and participatory democrats, they side with the pluralists and reject the view that democracy must be highly valued as an end in itself.[12]

To take the ideological belief in, and advocacy of, limited citizen involvement a step further, another former president of the American Political Science Association, Samuel Huntington, argues that the United States is currently suffering from too much citizen participation or, as he calls it, an "excess of democracy."[13] When the 1960s brought an upsurge in the degree and intensity of political participation by youth, ethnic minorities, and women, the increased demands created an overload on the Expanded Representative State. In Huntington's view, political leaders were faced with the public expectation that representatives were to respond to their desires or else lose legitimacy and authority. Huntington's analysis is that the attempts by political leaders to please the public led to increased government involvement in trying to solve society's problems, runaway inflation, and a severe economic and political crisis born out of too much citizen participation in a representative system that was not designed to respond to such volume.

His solution for the survival of democracy (in other words, survival of the Expanded Representative State) rests on the belief that "the effective operation of a democratic political system usually requires some measure of apathy and noninvolvement on the part of some individuals and groups."[14] Recalling John Adams' statement "There never was a democracy yet that did not commit suicide," Huntington says: "That suicide is more likely to be the product of over-indulgence than of any other cause. A value which is normally good in itself is not necessarily optimized when it is maximized. . . . There are potentially desirable limits to the indefinite extension of political democracy."[15]

Thomas Dye and Harmon Zeigler are very clear about who should be the active participants and who should not. Their claim is that "the irony of democracy is that elites [those with high educational levels, prestigious occupations, and high social status], not masses, are most committed to democratic values."[16] They believe that social science research backs their view that the American people are not committed to liberty and equality. Instead it is the elites in society who support free speech, free press, and "equality of opportunity." Therefore, they write, "If elites are to fulfill their role as guardians of liberty and property, they must be insulated from the antidemocratic tendencies of the masses. Too much mass influence over elites threatens democratic values."[17] The answer for the survival of democracy then is for the masses to be "absorbed in the problems of everyday life and . . . involved in groups that distract their attention from mass politics."[18]

There are other political scientists who study citizen participation in the United States, however, who do not narrowly define participation, who recognize the overemphasis often placed on the mere act of voting, and who do not demonstrate a clear bias against increased citizen participation. For instance, Sidney Verba and Norman H. Nie criticize "most studies of participation" for paying "little attention to the questions of the alternative ways in which citizens can participate" and for restricting their studies to representative-electoral politics.[19] They argue that to focus on elections, "which simplify the participatory influence of the citizenry into a choice among candidates rather than a choice among policies," is to consider participation as a "unidimensional phenomena."[20]

Verba and Nie's analysis of contemporary American citizen participation identifies six different categories of citizens based on different levels of participation. Their studies indicate the following categories:

1. *The Inactives* (22%) are citizens who take no part in political life. Not only do they not vote, but they do not take part in the communal activities of their neighborhoods.

2. *The Voting Specialists* (21%) are citizens who vote regularly but participate in no other political activity, either in their community or in political campaigns. They make no attempt to contact or influence government officials once they are elected. Verba and Nie point out that this group is not as large as many analyses of American politics lead one to suspect.[21] In other words, most citizens are involved in activities that frequently get ignored in studies of citizen participation that focus exclusively on voting.

3. *The Parochial Participants* (4%) are citizens who vote regularly but do not get involved in communal or campaign activities. They differ from the Voting Specialists in that they initiate contact with political leaders on matters that affect their personal lives.

4. *The Communalists* (20%) are citizens with a high level of community activity but low level of campaign activity.

5. *The Campaigners* (15%) are citizens who engage in almost no communal activity but are very active in political campaigns.

6. *The Complete Activists* (11%) are citizens who engage in all types of activity with great frequency.[22]

For political scientists who limit their studies to voting, the activities of one-third of the American public, according to Verba and Nie's classification, are being overlooked. In addition, the labeling of nonvoters as being either apathetic or immobilized by contentment ignores the increasing number of educated citizens who feel that the current contours of the American representative system do not truly represent them. As one nonvoting American political scientist, Lester J. Mazor of Hampshire College, has put it: "I am not apathetic. I do not believe that people who do not vote should be labeled apathetic. Many of us . . . do not want any of those who are elected ever to be able to say that they speak for us, that the things they do are what we authorized."[23]

But voting for representatives, and centering one's participation around the election of or influencing of them, remains the official ideology of the current American polity, an ideology that is spoken, written, and ardently defended by many of its articulate citizens; almost all of its practicing politicians at all levels of government; the overwhelming majority of reporters, anchorpersons, and commentators occupying key positions in the mass media; and most of its practicing political scientists. The Expanded Representative State is alive and well in its original, but modified, form. Those who speak out against it are far from legion, and those who theorize and research in the direction of greater citizen participation within its present structure, or who see and work toward a new kind of state in which citizen participation takes on new directions and new dimensions, are small in number. But their ideas and ideals have a long history in the United States and their ranks seem to be swelling.

As the previous chapter indicates, there always have been those in America who have attempted to make representatives more accountable and citizens more responsible for important governmental decision making. The democratic fervor that flourished in the Revolutionary Period has never disappeared and there always has been a dream and action for more democratic citizen participation that has manifested itself in occasional movements and spurts of oratory and writing. Furthermore, there always have existed some direct democratic forms of participation in the United States to sustain the passion for even more. The remaining sections of this chapter, therefore, will examine current theories and studies of citizen activity that promote more participatory democracy in the United States and offer a broad participatory civic role for all citizens rather than the narrowly defined Hamiltonian or Madisonian roles still in vogue.

POLITICAL SCIENTIFIC THEORIES OF THE PARTICIPATORY STATE

The analytic models of types of democratic states that I constructed in this chapter are original and, as far as I know, unique. I find them useful in helping explain the ideological, theoretical, and political struggles that have characterized North American politics through the centuries, to the present day, and probably into the future.

There was no problem in attempting to demarcate political science theorists who favored the Limited Representative State from those who preferred the Expanded Representative State because in this day and age, as we noted earlier, almost no one advocates a return to the original state of the Constitution and a revocation of all of the constitutional amendments that have led to the Expanded Representative State. What has been done is done and there is no call for a retreat to the past. The ideas and actions for reform among this group are limited to the goal of improving the representative function itself.

Trying to classify theorists, researchers, and practitioners who favor greater participatory democracy in America, however, is a more challenging task. The first key reason for this is that instead of two categories, there are three. There are those who favor: (a) the Participatory Representative State, who seek significant participatory reform—what could be called a major overhaul—of the Expanded Representative State; (b) the Representative Participatory State, who see a need for radical restructuring of the representative polity—what could be called revolutionary changes—that would make the system have much truer representation and increase the direct participation function; (c) the Full Participation State, who desire a complete abolition of the representative polity in all forms and degrees and its replacement by a total participatory citizenry.

The second key reason is that theorists of participatory democracy do not make the distinctions I have made. Most of them simply discuss the deficiencies of representative theory and the positive aspects of participatory democratic theory. The only way one can detect whether they are leaning more toward the Representative Participatory State or the Participatory Representative State is if and when and to what degree they favor particular methods of increasing and improving citizen participation in the process. This problem is even more pronounced when one deals with researchers and those who invent and implement new methods of participatory democracy. They rarely engage in theoretical discourse. Their goal is simply to improve citizen participation regardless of the type of democratic state in which it may be applied.

The next part of this chapter, then, will deal with some major political theorists who advocate a more participatory state and discuss why. The first group of them, who will be called the general participatory theorists, are notable for their theoretical discourse on the inherent inadequacies of the representative state and why a more participatory state is necessary—that is, its individual, social, and political benefits. The second group, who will be called the institutional participatory theorists, are notable for their attempts at constructing or reconstructing governmental structures that would promote direct participation in governance.

The General Participatory Theorists

To a minority of American political scientists, voting for representatives as a form of citizen participation is, as Ben Barber describes, "the least significant act of citizenship in a democracy."[24] To Peter Manicas, voting in the American representative process is not only insignificant, but is deceptive in that it "deludes the powerless into thinking they had their say."[25]

In addition, if one examines the high percentage of current members of the U.S. House of Representatives who are reelected each voting period (over 90% since Watergate and 98% in 1988),[26] one is inclined to give credence to David Schuman's assertion that voting in the United States "is not action, it is not politics; it is merely reaction, simply endorsement."[27] Meaningful citizen participation, in the minds of participatory democratic theorists, includes at the very least the following kind of political action described by Schuman: "One must help frame the issues; one works for those issues; and finally one must help carry out the results of those issues. Ideally, this is done openly and with others."[28]

A number of other important American participatory democratic theorists in the twentieth century have urged a form of politics in the United States that provides for the level and type of political participation advocated by Aristotle in which the individual is encouraged and supported to develop his or her capabilities to the fullest.

John Dewey was a democratic theorist who believed the primary challenge of democracy was how to maximize the common good and personal liberty at the same time.[29] But he also believed that it was imperative for a democratic state to seek ways to give each individual the opportunity for release, expression, and fulfillment of his or her distinctive capacities.

Through maximization of individual opportunity and growth, Dewey was convinced there would more likely develop a fund of shared values. Consistent with participatory democratic thought, Dewey viewed society as a process, with the state's role being a facilitator and enricher of the contacts human beings have with one another.[30] He realized that he presented an ideal that had not been achieved at that point in U.S. political history. Yet he sought new paths and exhorted experimentation with ways that would help achieve individual and societal political growth and fulfillment.

Carl Friedrich, a prominent American political scientist and a onetime president of the American Political Science Association, maintained that the public good for society cannot be attained by disregarding the public. His advocacy of citizen participation went well beyond the voting stage and insisted on plugging citizens directly into the policy-making process, of not only elected politicians but also career bureaucrats. He states: "Democratic planning, dedicated as it must be to achieving the greatest satisfaction for as many as possible, cannot neglect the reactions of all those whom a given policy affects."[31] What often happens, according to Friedrich, is that distrust of public opinion has resulted in putting "the experts on top, rather than on tap."[32]

Rather than arguing for citizen participation as an essential aspect of self-actualization, Friedrich's position is that the "common man collectively is a better judge as to what is good for him than any self-appointed elite."[33] Indeed, his brief is that the average person is much likelier than the political partisan to recognize and adhere to "a working scheme of cooperation among men of different views" and that the pursuit of interests "calls for a sense of mutual obligation."[34]

Peter Bachrach, whose advocacy of participatory democracy is consistent with Dewey's view that active participation in politics by individual citizens contributes to the individual and collective self-development among the citizenry, also is concerned with the survivability of the democratic components of the present American system. He insists that if there is not a revitalization of democratic participation, then one must accept the grim fact that future political decision making will have even less democratic control than it has now.[35]

Also concerned with means as well as ends, Bachrach defines political participation as

> a process in which persons formulate, discuss, and decide public issues that are important to them and directly affect their lives. It is a process that is more or less continuous, conducted on a face-to-face basis in which participants have roughly an equal say in all stages, from formulation of issues to the determination of policies.[36]

Bachrach's criticism of the present-day American political system—the Expanded Representative State—is that it has "failed to construct channels and institutions to facilitate and encourage people from the lower strata to articulate their interests."[37] The way in which the system has functioned has resulted in dominance by elites rather than guidance by them.[38]

At the center of the arguments made by many proponents of participatory democracy is the fundamental belief that most, if not all, decision making ultimately rests on one's value system, not on any knowledge of absolute right and wrong or on any particular set of facts or data. In this view, the role of elites should be to provide information, a variety of viewpoints, and perhaps recommendations on alternative policies, processes, and so forth. The decision making, however, should not be reserved to elites because their own subjective (and perhaps class) values ultimately guide their decision making.

Advocates of participatory democracy do not believe that "experts" or elites deserve any elevated rank in a hierarchy of decision making based on values. In fact, Thomas Jefferson, Jeremy Bentham, Carl Friedrich, and many other advocates of a more participatory democracy were more leery of decisions made by an unchecked elite than of decisions made by the average person. Jefferson stated, "I am not among those who fear the people. They, and not the rich, are our dependence for continued freedom."[39] To him, "the good sense of the people will always be found to be the best army" against "tumults" in America.[40]

The Institutional Participatory Theorists

Robert Dahl, whose description of the dynamics of the current processes in the Expanded Representative State is generally accepted as a potent defense of it, also has a body of work that appreciates the desirability of a more participatory polity. For example, according to Dahl, Jean Jacques Rousseau "was the last great democratic philosopher to advocate primary democracy in a literal sense."[41] Indeed, Rousseau wrote that "as soon as a people gives itself representation, it is no longer free."[42] While Rousseau thought it appropriate that the citizens allow a small group to administer the laws they made, it would be death to democracy and freedom to delegate lawmaking powers to any smaller group.

Dahl believes that Rousseau's vision of primary democracy is "one of the most beguiling utopias since Plato's republic."[43] While Rousseau's plan, according to Dahl, is completely impractical and totally unachievable, Dahl admits to being captivated by the vision of friends and neighbors settling their common affairs together. Guided by concerns of "Competence, Economy and Personal Choice," Dahl rejects Rousseau's primary democracy, yet seriously recommends the reinstitution of the lottery system in modern democracy.[44]

Under this system, citizens would be randomly selected to serve as representatives on advisory councils to every elected official of the "giant polyarchy"—from mayors of large cities to governors, members of Congress, and the president. Believing that making national decisions on complex issues regarding appropriations, revenues, foreign affairs, and so forth requires much more thought and time than most Americans could or would apply, Dahl argues against making the randomly selected bodies more than advisory. He does not argue that elected officials are more capable to do the research or the necessary deliberations. But he does believe they are definitely more motivated. What they need, however, is much more guidance by a much more representative citizenry.

Subsequently, in 1972 three Cornell University professors (Dennis C. Mueller, Robert D. Tollison, and Thomas D. Willett) offered a design for the Representative Participatory State that also addressed Dahl's concerns about "Competence, Economy and Personal Choice."[45] They proposed a combination of an elected legislative body and a randomly selected legislative body. Under their scheme, one house would be composed of about 20 senators elected at large throughout the country. This house would only initiate legislation that would then be passed on to the random house, chosen from the adult citizenry, to enact the legislation if it saw fit to do so.

The Mueller–Tollison–Willett system serves somewhat to institutionalize national referenda since it permits laws to be enacted from a body of citizens that truly represent all demographic and political groups in the country, because that would roughly be the consequence of a nationwide random selection process for a lawmaking body. The three professors do not choose to abolish election altogether because they wish to allow some degree of "political entrepreneurship" to flourish in the United States. Elections encourage the development of some leadership qualities, which is seen by them as having substantial value to the political system.

This dual legislative system, one house elected by the people and one selected at random from the people, was endorsed in 1976 by Theodore L. Becker[46] and in 1985 by Ernest Callenbach and Michael Phillips.[47] Political scientist and futurist Jim Dator goes even further and states he believes "all political figures should be chosen by lot, as jurors are."[48] Those advocating random legislatures all agree that no other way can possibly produce a truly "representative" legislature. They take literally the definition given by our second president, John Adams, of a representative assembly, which is described in Chapter 2. It "should be an exact portrait, in miniature, of the people at large, as it should think, feel, reason, and act like them."[49]

Becker wonders why there is such popular acceptance of the fact that life and death decisions can be made by randomly selected juries, yet there is such widespread incredulity over a system that also would trust citizens with legislative matters. Using 1976 data, he pointed out that 50 to 60 percent of congressmen were lawyers, 20 percent were millionaires, 96 percent were white, and 97 percent were male. There is no way, he believes, this very homogeneous body can ever truly reflect the viewpoints of the citizenry at large or share the same values and interests.[50]

Callenbach and Phillips also note that a lottery system existed for almost 200 years in Athens. Some 500 randomly selected legislators served one-year terms in an institution called the "boule." This lawmaking body performed some judicial functions as well.

Of course, advocating a randomly selected legislature, even at all levels of government, in every state and in every city and town in the nation, is still a vote in favor of a representative polity. Yet its goal is broader. Such an institution would emphasize participation by all segments of society in the lawmaking process, albeit through representative bodies. Advocates of random legislature, then, are moving in the direction of a Representative Participatory State because they emphasize the legislative capacity of the ordinary citizen and want new institutions that foster such.

While the actual number of citizens who would be serving as congressmen, state legislators, and city councilpersons under the random system of selection would still be only a small minority of the entire population, larger and larger numbers of citizens would become involved in these roles over the years. The level of education and awareness developed through such service would likely enhance and increase other citizen interest and involvement. Moreover, the government process would no longer appear to be so removed and alien from their own experience. And finally, the representatives of the people would more accurately reflect the people in their values and attitudes; for example, the broadest base of the population's value system would actually be participating in the political system.

Seeking to address the dilemmas discussed earlier of a totally involved citizenry on all issues at all times, these proposals place participation of the citizenry at the center, but allow that participation to be on a rotating basis through the representative system. Hence, these proposals fit within the ideological framework of the Representative Participatory State.

National initiative, referendum, and recall, or a nationwide form of the traditional American town meeting, are institutional changes that would maximize citizen participation in lawmaking throughout the nation. This concept has had several important advocates in recent years. These structural alterations also would be key components in any move toward the Representative Participatory State. Taken together they would embody a strong participatory polity with some elements of the representative state. The crucial instrumentation that would facilitate such a major structural change in this day and age is modern communications and information processing technologies.

An early advocate of such a nationwide system of direct democracy was the famous psychologist Erich Fromm. In his book *The Sane Society*, he discussed the many ills of modern industrialized society, social maladies that most definitely included a sense of alienation and helplessness in persons about how they could control important events in their lives, including their economic and political welfare.[51] This psychological malaise permeating society created, in Fromm's view, a relatively insane societal situation. Among the many methods Fromm devised to help remedy some of the sense of political alienation that characterized modern society was national electronic voting.

According to Fromm, the whole population should be divided into small groups of 500 or so according to residence or place of work. These groups would meet regularly, such as once a month, to discuss political issues of national and local concern. In order to have meaningful discussion, Fromm argues that citizens would need to be informed. He proposes a cultural committee of outstanding individuals noted for their integrity in the fields of art, science, religion, business, and politics to provide factual information to the citizens. After the groups discussed the issues in their face-to-face meetings, they would vote "with the help of the technical devices we have today."[52] Fromm states these groups would constitute "the true 'House of Commons,' which would share power with the house of universally elected representatives and a universally elected executive."[53]

R. Buckminster Fuller, a noted thinker and inventer, agrees with Fromm that "democracy must be structurally modernized . . . to give it a one-individual-to-another speed and spontaneity of reaction commensurate with the speed and scope of broadcast news."[54] Fuller argues that America is now ready to try democracy for the first time. What makes the time right for America is not only her experience and intellectual development, but also modern technology.

Fuller calls for daily nationwide voting on issues through the use of television, computers, and other available technology that could record votes instantaneously. He believes there are several advantages to this system, which is the product of centuries of human progress and development. Included in his list of advantages are efficiency in decision making; popular cooperation in carrying out decisions of the public; possible continuous correction if expenses indicate the need; more unification against foreign forces because all citizens have been allowed to take responsibility for acts of the United States; other countries' envy of the U.S. democracy; and being an evolutionary process of reform that guards against revolution. In terms of voter fraud or cheating, Fuller maintains that technology is so advanced that a system can be devised to make the "effective abuse through cheating" to be virtually nil. If this modern electronic democracy he advocates is tried and proves to be inferior to other methods as a survival means, then citizens will learn and can turn to superior methods. However, he argues, if direct democracy is not tried now, future generations will champion it again and again and wars will be fought until it is finally given an "adequate trial."[55]

Becker also advocates a national initiative and referendum process. For "highly critical and very important legislation" that deals with "society-wide problems" he calls for the use of national, home-TV referenda to bring the entire population into an electronic town meeting discussion and deliberation of national issues. Becker addresses broadening citizen participation not only within the legislative branch, but also within the judicial branch. Pointing out that such disparate countries as England, Denmark, Cuba, and the Soviet Union have found ways to use nonlawyers as judges in their legal systems, Becker calls for a system of lay assessors to supplement the legally trained judges. The argument he makes is that laypersons should not be limited to finders of fact (as the jury in the United States is), but also should be involved as deliberators on how the facts should be interpreted according to the law. The rationale for this is his view that judges interpret the law not according to some universal standard or truth, but according to their personal views of what the law means. In addition, these personal views are certainly influenced by class, education, and status in society. Although Becker does not advocate abolishing the requirement of a legal education for judges, he believes all trials in which juries are not involved should be presided over by a tribunal of three judges and supplemented by two lay assessors. This system also would apply at the appellate level.[56]

Alvin Toffler addresses Becker's random legislature plan and arguments in his book *The Third Wave* and offers a proposal for consideration that combines both Becker's and Fuller's views. Rather than transporting the randomly selected branch of the legislature off to Washington, Toffler suggests using computers, advanced telecommunications, and polling methods to allow the random House to operate out of their homes. This dispersal of the legislators would, he argues, "strike a devastating blow at the special interest groups and lobbies who infest the corridors of most parliaments. Such groups would have to lobby the people—not just a few elected officials."[57]

FROM THEORETICAL DISCOURSE TO THEORY TESTING

Thus the struggle of words, ideas, concepts, theories, philosophies, and ideologies perseveres to this very day—and promises to continue into the indefinite future. As I have tried to demonstrate in this chapter, beneath the ostensibly objective theoretical position of those antagonistic toward or in favor of a participatory-based state are beliefs about human nature. Sometimes, too, there are beliefs about the physical universe and the relationship that exists between the humans and their universe that provide a theoretical guide for political theory. Different theoretical approaches, guided by different value systems, produce different types of studies and different answers to similar questions.

For many of the theoreticians, however, at least partial answers to many seemingly intractable social, economic, and political problems in the world and in the United States lie in the further "democratization" of political structures (toward more participatory systems). Some of them have devoted their research activities toward experimentation with and development of novel devices and approaches that are capable of promoting, stimulating, and inducing—and measuring—citizen participation.

Although many of these researchers and coordinators of improved citizen participation action projects do not identify themselves as partisans of the Representative Participatory State, they are allies of those who do. For their works, whether successful or not, provide important knowledge as to what does or does not provide a greater degree or higher quality of interactive feedback among citizens and between citizens and those occupying policy-making, planning, or administrative positions.

The next chapter will select several major studies of the past few decades that have integrated modern communication and information technologies and techniques in a quest to provide the technical infrastructure of either the Participatory Representative State or the Representative Participatory State. These works all were instrumental in the development of the Televote method, which I consider to be a major, central component of a political system that successfully blends representation and participation, Newtonian theory and quantum theory.

NOTES

1. Gabriel Almond, "Separate Tables: Schools and Sects in Political Science," *Political Science* (Fall 1988): 828–842.

2. Margaret Conway, *Political Participation in the United States* (Washington, D.C.: Congressional Quarterly Press, 1985), pp. 53–56.

3. Ibid., p. 46.

4. Ibid., p. 5.

5. *Congressional Quarterly*, 21 January 1989.

6. F. Christopher Arterton, *Teledemocracy: Can Technology Protect Democracy?* (Newbury Park, Calif.: Sage, 1987), p. 49.

7. Frank B. Feigert and Margaret Conway, *Parties and Politics in America* (Boston: Allyn & Bacon, 1976), p. 85. Having examined citizen participation studies and published two books on the subject, Conway concluded: "Only a few studies have examined participation in and support for unconventional political activity in the United States and hardly any of them have been based on data from national samples. More research has been conducted in other countries where unconventional participation occurs more often" (Conway, *Political Participation*, p. 138).

8. David B. Truman, *The Governmental Process* (New York: Alfred A. Knopf, 1951).

9. Robert A. Dahl, *Polyarchy: Participation and Opposition* (New Haven, Conn.: Yale University Press, 1971).

10. Lester Milbrath and M. L. Goel, *Political Participation* (Chicago: Rand McNally, 1977), pp. 151–152.

11. Ibid., p. 153.

12. Ibid., p. 149.

13. Michael Crozier, Samuel Huntington, and Joji Watanuki, *The Crisis of Democracy* (New York: New York University Press, 1975), p. 113.

14. Ibid., p. 114.

15. Ibid., p. 115.

16. Thomas R. Dye and L. Harmon Zeigler, *The Irony of Democracy* (Monterey, Calif.: Brooks/Cole, 1984), p. 14.

17. Ibid., p. 15.

18. Ibid.

19. Sidney Verba and Norman H. Nie, *Participation in America: Political Democracy and Social Equality* (New York: Harper & Row, 1972), p. 44.

20. Ibid., p. 45.

21. Ibid., p. 79.

22. Ibid., pp. 82–101.

23. Lester J. Mazor, letter, *New York Times*, 23 October 1980.

24. Benjamin Barber, *Strong Democracy* (Berkeley: University of California Press, 1984), p. 187.

25. Peter Manicas, *The Death of the State* (New York: G. P. Putnam's Sons, 1974), p. 177.

26. Richard Wolf, " 'Incumbent Party' Keys House Seats," *USA Today*, 27 October 1988, p. A1.

27. David Schuman, *A Preface to Politics* (Lexington, Mass.: D.C. Heath, 1977), p. 115.

28. Ibid., p. 113.

29. John Dewey and James H. Tufts, *Ethics* (New York: Henry Holt, 1932), pp. 377–414.

30. John Dewey, *Reconstruction in Philosophy* (Boston: Beacon Press, 1957), pp. 187–213.

31. Carl Friedrich, *The New Belief in the Common Man* (Boston: Little, Brown, 1943), p. 217.

32. Ibid., p. 216.

33. Ibid., p. 113.

34. Ibid., p. 123.

35. Peter Bachrach, *The Theory of Democratic Elitism* (Lanham, Md.: University Press of America, 1980), p. x.

36. Peter Bachrach, "Interest, Participation, and Democratic Theory," in *Participation in Politics*, edited by J. Roland Pennock and John W. Chapman (New York: Lieber-Atherton, 1975), p. 41.

37. Ibid., p. 40.

38. Bachrach, *Theory*, p. 4.

39. Thomas Jefferson, "Letter to Kercheval," 12 July 1816, in *Jefferson Writings* (New York: Literary Classics of the United States, 1984), p. 1400.

40. Thomas Jefferson, "Letter to Edward Carrington," 16 January 1787, in *Jefferson Writings*, p. 880.

41. Robert A. Dahl, *After the Revolution?* (New Haven, Conn.: Yale University Press, 1970), pp. 79–80. Dahl describes "primary democracy" as governments based on the town meeting model where all citizens are allowed to participate in making laws.

42. Jean Jacques Rousseau, *The Essential Rousseau* (New York: New American Library, 1974), pp. 78–80.

43. Dahl, *Revolution*, p. 80.

44. Ibid., pp. 149–153.

45. Dennis C. Mueller, Robert D. Tollison, and Thomas D. Willett, "Representative Democracy Via Random Selection," *Public Choice* 7 (Spring 1972): 60–61.

46. Theodore L. Becker, *American Government: Past, Present, Future* (Boston: Allyn & Bacon, 1976).

47. Ernest Callenbach and Michael Phillips, *A Citizen Legislature* (Berkeley, Calif.: Banyan Tree Books, 1985).

48. James A. Dator, "Rethinking Honolulu City Governance," City and County Charter Commission Retreat, Honolulu, 19 August 1981.

49. Gordon S. Wood, *The Creation of the American Republic, 1776–1787* (Chapel Hill: University of North Carolina Press, 1969), p. 165.

50. Theodore L. Becker, *Unvote for a New America* (Boston: Allyn & Bacon, 1976), p. 184.

51. Erich Fromm, *The Sane Society* (New York: Rinehart, 1955).

52. Ibid., p. 342.

53. Ibid., p. 343.

54. R. Buckminster Fuller, *No More Secondhand God* (Garden City, N.Y.: Doubleday, 1971), p. 9.

55. Ibid., pp. 12–13.

56. Becker, *American Government*, pp. 488–489.

57. Alvin Toffler, *The Third Wave* (London: William Collins Sons, 1982), pp. 434–435.

4

Toward the Representative Participatory State: Research and Action Projects

A s with American political theorists, the agendas of American political scientists who engage in empirical research or research-action projects are driven, to a large degree, by their own political values and ideologies. So it is not surprising to discover that most of the American political science empirical research is founded on a deep-seated belief in, or adherence to, the values inherent in the Expanded Representative State. As goes the overwhelming majority of American political theorists, so goes the overwhelming majority of American political researchers.

Political scientists have been concerned for quite some time about the legitimacy or efficacy of American representative democracy when large numbers of U.S. citizens choose not to vote. So it is quite understandable that one of the first modern political scientific experiment-action projects was avowedly undertaken to help improve the American representative system. A research team from the University of Chicago had an idea about how to generate greater voter turnout. Led by Professor Harold Gosnell, a field experiment was conducted whereby an experimental group of citizens was given leaflets containing information on voter registration and a similar control group was not. The object was to see to what degree information provided in the leaflet would induce citizens to register to vote. The experiment was "successful" insofar as 9 percent more citizens in the experimental group registered to vote than in the control group.[1]

Political scientists partial to a well-functioning, legitimate representative system have an abiding interest and concern with high voter registration and turnout. This is also consistent with the rhetoric of most government officials and many political party officials in the United States. Therefore, a great deal of study is made of who registers to vote and who does not, and who votes and who does not. Well within that tradition is the work of the Survey Research Center at the University of Michigan with its finding that "one of the greatest limitations on civic participation [voting] is imposed by sheer ignorance of the existence of major social and economic problems. From the viewpoint of social action [getting out the vote] the problem of creating familiarity with issues is the first task."[2]

A very recent American political scientific examination into why there is such a low voting turnout in the election process of the United States also was aimed at devising a strategy to increase the number of citizens selecting representatives. Francis Fox Piven and Richard A. Cloward, in their *Why Americans Don't Vote*,[3] came to the conclusion that the major factor in nonvoting was impediments to registration. Looking at past American standards for registration, as well as those in current European systems, they concluded that the contemporary American process was consciously designed to discourage registration, and thus voting. Their solution: to seek political reform that makes voter registration an important public policy to be implemented by government through a variety of ways that facilitate the registration process, and to see that voter registration drives are conducted where poor people do their business so that registration efforts reach the traditional nonvoters.

Recommendations for registration reform in the United States have been advocated for quite some time and are intended to swell the percentage of voter participation in an electoral system that falls far short of the public involvement of almost all other Western representative systems. Suspicions exist among participatory democratic theorists, however, that reforms aimed at increased citizen voting without opening other avenues for citizen involvement in decision making are merely techniques to obfuscate the fact that the American system of representation has been designed and redesigned to discourage participation and always has accomplished that purpose substantially.

Therefore, over time, there have been a growing number of empirical researchers who have been developing and testing ways to improve the quality of citizen participation, in general, consistent with a wide variety of political structures. Some of the research has been designed merely to strengthen the Expanded Representative State. Other research has constructed means to provide a new level and/or new types of citizen participation consistent with developing a new form or level of representative government as well, in other words, the Participatory Representative State.

In a few cases, the research and the ideas are consistent with the more revolutionary concept of the Representative Participatory State. In the latter two instances, the citizen participation projects are aimed at making the system more representative of excluded or traditionally under-represented groups. They also are characterized by developing new ways by which citizens become more and better informed and interact more freely and comfortably with one another. In these projects, the nature of the citizen involvement is richer than a simple, silent vote for representatives and other political figures who reign rather than serve.

Defenders of the status quo, and various skeptics, belittle such efforts as being either something that the Founders correctly dismissed (an appeal to the authority of American tradition and the tradition of American authority) or something that cannot work in a nation even the size of the original 13 states, much less the size of modern America. Today's participatory democratic researchers, however, are impressed by the potential inherent in advanced communications technology to overcome great physical distances and facilitate interaction between huge masses of people that make possible forms of participation that the Founders never could imagine. Furthermore, they are more impressed by the dynamic process of revolutionary and inventive thinking of the Founders than they are by the static, historical substance of it. For example, an ardent advocate of political innovation and change, James Madison, once wrote:

> Hearken not to the voice which petulantly tells you that the form of government recommended for your adoption is a novelty in the political world; that it has never yet had a place in the theories of the wildest projectors; that it rashly attempts what is impossible to accomplish. No, my countrymen, shut your ears to this unhallowed language. . . . Is it not the glory of the people of America that, whilst they have paid a decent regard to the opinions of former times and other nations, they have not suffered a blind veneration for antiquity, for custom, or for names, to overrule the suggestions of their own good sense, the knowledge of their own situation, and the lessons of their own experience? To this manly spirit posterity will be indebted for the possession and the world for the example of the numerous innovations displayed on the American theater in favor of private rights and public happiness.[4]

This chapter will center its attention on the inventive tradition established by the Founders of the U.S. Constitution and examine and analyze a number of research and action projects that have tested some technologies and techniques that could prove useful in the functioning of a Representative Participatory State. Some of them sparked and informed the development of the Televote method of public opinion polling and improved citizen participation, the major focus and final section of this volume. The first part of this chapter will analyze some "small-scale" experiments that delve into the microdynamics of citizen participation, specifically, how to develop more informed and higher quality interaction among citizens as they learn about and deliberate issues.

SMALL-SCALE EXPERIMENTS: THE MICRODYNAMICS OF CITIZEN PARTICIPATION

James Dator, who has written extensively on the antiquated American political system, observes that it was created in a period devoid of "the railroad, the telegraph, the telephone, automobile, airplane, television, [and] satellite"[5] and that it gave little power to ordinary citizens who were considered to be "illiterate, isolated, and provincial" by the Founders.[6] The surge into the postindustrial society, the Information Age, the Third Wave, or the New Age has intensified the need for and constructed the instruments for an informed and involved public. Jerome Glenn voices the view of democrats through the centuries who emphasize, "the keystone of a democracy's survival is an educated public."[7] The communication and information technologies of the twentieth century have created the possibilities for the blossoming of a "strong democracy."

Along with the quantum leaps in scientific knowledge and inventions has come a dramatic increase in alternatives available. For many of those concerned with more participatory democracy there is the concern to create "a more conscious awareness of the range of alternative futures and their implications [so] citizens [can] make better informed decisions."[8] Glenn, whose work focuses on involving citizens in policy planning for the future, has studied a number of techniques designed to inform citizens, encourage interaction, and promote participation. Most of them are versions, or include aspects, of the twentieth-century art and science of public opinion polling.

Delphi

One such technique is *Delphi*, a series of questionnaires sent to individuals in an effort to develop consensus. After each round of questioning, each participant in Delphi is provided the results and is allowed the opportunity to change her or his opinion. A distinctive feature of Delphi is that it intentionally keeps the form of communication in a written medium in an effort to keep the focus on ideas rather than on the personalities of the participants. It is a relatively inexpensive and flexible method. It can, however, be tedious and monotonous to individuals who prefer person-to-person contact rather than the isolation inherent in the Delphi method. It also has been used primarily among those with a great deal of education and/or expertise in some field, which has apparently limited its contribution to more inclusive participatory democracy systems. However, the idea of a series, or rounds, of votes and/or opinions as a method of developing consensus would seem to be a useful means to generate a meaningful dialogue and discussion among a larger and/or more diverse group of citizens over time.

Charrette

Another technique, *Charrette*,[9] was created to bring people from various segments of society—the general public, government agencies, universities—to participate together in a series of discussions in an effort to reach a consensus. Small groups, including a wide variety of participants, talk about various aspects of a problem and then report periodically to the whole group, which responds to their ideas. The process moves back and forth from small group discussions to meetings of the entire group until a deadline is reached.

Charrettes come in all sizes with the average consisting of approximately 500 members broken up into five groups. The goal of the charrette is to eliminate distinctions between so-called experts and members of the public. What is made clear is that participation means representing oneself and that hierarchies are not to be established.

Syncon

Another technique aimed at consensus building is the *Syncon* (Synergistic Convergence) created in 1971 by John Whiteside and Barbara Marx Hubbard. Its goal is to bring together people from all walks of life and professional backgrounds to discuss global policies for the future—25 to 100 years ahead. Syncon, which usually consists of about 250 persons, begins with small groups that then merge into groups of intermediate size and then into one large group. The smaller groups discuss functional areas of a culture, while the larger groups discuss areas of new potential (in other words, a merging of functional areas in new patterns).

The Syncon process is intended to be made available on television, allowing home viewers to participate by telephone. PBS broadcast the Los

Angeles Syncon in 1971. This increased its value as an educational device for the general public, but it did not result in any legislative or policy impact. Because Syncons have not been directly related to state or local policy processes, their conclusions rarely are implemented.

Problem/Possibility Focuser

One process that does not strive for consensus, but instead seeks to clarify the agreements and disagreements surrounding a specific issue, is the *problem/possibility focuser* created by Robert Theobald. This begins with a group delineating all the areas of agreement, and then all the areas of disagreement, on the issue at hand. The next step is to develop ideas to settle disagreements. The last step before preparing a report on the process is to list the resources that may help to clarify the nature of the disagreements listed. Theobald states: "The object of a problem/possibility focuser is to increase the agreements and to limit the disagreements surrounding an issue so that those who make policy have the best possible guides to understanding the world within which they must act."[10] He views this method as a continual process, one to keep the public and policy makers informed about new developments relating to the issue.

Computer Conferencing

Computer conferencing is a technique that allows instantaneous communication between a large number of participants all over the country. Messages are typed into a computer, which allows them to be stored and retrieved by participants at their own convenience. It provides a relatively inexpensive means of organizing a conference to discuss a topic without individuals having to travel to a meeting place from various parts of the country. As computer terminals (PCs, laptops, and so forth) become more available and accessible to the general public, computer conferencing can develop into an important component of what Ted Becker has termed the "Electronic Town Meeting."[11] Citizens would have rapid access to substantial data bases and could, in turn, communicate their ideas in an efficient and convenient manner, and utilize Delphis and all other techniques of informed consensus building, via computer networks.

Projects designed to involve citizens in ways to improve the quality of political agenda setting and/or policy-making processes, which use the techniques described above or similar activities, have been experimented with repeatedly all over the United States. The results of these studies have been overwhelmingly positive; that is, new techniques constructed to encourage informed interactions between citizens with varying degrees of knowledge and from diverse backgrounds produce deliberative and informed judgments and occasional consensuses on important and complex public agendas and policies.

In addition, over the last two decades or so, experiments or projects involving large-scale citizen participation in, with, and/or adjacent to government have been plentiful and varied. Some have been shoestring operations and privately sponsored, while others have been major undertakings with significant financial resources and governmental backing aimed at increasing the participation of citizens in a wide variety of governmental functions at all levels of governance. In all cases, the new systems have increased and improved citizen participation from what could have been expected without the use of these techniques and technologies.

LARGE-SCALE EXPERIMENTS: LINKING CITIZENS TO GOVERNMENT

Although the research being conducted on a small scale is important and essential to an understanding of the factors leading to increased and improved citizen participation, as well as the impact of citizen participation, the emphasis here is on relatively large-scale projects that have either a formal or informal relationship with governmental officials in an effort to involve citizens in actual agenda setting, planning, and/or policy making. The components of each of these participatory democratic projects include: (1) an initial openness to all adult citizens in the area; (2) methods to educate citizens; (3) procedures to obtain citizen views; (4) encouragement and provision of ways to interact among citizens; and (5) means to link the citizen participation to planners, policy makers, administrators, and so forth.

Since the projects I am focusing on in this book are all efforts that had direct support from and linkage to either a national, state, or local government, they all have as a goal, either expressed or implied, the desire to strengthen citizen participation in an actual representative system and thus are clearly supportive of the Expanded Representative State and/or the Participatory Representative State. However, many of their techniques, technologies, and theories are compatible with the development of a Representative Participatory State, as are their findings. For example, all of them utilize interactive communications techniques, and all but one (Berks County Television) utilize random methods. Finally, all try to develop new techniques to enable substantial factual and balanced information and opinion to be presented to the public.

Alternatives for Washington

One of the first and most extensive projects aimed at involving citizens in major public planning is Alternatives for Washington (AFW), which ran for two years in the state of Washington.[12] Not only did this pioneering effort link citizens with government, but it was sponsored and funded by the Washington governor's office during Gov. Dan Evans's tenure. Its goal was to involve as many Washington citizens as possible in a process of identifying the major problems the state needed to address and determining the preferred alternative futures to guide state policy. Strong support for participatory democracy came from the state's top official when Governor Evans initiated the program with the statement:

> Our future need be imposed neither by the personal interests of an elite nor the impersonal force of history. It can be determined by all of the people of the state if they are willing to . . . devote the effort to the task. . . . I believe the citizens of this state can, in an orderly and rational manner, determine their future and assure such a privilege will also be available to generations to come.[13]

The project was separated into two phases. The first year's processes sought to portray various future scenarios for the state of Washington and the preferred policies of each of those futures. The second year's processes evaluated the pros and cons of the various policies selected in the first phase.

There were many ways that this project recruited citizens from all walks of life to participate in it, to educate those involved, and to generate and expedite interaction between them. For example, the project included contributions from the state's major newspapers and public television. Activities ranged from small, face-to-face group discussions to thousands of individuals responding to a questionnaire from the privacy of their own homes.

Components of the project, which were tightly coordinated and well integrated, included: (1) a statewide task force of 150 individuals, selected from 4,000 nominees, to oversee the project and to identify the alternatives from the information obtained from the public. A strong emphasis was placed on choosing members of the task force who would be closely "representative" of the population in socioeconomic status, geographic distribution, race, and profession. (2) A Delphi questionnaire was conducted in a three-part series with 2,500 citizens participating to determine trends within and outside of Washington and to judge their effects on the state. (3) Area-wide conferences took place in ten areas of the state and were comprised of 150 to 200 citizens (selected by the governor) to supervise the work of the task force so as to prevent it from becoming too centralized and removed from those they supposedly represented. (4) Television programming sought to educate the public on the evolution of the process and to obtain substantive feedback through call-ins. (5) Newspapers statewide featured lengthy mail-in questionnaires that described 11 futures and asked citizens to respond with their own preferences. Over 26,000 responses were received. (6) Random sample telephone and mail surveys were sent to 6,000 citizens to gain a representative sample of the population's views to the questionnaire published in the newspapers. Two-thirds of those surveyed responded.

While there were many problems in the AFW project, including financial limitations, lack of involvement and support by the state legislature, and tensions between the governor and the legislature, the designers and organizers were able to directly involve over 60,000 Washington State citizens in the various activities. They concluded the program demonstrated that the people have the capacity to participate in the development of policy whether at the local, state, or national level.[14] Criticisms can be and have been made of the failure of the project to prove that all or most citizens are eager to participate or express views when given the opportunity to do so. After all, the newspaper distribution was over a million—why did only 26,000 respond? At the same time, one could ask a different question: When is the last time over 60,000 citizens in any state responded to calls for participation in setting the future agenda for their state—whether the participation involves thinking through philosophical visions of one's future or responding to intensely debated questions of future public policy?

It was particularly interesting that in Washington so much participation could be aroused even though the legislators were obviously ignoring the project. After all, if a citizen is merely using a cost-benefit analysis, what is the likely benefit of participation in a project in which his/her "representatives" are either openly hostile or noticeably aloof?

There are no scientifically determined answers to these questions about the Washington experience. However, the AFW results raise other questions. What would have been the participation rate if (1) the legislature embraced the project; (2) the results of the two-year project determined public policy; and (3) resources and means were available to all those who desired to participate?

F. Christopher Arterton, who studied 13 "policy neutral," "tele-democracy" projects,[15] criticized the AFW project for its unrepresentative samples and maintains that the participants did not necessarily reflect the views of the population at large.[16] He cites the selection process for many of the groups as choosing those who are already politically active and aware and thus not including the views of the traditional nonparticipants. And even though much energy was spent on composing the task force group with emphasis on nonpartisanship and balance according to sex, age, race, and geographic areas, Arterton says the average income of the members was well above the median income of Washington residents.[17]

In spite of these criticisms, Arterton concedes that "involving 65,000 citizens in the public policy process is quite an accomplishment."[18] In fact, it is estimated that a third of the state's 3.5 million residents were contacted in some way to discuss planning goals for the state.[19] Such extensive citizen awareness and participation also had long-term impact. Many of those who got involved, Arterton's study concludes, "went on to further involvement with planning, state government, and citizen activism. Liaisons that developed among citizens, community leaders, and government officials lasted well beyond the life of AFW. And the value of public input was made apparent to both citizens and the government."[20]

Some other impacts of the AFW project include:[21] (1) AFW was viewed as conveying the importance of controlled growth and conservation to citizens who were not sensitive to these issues before the project. Several conservation measures passed after the discussion of them in AFW. (2) There was a realization that the media was willing to cooperate in providing substantive information to the citizens and government on controversial issues. Many activists developed very good relations with the media during and after AFW. (3) The local NBC affiliate began to provide several programs dealing with local and national issues and worked with the League of Women Voters and newspapers to publicize the programs. (4) The transportation authority in Seattle began a cable television program to provide information and seek call-ins from citizens. (5) Even though the legislature was unfriendly and unreceptive to the project, Arterton's study found "many of its recommendations subsequently worked their way into state policy and the project legitimized innovative ways of gauging citizen opinion to inform the policy process."[22]

Berks Community Television

A project which began at the same time AFW was ending provides an excellent indication of the results that can be obtained when the "representative" body is responsive to public input. In 1976 the New York University Media Center received support from the National Science

Foundation to develop a video communications network in Reading, Pennsylvania, in order to promote the social welfare of senior citizens and shut-ins.[23] The system, called Berks (County) Community Television, began as a program that allowed senior citizens to communicate via video with city officials since they were unable to attend public hearings.

The participation of these citizens in the program was so much better than expected that the city government decided to try to increase general citizen participation in government by expanding the program. All budget hearings and Community Development Block Grants hearings were then aired "live" over two-way cable television. All citizens were then able to participate on-camera by visiting neighborhood centers equipped with interactive video that utilizes a "split-screen" technique. Citizens also could telephone in from their homes while watching the hearings on television.

When the expansion of the project first began, the average number of citizens who attended budget hearings in Berks County was two or three.[24] At the first interactive television budget hearing, more than 50 citizens participated in providing input either from their homes or via the video equipped neighborhood centers. The process allows citizens to propose alternatives, disagree with city-sponsored proposals, or simply ask questions for more information.

Currently there is a weekly dialogue among the mayor, one or more city councilpersons, and the public. In addition, if a major community crisis arises, electronic town meetings are established to bring citizens into the discussion of the problem and determination of how to solve it. Rather than turn their backs on the eagerness of many citizens to participate, the city officials in Reading, Pennsylvania, have acknowledged its value and expanded the opportunities. Ben Barber argues that the project's success in providing access to information and stimulating participatory debate "suggests ways to overcome the problem of scale and to defeat technological complexity by putting technology to work for democratic ends."[25] The results of the ongoing project are highlighted by a dramatic increase in citizen participation.[26]

Not only did citizen participation dramatically increase in Reading, but Arterton's study reveals qualitative improvements in the participation for both citizens as well as government leaders.[27] As time went by, the citizens began to show a much better understanding of how city government operated. When the project first began, citizens asked questions about services the city did not provide and showed a confusion about which functions were performed by various departments. They not only began to understand more about the functions of their government as programming continued, but also began to ask follow-up questions, which demonstrated an analytical approach to the issues being discussed. The mayor and city council members also became more sophisticated in interacting with the public. Some of them showed their own lack of knowledge or understanding of political problems. Through increased interaction with citizens, they began to be less ignorant of issues and functions and more responsive to citizen concerns.

Arterton's conclusion is that "BCTV has improved the accountability of local officials to those whom they serve.... BCTV has exposed city government to the real concerns of the people."[28] The mayor of Reading, who came to power as a strong supporter of BCTV, believes that "as citizens become better acquainted with how local government works and what it can accomplish, they have also become less cynical about local politics."[29]

Alaska Legislative Teleconference Network

An example of obtaining input from citizens on an even larger scale than Reading, Pennsylvania, is how the Alaska legislature designed a system to allow the citizens in the nation's geographically largest state to obtain information on legislation from the government and then to communicate their ideas and views in legislative committee hearings.[30] Their system began in 1977 in response to the repeated complaints that Juneau, the state capital, was too isolated, which made it extremely difficult for Alaskan citizens to appear in person to speak at public hearings. An experimental statewide public hearing was broadcast live by the state's public television and radio stations, as well as by some commercial broadcasters. Citizens were given toll-free numbers so they could call in with comments and questions.

Steve Smith maintains that "the success of this experiment, fear of a capital move by Southeast legislators, interest by rural legislators in connecting their constituents with the rest of Alaska, and a bulging state pocketbook (due to oil revenues) led to the formation of the legislative teleconference network (LTN)."[31] It originally began with teleconferencing centers that connected citizens to legislative hearings. Since that time the number of teleconference sites has expanded to over 60 operating in several Alaskan cities. The LTNs are available for use 24 hours a day and not only serve citizens through increased access, but facilitate research by legislators and other government officials who can communicate more easily without having to travel as frequently to obtain information from experts and citizens.

While the LTN has been met with enthusiasm by citizens, not all legislators have been pleased with it. Prior to its existence, there was little news from remote Juneau during the legislative sessions. After a few years of the LTN and increased awareness of state functions, there were reporters from the major newspapers, television stations, and radio stations covering events all over the state capital. The watchful eyes of the media hawks made many legislators anxious. Thus at one point the Alaska House of Representatives suspended its coverage of hearings but resumed when the senate failed to follow suit. Smith also points out that there has been no research conducted to determine the impact of the increased citizen involvement on legislative policy making.[32]

Arterton's study demonstrates the increasing local popularity and citizen interest in the LTN of Alaska. His data shows that from 1981 to 1984 the number of teleconferences increased from 412 to 715 and the number of citizens attending the teleconferences increased from 8,745 to 17,661.[33] The LTN has become so popular that the network usage reached saturation levels during the 1984 legislative sessions, forcing the system operator to establish priorities by which to choose between competing users for the valued air time.[34]

While many of the legislators were originally worried that the system was somehow an attempt to erode their power, most have become users of the system. They discovered in a very short period of time that "Alaskans wanted a greater voice in government and were willing to use the network."[35] Even though some legislators see its value as an informational tool for themselves as well as the citizens, they also recognize the political wisdom of continuing the LTN. As research indicates, the citizens want to participate and legislators fear the reaction of citizens if they are no longer included in this process.[36]

As in Reading, Pennsylvania, Arterton's study concludes that the LTN "has exerted an important influence on government accountability of Alaskan politics."[37] It also has increased the sophistication of citizens and produced the same understanding of government and complexity of issues that the BCTV programming has produced over time.[38] As a result, lawmakers in Alaska are now seeking opinions from a cross section of the Alaska population.[39]

Alaska Television Town Meeting

Another impressive citizen participation innovation in Alaska was the 1980 Alaska Television Town Meeting (ATTM). It was a series of modern-day electronic town meetings sponsored by the Alaska Department of Transportation in order to determine how Alaskans wished to spend transportation tax dollars and to obtain their ideas on long-range planning and other general fiscal matters.

The ATTM was conducted over a ten-day period in seven urban centers around the state. Prior to the start of the programming, a baseline survey was conducted to provide a framework of issues for each television town meeting. The questionnaire was developed in consultation with state officials and was utilized in a survey of randomly selected homes. The purpose was to obtain data on the trends in the use of transportation and communication facilities. In addition, extensive advertising took place in order to spur interest and participation in the shows. Thirty-second public service announcements (PSAs) were broadcast on local television stations, radio commercials were aired, and newspaper advertisements were run in local newspapers.

In order to increase participation, experiment with new forms of technology, and expand public-opinion gathering capacity, the organizers felt they also could create a dynamic public hearing by designing three different groups of participants from the viewers in each urban area. The first group was a *telephone group*, which was randomly selected, that called certain numbers to record their vote and a computer automatically tallied the votes in two to four minutes. The second group was the *consensor group*, which met at a central location in each community. This group also was randomly selected from telephone listings or random digit dialing. Each participant was given a consensor, a hand-held electronic device rigged to a computer, and could respond to questions by turning to a numbered dial on the consensor. The results were tabulated by the computer in three to four seconds. Finally, the rest of the audience was encouraged to respond as individual callers to ask questions or make comments live on the air. For those whose calls were not aired live, they would receive a written response, if requested, from the appropriate state or local agency.

An evaluation survey conducted the day after each show in each community indicated around 95,000 people watched the programs (attended the hearings) and over 4,000 of them participated as part of one of the three groups. Public response to the program was quite favorable. The more involved the participants were, the more they rated the experience superior to the conventional public hearings. The viewing audience preferred the television town meeting with a 66 percent majority, the consensor group with a 71 percent majority.

One of the major drawbacks of the ATTM experiment from the perspective of representative participatory democracy, however, is the over-representation of college-educated participants. In all cities, well over a majority of participants had some college education. In Juneau it was 87 percent and Anchorage had 80 percent. A full 59 percent of the participants in Juneau had college degrees.[40] It is clear that large segments of the population—the ones traditionally left out of the political process—did not get involved. Nevertheless, of those who viewed, nearly half had never attended a public hearing, so this process afforded them an opportunity for involvement that increased the likelihood of their participation. The organizers of the project concluded:

> The main discovery of the Television Town Meeting Project was that a new form of public participation could be produced. New technological tools were combined with television to enable more people to take part in a town meeting. . . . The project resulted in a design for low-cost, high-efficiency public participation. The design can now be used to procure large-scale public participation in appropriate projects.[41]

These participatory democratic government affiliated projects have demonstrated the following: (1) Large segments of the population are willing to participate in ways they never have before. (2) Attempts to educate the public on issues, processes, and functions of government are successful. (3) Citizens not only become better informed through attempts to involve them in public discussion and interaction, but begin to understand complexities and approach issues more analytically. (4) When legislators are involved, they become better informed on problems and issues. (5) Legislators become more accountable as public awareness and sophistication grow. (6) Citizens want more, not less, access and responsibility.

As Arterton points out, however, each project failed to significantly include the poor and uneducated. None of them came close to approaching universal participation. While the lack of participation by those who regularly are excluded or not represented in the system is a dilemma participatory democrats must face, they also have to work within a system with a structural bias against, distrust for, and contempt of massive political participation. There are many obstacles participatory democrats face in demonstrating the capacities of the people and the technology for a more representative and participatory democracy. Although these projects neglected to design appropriate means for reaching and involving the undereducated and poor, their results certainly challenge the view that citizens are unable and unwilling to play a greater and more responsible role in government and provide a foundation for extending their research and designs to include even greater diversity in citizen participation.

The final parts of this chapter, building on the knowledge gained from previous participatory democratic experiments, present a model, designed by Canadian researchers, that offers a view of how such a system might function. It concludes with an introduction of the Televote system, which has been designed as a tool to be utilized in a more participatory and more representative state.

A MODEL FOR CITIZEN PARTICIPATION IN A REPRESENTATIVE AND PARTICIPATORY STATE

In 1982 a group of Montreal researchers, called the Gamma Group, published the results of an international study of citizen participation projects. The purpose of the research, which was commissioned by the United Nations Educational, Scientific, and Cultural Organization (UNESCO), was

> to develop a theoretical model of democratic and horizontal com-
> munication on the basis of maximum public participation in the
> decision making process. In effect it provides a conceptual and logical
> framework concerning the hypothesis that modern communication
> technology may lead to "telecommunitary democracy" where inter-
> active devices will allow both intracommunity and intercommunity
> involvement in the political process.[42]

The Gamma Group evaluated projects on the basis of how well each addressed the problems of political alienation by designs that encourage and increase citizen participation within the present confines of the rep-resentative state. The theory behind the design of the study is that as institutions become larger and more powerful, they also become more impersonal, which makes citizens feel smaller and less useful. This in turn leads to massive frustration and alienation. At the same time citizens are developing this "inferiority complex," they begin to pull away from accept-ing responsibility for human action. Big government then steps in and becomes more involved in social activities and increases its impact on the lives of citizens. The danger of this disengagement of the citizen from public affairs combined with the interference of the state in social life is the establishment of totalitarian elitism where a small minority governs all aspects of society. In addition, "advances in science and technology make it easier to centralize control and manipulate people."[43]

The solution advocated by the Gamma Group is to build confidence in the individual and to promote citizen responsibility in politics. Their hypothesis is that "increased politicization of people decreases alienation and makes far more responsible and legitimate government."[44] Rather than being ruled or controlled by modern technology, the goal is to use

Figure 4.1
Political Underdevelopment

Political Underdevelopment	Political Development
Symptoms	Cure
Colonialism	Sovereignty
Elitism	Equality
Irresponsibility	Accountability
Oppression	Free Speech
Violence	Peace
Anomie	Rule of Law
Alienation	Legitimacy
Apathy	Participation
Atomism	Civic spirit
Secrecy	Knowledge

information and communication technologies to enhance the power of citizens. Their pursuit is what they term "Telecommunitary Democracy" (TCD), a participatory alternative to the technocracy of modern society.

Telecommunitary Democracy is seen as a prescription for the ills of modern governments—political underdevelopment. Figure 4.1 indicates the problems that may occur within governmental systems and solutions sought by TCD.[45]

The formula for Telecommunitary Democracy is: Political Development + Information Technology. In TCD there are three kinds of actors: (1) government officials, (2) citizens, and (3) mediators. The mediators are those individuals or groups who facilitate contact among the other actors and who produce and distribute information. Traditional mediators in society have included experts who produce or transform knowledge, such as researchers, inventors, scientists, consultants, or the media communicators of information—journalists, publishers, broadcasters.

The crucial role of the mediators, who are labeled "technics" in the TCD policy-making flow model, is simply to distribute knowledge and information and facilitate communication between the citizens and government officials. The technics are not to make judgments. Their knowledge will be available by all to use in their own evaluations and decision making. In the participatory democratic mode, the technics will place the experts where Friedrich says they should be—on tap, not on top.

The political process as envisioned by the Gamma Group is laid out in their policy-making flow model (see Figure 4.2).[46] Activities of the three groups in the society go through three states: inputs, throughputs, and outputs. The Gamma Group describes the political process generally as a process in which disagreements turn into agreements. The model provides for interaction between citizens and government officials at every stage. The technics are responsible for the flow of information not only between groups, but also as the process moves from one stage to another. In the process of each stage, the technics present information that includes not only undisputed facts, but also pro and con arguments. They promote debate as well as consensus building. The debate is not a means to polarize in this process, but a means used in evaluation that can lead to informed and deliberated decision making in a participatory democratic system.

The TCD model is not reliant upon a highly industrialized, economically developed nation. Case studies included in the Gamma Group study include those originating in such diverse countries as Mexico, Yugoslavia, India, and Ecuador and they indicate how the educational system or elementary media devices such as newspapers or radios can function to promote participation by citizens. The model, however, is reliant upon independent mediators. If information is owned, screened, withheld, or distorted for the benefit of any group in society, this taints the entire process. The Gamma Group researchers provide no concrete panaceas as to how mediator independence is achieved, rather an ideal to be pursued, offering brief evaluations of the successes and failures of 20 TCD case studies from various nations that to some degree work toward the ideal. The two projects that the Gamma Group researchers found to most closely fit the TCD model were *Televotes* conducted in Hawaii and New Zealand.[47]

In answering their question "Is telecommunitary democracy a utopian vision or probable future?" the Gamma Group concludes from their research that it is both possible and desirable.[48] Their study of 20 projects across the globe convinces them that the use of technology to promote democracy already is being demonstrated. They add to that the fact that the international community through the United Nations has "implicitly or explicitly called for increased popular participation in policy-making as a fundamental aspect of the development process."[49] While vested interests of powerful groups will resist efforts to increase democracy, the Gamma Group believes that the "consciousness-raising and rising expectations of people everywhere increases social demands and political pressures which

Figure 4.2
TCD Policy-Making Flowchart

POLITICAL PROCESS

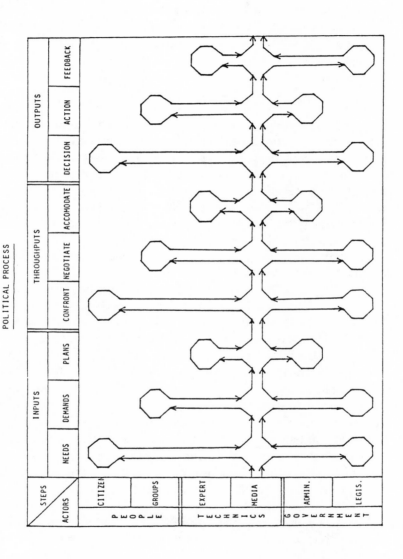

cannot be ignored indefinitely."[50] Given the demand for more participation and the technological capacities now available to facilitate it, the
Canadian researchers call for serious thought about the implications and
the implementation of more citizen participation. Their TCD model is
their effort to address this next step. The research conducted by the Televote
designers continues the research process.

TELEVOTE: INCREASING CITIZEN PARTICIPATION
THROUGH EDUCATIONAL PUBLIC OPINION POLLING

Televote is a phrase coined by Vincent Campbell, a psychologist, who
places himself in the category of a "democratist" who seeks to maximize
direct public control. The purpose of the Televote design was to create an
innovative system of "civic communication" that could lead to the implementation of effective methods of citizen participation. Campbell
received a National Science Foundation grant in 1973 to provide a means
for involving parents and students in the determination of public school
policy in San Jose, California.[51]

From the beginning stages, parents, students, and public officials
participated in working with the Televote researchers to decide the
issues that would be the subject of Televote questionnaires. After the key
issues were determined, the Televote staff conducted research on them
to obtain factual information as well as arguments for and against
various alternatives in dealing with them. All the material was refined
to be included as a part of each questionnaire. Campbell stresses that
"the most critical function of the [Televote staff] is to insure that all
sides of each issue are stated well and fairly, so that citizens' judgments
are informed from all major perspectives."[52] The Televote staff was so
conscientious in its task of providing unbiased information to questionnaire respondents (Televoters) that "complaints of bias in the final issue
statements were almost nonexistent."[53] This is the sort of role definition
that fits well within the requirement of successful "technics" in the
Gamma Group model. The original Televote experiment showed that it
could and did work well.

The major emphasis in the project was placed on maximizing citizen
participation, particularly reaching out to those who traditionally were less
likely to participate. For instance, Mexican-Americans were sent Televote
information in both English and Spanish. An extensive outreach campaign
took place through newspapers, cable television programming, commercial television spots, and radio announcements in an effort to get citizens
to become Televoters.

The process worked as follows. After citizens learned of the project through the media, which also distributed the list of issues to be voted on, anyone interested in participating—students included—registered as an official Televoter by mailing in his or her name and some personal information, sending it through the San Jose inter-school delivery system, or phoning it in.

Once registered, each Televoter received a personalized registration number and detailed information on each issue, which included the relevant undisputed facts and pro and con arguments. Televoters were given several days to think about the responses before casting their tele-ballots. The actual voting process was a technologically sophisticated system designed to minimize the inconvenience and maximize the time efficiency for both the Televoters and Televote staff.

Televoters had two options for voting. One option was to call during an eight-hour period on weekdays and record their vote with an operator, who answered the Televote "hotline." In placing his or her vote, the Televoter provided the personalized registration number and then responded by stating the number of the preferred choice. (Each alternative had been assigned a number on the questionnaire that allowed for instantaneous recording of responses.) The other option made full use of the advanced technology. Citizens could place calls to the central office where an answering machine allowed them to dial their Televote registration number and then their answer numbers. A computer program attached to the answering equipment tallied the results automatically. Within a few days of the televoting, the results of the Televotes were mailed to the school officials, the media, and the school-parent associations. During the 1973 to 1974 school year, nine Televotes were conducted.

In evaluating the project, Campbell examined level of participation, impact on policy making, attitudes regarding communication, and user satisfaction with the process. While he was impressed with the 5,500 individuals registering to participate in the demonstration project, the actual participation in any given Televote was only about 15 percent of those registered. There are a number of factors that Campbell feels contributed to this low turnout, including the requirement that Televoters register and the fact that participation did not guarantee results. In other words, the vote did not carry the weight of law. Also the self-selection resulted in a demographic disparity with ethnic minorities greatly underrepresented.

Did the Televotes have an impact on policy making? The results indicated if the issue was already on the policy agenda of the San Jose school district officials, it had a much greater chance of being dealt with. It was determined that out of seven issues already on the agenda, four apparently had some impact. However, if the issue was one initiated by students, parents, or the Televote staff, Campbell concluded there was no "tangible impact on district policy or decisions as a result of those Televotes."[54]

Follow-up surveys indicated that the level of public awareness could be increased by Televote. They found that the public awareness of school issues tended to increase during the Televote period. However, level of awareness was highly correlated along ethnic and socioeconomic lines. The Televote was not sufficient to overcome the feelings of approximately half the follow-up survey respondents that either government officials don't care what people think or that government is too complicated for them to understand.[55] But it did encourage over 5,000 people to participate in a process of thinking about and acting on major educational issues—which is radically more than would have participated without the Televote system.

An important finding of the Televote experiment for those interested in participatory democracy is the post-test survey results that indicated 95 percent of the Televoters would be interested in participating again and expanding the project to include other governmental bodies as well as the school district. In addition, a random survey of the registered Televoters found that 73 percent were willing to pay for the system of participation.[56]

Televote is a political design that fits well within the TCD model. It offers an unbiased, independent mediating role between government and the citizens in order to produce an interactive decision-making process that offers great potential for a truly representative participatory democracy. Campbell created the design and provided essential information for those promoters of expanded citizen participation. He demonstrated that (1) citizen awareness and knowledge can be increased through the use of modern communications; (2) many citizens are willing and eager to take on more responsibility; and (3) participation can be increased. His research provided a foundation for others who adapted the Televote system to create even greater potential for citizen involvement in the United States. The next chapter will examine a series of Televotes conducted in Hawaii, Los Angeles, and New Zealand to see how Televote has been revised to expand citizen participation in a representative participatory democracy.

NOTES

1. Harold Foote Gosnell, *Getting Out the Vote* (Chicago: University of Chicago Press, 1927).

2. Angus Campbell, Philip E. Converse, Warren E. Miller, and Donald Stokes, *The American Voter* (New York: John Wiley & Sons, 1968), p. 170.

3. Frances Fox Piven and Richard A. Cloward, *Why Americans Don't Vote* (New York: Pantheon Books, 1988).

4. James Madison, "Federalist Paper No. 14," in Alexander Hamilton, James Madison, and John Jay, *The Federalist Papers* (New York: New American Library, 1961), pp. 99–105.

5. Some examples are the following articles by James A. Dator: "Futuristics and the Exercise of Anticipatory Democracy in Hawaii," in *Political Science and the Study of the Future*, edited by Albert Somit (Hinsdale, Ill.: Dryden Press, 1974), pp. 187–203; "Reforming American Government: Within-System Tinkerings," unpublished manuscript, 1972; and "The 1982 Honolulu Electronic Town Meeting," in *The Future of Politics*, edited by William Page (London: Frances Pinter, 1983), pp. 211–220.

6. Dator, "Futuristics," p. 197.

7. Jerome C. Glenn, "Social Technologies of Freedom," in *Anticipatory Democracy*, edited by Clement Bezold (New York: Random House, 1978), p. 251.

8. Bezold, p. xxvi.

9. Charrette is a French word meaning "little cart." It has come to mean feverish work to meet a deadline with some public input (Glenn, p. 259).

10. Robert Theobald, "The Deeper Implications of Citizen Participation," in *Anticipatory Democracy*, p. 314.

11. Theodore L. Becker, "The Constitutional Network: An Evolution in American Democracy," in *Anticipatory Democracy*, p. 297.

12. Information on Alternatives for Washington is obtained from Robert L. Stilger, "Alternatives for Washington," in *Anticipatory Democracy*, p. 88–99.

13. Ibid., p. 88.

14. Ibid., pp. 98–99.

15. F. Christopher Arterton, *Teledemocracy: Can Technology Protect Democracy?* (Newbury Park, Calif.: Sage, 1987). He defines teledemocracy as "the use of communications technology to facilitate the transmission of political information and opinion between citizens and their public leaders" (p. 14).

16. Ibid., pp. 149–151.

17. Ibid., p. 150.

18. Ibid., p. 155.

19. B. M. Orton, "Media-based Issue Balloting for Regional Planning," dissertation, Rutgers University, 1980.

20. Arterton, p. 154.

21. Ibid., pp. 154–155.

22. Ibid., p. 158.

23. Information on the Reading, Pennsylvania, project is obtained from Theodore L. Becker and Richard Scarce, "Teledemocracy Emergent: State of the American Art and Science," in *Progress in Communication Sciences*, edited by Brenda Dervin and Melvin Voight (Norwood, N.J.: Ablex, 1986), pp. 263–287; and Benjamin Barber, *Strong Democracy* (Berkeley: University of California Press, 1984), p. 276.

24. Becker and Scarce, p. 276.

25. Barber, p. 276.

26. Ibid.

27. Arterton, pp. 101–102.

28. Ibid., p. 104.

29. Ibid., p. 102.

30. Information on Alaska's LTN and Television Town Meeting is from Becker and Scarce, pp. 276–277; Steve Smith, "Alaska Communications, Development and Democracy," in Majid Tehranian, "Electronic Democracy: Information Technologies and Democratic Prospects," Honolulu, report given to UNESCO, 1985, pp. 139–172; and Alaska State Legislature, Division of Public Services, *Providing a Participatory Legislative Environment* (Juneau: Alaska State Legislature, 1982).

31. Smith, p. 156.

32. Ibid., p. 157.

33. Arterton, p. 109.

34. Ibid., p. 106.

35. Ibid., p. 108.

36. Ibid., p. 109.

37. Ibid., p. 111.

38. Ibid.

39. Ibid., p. 112.

40. Data from Alaska, Office of the Governor, *Report on Alaska Television Town Meeting of the Alaska Public Forum* (Juneau: Office of the Governor, 1980), pp. 9–11 and 44.

41. Office of the Governor, p. 44.

42. P. J. Arnopoulos and K. Valaskakis, *Telecommunitary Democracy: Utopian Vision or Probable Future* (Montreal: UNESCO, 1982), preface.

43. Ibid., p. 1.

44. Ibid.

45. Ibid., pp. 4–5.

46. TCD Policy-Making Flowchart is a reproduction of a chart presented in Arnopoulos and Valaskakis.

47. Arnopoulos and Valaskakis, p. 56.

48. Ibid., p. 45.

49. Ibid.

50. Ibid., p. 46.

51. Information on the original Televote project from Vincent N. Campbell, *The Televote System for Civic Communication: First Demonstration and Evaluation* (Palo Alto, Calif.: American Institute for Research, 1974).

52. Ibid., p. 8.

53. Ibid.

54. Ibid., p. 17.

55. Ibid., pp. 31–32.

56. Ibid., pp. 36–37.

5

The Hawaii Televote Model:
Applying Techniques,
Learning Lessons,
Realizing the Future

The success of Campbell's innovative Televote system came to the attention of researchers at the University of Hawaii who were pondering how to get the citizens of the state involved in a statewide constitutional convention to be convened in summer 1978. Constitutional conventions, despite their significance and revolutionary potential, are not known to stimulate much excitement—or participation—among the citizens of any polity. Ordinary exhortations and normal methods of publicity usually fail to alleviate citizen apathy toward such events. Extraordinary and novel means were needed—and Televote seemed an excellent way to go. In addition, it seemed to be an excellent prototype of technology and technique for a much more participatory government.

There were problems and/or questions we had, however, about Televote's usefulness as a technique to generate quality participation (among all segments of the state) and to deliver informed input on the public's views to the delegates of the Constitutional Convention (CONCON). First, there was the big question about how a more representative group of citizens could be induced to become Televoters and actually participate in the whole process. Second, there was the problem of how an independent organization could be formed, trained, and run without large sums of money (not easy to come by and always a problem remaining free of its influence). Third, what kind of system could be developed, with what democratically sensitive roles, that would minimize bias in the information dispensed to the public? Fourth, would this system work? Would the provision of data and opinion actually educate the respondents and help them decide questions that were previously beyond their interest and/or understanding? Fifth, how could the information on the public's views be best distributed to the CONCON delegates, or any representative government officials, and to what extent, if any, would that information be used? And finally, how sustainable was this new system? Would the public find it satisfying enough to want to use it, participate in it, more than once?

THE HAWAII TELEVOTE MODEL

After discussing the situation, and the pros and cons of Campbell's Televote system, Ted Becker, Richard Chadwick, and I devised a new model of Televote, which we called Hawaii Televote, and invited Campbell to Honolulu as a consultant on the project. He came and helped us revise his system.

How to Recruit Representative Samples of Televoters

Rather than rely on a self-selected group of citizens to participate in the system, as Campbell did, we chose to seek a representative sample of the population by using the conventional telephone survey method called "random digit dialing" (RDD). In addition, we applied other scientific survey methods so that our results could reflect the general population's views within a given margin of error. By doing this, we could help avoid the heavy demographic skews that characterized Campbell's Televotes.

However, even though this RDD methodology reaches a random and representative portion of the population (including those with unlisted telephone numbers), we were concerned about how to convince the people who answered the phone (or those whom we sought) to spend their time on such a lengthy and complex (Televote) process and how to increase the chances that a representative sample would complete the process. Also, how could we best ensure that citizens would actually read the material and not discard it upon reception?

It was decided that a necessary requirement was to make the Televote brochure visually attractive. We did this by using quality paper, multiple colors, an attractive logo with a catchy slogan, and artistic illustrations. We also stamped our envelopes with the slogan "Televote: Your Hotline to Government." Another necessary component was the use of a combination of telephone and mail survey techniques in the Hawaii Televote model.

From the start, we planned to use the telephone to recruit Televoters for a number of reasons. First, with over 95 percent of Hawaii households having telephones, it was believed that random digit dialing would offer an excellent chance of attracting a representative sample of the population without the added costs and difficulties associated with door-to-door interviews. Second, the telephone contact would offer more personal contact and better opportunity to recruit Televoters than a simple mail survey. In addition, we were aware of the advanced technology and potential of instantaneous recording of votes if one were to use the telephone, rather than mail-in questionnaires, to respond. Although the Hawaii Televote project did not have the funds or technology available to Campbell, we felt his model could be applied at basic (person-to-person), as well as sophisticated (person-to-computer), levels.

From a computer-generated list of random numbers we called to enroll Televoters. All businesses and foreign speakers were weeded out. When we found an eligible respondent, we explained who we were and what we were trying to do and asked for their help. If the individual was reluctant, we stressed the importance of his/her participation in order to lend scientific validity to our system. Some of our efforts to solicit respondents were hindered—though not significantly—when we asked the respondents for their names and addresses in order to mail the Televote brochures to them. Most of those who objected to this request expressed suspicion that we were trying to sell them something or that we were part of a commercial gimmick.

During our initial introduction, however, we emphasized that we were university-based. When suspicions arose, we gave our university telephone number and, if requested, the names of professors in charge. A few individuals were fearful that their responses would somehow be used against them. In those cases, if our assurances of confidentiality were not enough, we were willing to send the questionnaire to Mr., Ms., or Mrs. Resident at the designated address.

Willingness to participate varied somewhat from survey to survey. Generally, approximately 50 percent to 65 percent of those eligible to participate agreed to do so.[1] For most polls we sought 550 participants, expecting to "lose" approximately 25 percent, leaving us with around 400 who actually responded.

The instructions we gave the participants at the time of recruitment included requests to read the information we sent; talk to their friends, relatives, and others about the issue; and to think about it before making up their minds. In our early Televotes, we told them to call our hotline number to convey their results. We were open seven days a week for several hours a day. Those who did not call us within a week of receipt of the Televote were called by our office—sometimes several times—to record the responses. Only 10 percent to 15 percent of the Televoters actually initiated calls to our office. This small percentage is quite consistent with the initial response rate to most mail questionnaires. In later Televotes, rather than keeping the office staffed for many hours a week to handle only a few calls, we began to make appointments with our Televoters at the time we recruited them for a time to call them back for their answers that was convenient to them. Utilizing this method, we would note on the first page of their Televote the day and time we would be calling them back for their responses.

Our call-back process lasted two to three weeks, resulting in an average response rate from those who had received the materials of approximately 75 percent to 80 percent (although we often stopped calling soon after reaching our baseline number). There were problems of incorrect addresses and questionnaires not being received or being misplaced, which prevented some of the respondents from being prepared when we called. Every day of the data collection we re-mailed several questionnaires to Televoters. In each of our Televotes, we were able to obtain the minimum number of Televoters we needed.

How to Support and Sustain Political Independence and Neutrality

Campbell's design established a neutral, independent organization whose role was to serve as an impartial intermediary between the public and the government. The money to pay the staff to do this came from the National Science Foundation in the form of financing a pilot or demonstration project. It worked. But it was not an organization that was to continue. It had a limited time with limited funding.

So a big question remained: How can one establish an ongoing organization that would be (relatively) free of a structural bias or manipulation of the data and/or process? The Gamma Group in Montreal did an excellent job of describing the role of the "technics" in facilitating "Telecommunitarian Democracy," but it failed to explain how such an entity can be born and live in the real world of powerful competing and co-opting interests.

The Hawaii Televote group came up with a design, not a perfect one, but a design that seemed to hold substantial promise. The American-style university is, itself, one of the most independent institutions in the society—but only at the curricular level. Administratively, it is dependent on (and strongly influenceable by) a wide variety of economic and political power sources. Due to the long tradition of "academic freedom" that pervades the American higher education establishment, professors and researchers have substantial degrees of freedom to say and do what they desire in the classroom and laboratories of the U.S. university system.

While, admittedly, professors can be just as biased as any other individuals in society and they can feel the subtle (and sometimes not so subtle) pressures to comply with powerful political or funding interests, their training has conditioned them to a self-critical approach in developing their theories and conducting their research. And if a professor should fail in seeing his or her bias or error, or neglect the standards demanded by the academic profession, it is likely that the professor's colleagues would provide the criticism to reveal the flaws. University research is usually subject to review, evaluation, and critique by skilled professionals utilizing a variety of approaches and perspectives. Trade secrets and undisclosed methodologies that may exist in private laboratories and institutes, or even some governmental institutions, are not tolerated in academia (except when research is "classified").

Of course, critiques of academic work do not end all problems of bias or misuse of information. In fact, the critics of research may themselves be guilty of prejudices or sloppy research. The value of work that is subject to the examination of other trained professionals, however, is that information distortion and manipulation are much less likely to occur successfully than under conditions that do not lend themselves to such exposure and review.

Another advantage of the university-based Televote is the low overhead of operation if existing resources at the university are maximized. In our case, the Televotes were conducted in methodology classes that allowed students hands-on experience in all aspects of the Televote process as they learned the rigors of scientific polling methodology.[2] Salary costs for directors, coordinators, and staff can be greatly reduced if the Televote process is employed as an educational tool while serving an intermediary function between the public and the government. In addition, support services, such as telephones, photocopying, office equipment, and stationery, can be funded out of the academic instructional budget (with the cooperation of the department chair or head). Educational benefits for students also are enhanced as they interact with government officials in the designing of the Televote brochure and in distributing the results to elected representatives.

The Hawaii Televote research project did need some start-up funding in addition to regular university resources. The vice-president for academic affairs at the University of Hawaii provided a small grant to cover the costs of some computers, designing and printing the Televotes, consultants (Campbell), and so forth. He was excited about the project as an innovative teaching tool. As will be discussed in greater detail later, our experiences taught us that the university is not an impermeable membrane against pressures that try to interfere with political impartiality and the sustainability of the operations. Yet after many years of experimenting with Televote, we believe that procedures can be designed and safeguards implemented that allow the university to successfully house "technics" in a Telecommunitarian Democracy.

How to Minimize Bias in Information Gathering and Distribution

As noted in Chapter 4, one of the greatest dangers in all forms of polling is the tainting effect of bias. We realized that this was something we had to take great pains to minimize and, if possible, avoid. At every stage of our process through research, design, execution, and analysis, we had to question our motives and actions, seek impartial sources of data, and obtain outside input to guard against personal views affecting the entire Televote process.

In our research stage, after an issue had been chosen, we decided to seek three kinds of information. The first was *undisputed, objective information.* For instance, if the issue were tenure of office for the governor, we would find out the present constitutional provision (unarguable legal data). We also would get *historical facts* on how long the provision existed and if it had ever been otherwise. Then we would seek *comparative data* from other states: How many states had the same tenure for governor? What other options were practiced in different states?

The next step would be to offer several alternatives to the current system. Finally, we would seek arguments for and against the various alternatives. In conducting the research in the last two phases we decided to be as broad-based as possible. We would read social science literature, editorials, letters to the editor, and campaign materials. We would solicit ideas from politicians, organized groups, professors, and interested citizens. Ideas were to be sought from diverse political perspectives. It was not assumed that the two major political parties, Democrat and Republican, fully represented the preferred choices of the public at large. Indeed, these two parties' differences are actually the boundaries of the American political center and more innovative and/or extreme positions and alternatives must be sought out and expressed in order to minimize the status-quo bias in any and all participatory democratic methods, including Televote.

In addition, because we were providing respondents education on the issue, we had to be extra careful that the material we chose to include did not show a prejudice in favor of one viewpoint over another. After going through our information and questions several times to correct for bias and errors, we took our draft to individuals who were advocates for various alternatives to be sure we had accurately conveyed their positions and that they also agreed that the data we included in the Televote was indisputable. We even went so far to insure that the pro and con arguments on any alternative were almost the exact size in the number of words used and appeared to be the same size and contour in the Televote brochure.

Next, our students conducted pre-tests with relatives and friends in an attempt to try to find any overlooked problems with confusing or overly complex verbiage or questions. Once we satisfied ourselves and our opinion contributors, we took the questionnaire to a respected professional polling firm, Survey Marketing Services, for a final check. We believe that this multistage process helped minimize the problems of providing exhaustive (but mutually exclusive) alternatives, avoiding double-barreled questions, using double negatives or confusing sentence structure, employing overly sophisticated wording, determining appropriate question order, and making instructions clear. Eliminating these errors in questionnaire construction is closely related to minimizing bias, since it can be cloaked behind these flaws in questionnaire design.

How to Increase Televoter Interactivity

Citizen participation can be a lonely business, for example: voting in solitude, writing a letter to a congresswoman, or reading a newsmagazine. It also can involve a great deal of interaction with others, for example: taking part in a demonstration, testifying at a hearing, or campaigning door-to-door. In the Campbell model, there was little interactivity between the Televoters and/or with any other citizens. The only interaction in the design came in the staff's distribution of the cumulative results to the San Jose school board. And that is not much interaction at the individual citizen level. We felt that we wanted to increase Televoter interactivity at least to some degree.

One of our ideas to increase citizen interaction in the Televote process was to encourage the Televoter, not only to read and think about the material in the brochure before deciding her/his opinions, but to discuss the material and the issues with others. We described this aspect of the Televote process when we recruited participants over the phone. We also included this as an instruction in all our Televote pamphlets. The idea was to spark interaction between the Televoter and her/his family, friends, co-workers, neighbors, and so forth. It was our view that the Televoter not only should be a demographic representative, but also should enrich her/his views through interaction with others and, in a sense, represent an opinion even wider than her/his own personal perspective. We also decided to encourage interaction among Televoters by sending the final results of the Televote to each participant. That would inform them of their relative position in the Televote sample and would be a necessary interactive step if we ever did a "Televote Delphi."

Another way that we decided to increase Televoter interactivity was to utilize this technique as a centerpiece in a larger, more expansive type of citizen participation—"Electronic Town Meetings" or ETMs. These projects will be described in greater detail later in the chapter. Not only did the Televote provide a scientific baseline of informed and deliberated opinion on the issues involved in the ETMs, but it also utilized the ETM as a method of involving Televoters and other citizens in a lateral information exchange, functionally equivalent to what occurs in face-to-face town meetings.

Finally, as Campbell had done before us, we conceived a number of ways to link the information gleaned from our Televoters to government officials. A major part of that linkage was the mass media, who always published the results of the Televotes within the confines of a major news article and, also, on several occasions published the entire Televote in the newspaper and once simultaneously solicited their readers' response to the Televote. Television and radio were also very intrigued by Televote and cooperated in airing information about the ongoing Televotes (on occasion) and often aired Televote results as a major news story.

Finally, since our project, from the outset, had not been developed in collaboration with any government officials as had Campbell's, we had to think of direct ways (in addition to their learning the results from television, radio, and the newspaper) to convey Televote information to specific officials concerned about whatever issues the Televote treated.

For our demonstration project, we discussed with a number of the newly elected CONCON delegates the possibilities of setting up a "Televote Room" in the building housing the state constitutional convention. Fortunately, enough of them were interested and the officials in charge of the day-to-day operation of the convention provided us a Televote Room where our staff could collate the data and route it on a regular basis to the delegates. The state legislature was not as cooperative subsequently. No such cooperation was extended to us. So, in all other Televotes done in Hawaii, we simply took the results from the Televote office at the university to the state legislature and dropped off the information in each representative or senator's office (if they were not available when we hand-delivered the results). In the two Televotes that were sponsored by quasi-governmental agencies, New Zealand Televote and Los Angeles Televote, the information was relayed to responsible government officials by the agency itself.

This, then, was the Hawaii Televote model, one conceived to improve upon the pioneering work done by Campbell. The remainder of this chapter will trace the history and describe the substantive content of what each Televote experiment was about, what we learned about our process from each Televote, how we refined the instruments and model over time, and most importantly, what new questions popped up after each Televote and led us to try something new each time. This is the essence of the Televote Odyssey: techniques applied, lessons learned, and the slow but steady realization of a future feature of the participatory system I call the Representative Participatory State.

HAWAII TELEVOTES 1 AND 2: INVOLVING CITIZENS IN CONSTITUTIONAL ISSUES

Getting a feel for the public pulse on issues related to the constitutional convention in Hawaii began several months prior to the election of delegates to the convention. As indicated earlier, there was some confusion on the part of voters about the nature and function of a constitutional convention. One poll conducted for a major Hawaii newspaper, the *Honolulu Advertiser*, found that only 39 percent of the respondents felt the major purpose of the CONCON was to make changes in the basic structure of government, while 29 percent said its job was to solve major issues such as unemployment and crime.[3] Nevertheless, as early as January 1978, the media and pollsters began to raise some major structural issues that might well be dealt with at the CONCON. Citizens were asked about their views on issues such as unicameralism; an elected attorney general; and initiative, recall, and referendum.

For many months leading up to the CONCON, issues such as these were presented and discussed in the news media; at neighborhood boards (bodies of elected citizens at the neighborhood level, who acted as advisors to city government); in public debates; in university seminars, symposia, and simulations; and so forth. The low starting level of citizen awareness and the cumulative effect of public discussion are apparent when one looks at the results of polls on two constitutional issues that were conducted in January, April, and July/August.

Televote 1: Testing the Hawaii Televote Model

Six months prior to the convention, a CONCON poll was conducted by a Hawaii polling firm for the *Honolulu Advertiser*. It asked the respondents simply: "Should initiative and referendum be included in the Hawaii Constitution?" Thirty-nine percent said "yes" and only 7 percent were opposed. But a clear majority (54%) were uncertain or had no reply! In the newspaper analysis of the poll, which was highlighted on the front page of the paper, definitions were provided as well as some historical background on these citizen lawmaking processes.[4]

Three months later, after increased public discussion and political campaigning on issues to be addressed at the convention, the CONCON poll was conducted again for the same newspaper. This time, however, the pollsters provided simple explanations of initiative and referendum to the respondents over the telephone. On the question regarding initiative, the respondents were told: "Initiative is a system whereby voters, by petition, can have a proposed law placed on the ballot. Some people favor this. Others say that it bypasses the Legislature and requires voters to say 'yes' or 'no' to complex issues. How do you feel?" In spite of the clear negative weighting in the information provided, which gives an argument against initiative but does not provide an argument in favor of it, this time 53 percent of the respondents favored initiative. The "uncertain" or "no reply" group decreased by almost half, down to 28.5 percent. The "opposed" group increased to 18.5 percent.

On referendum, the respondents received the following information: "Referendum is a system which permits voters, at a General Election, to approve or disapprove laws proposed by the Legislature. Some people favor this. Others say this is why we elect legislators. How do you feel?" Again, with a similar negative slant evident in the question, the respondents overwhelmingly (61%) favored referendum. Sixteen percent were opposed. The "uncertain" and "no reply" group shrunk by more than half, down to 23 percent of the total.

As is plain to see, the second CONCON poll allowed for more informed and discriminating choices for the respondents. In his analysis, the city editor of the *Honolulu Advertiser* pointed out that the results of the first poll (showing 54% uncertain or not replying) presented a picture that the public was "either confused or ignorant about the two 'populist' concepts invented early in this century."[5] Therefore, the pollsters chose to explain the concepts and provide useful information and this probably had a marked influence on the results in the second poll. In addition, in the first poll, initiative and referendum were lumped together into one question, allowing no distinctions to be made by the respondents. When distinctions were allowed, referendum was preferred by 8 percent more of the citizens than initiative. Already a picture of a more enlightened public began to emerge, their views being illuminated in part by the continuous public debate but probably more so by the data, opinions, and greater sophistication of the polling instrument itself.

When we conducted our first Televote in July, the constitutional issues already had been a part of the public debate for six months. The delegates had been selected and most had taken public positions on the various issues, with initiative and referendum emerging as one of the key issues to be decided at CONCON. It had been a genuine grassroots campaign with hundreds running for office for the first time. Only one then-current legislator was elected as a delegate while several students, some retirees, and a number of community activists were elected. Although mostly political unknowns prevailed in the election, many of them were backed by labor unions or were aides to legislators or other political leaders. The perception of the public, who had favored a CONCON controlled by "ordinary working people" in an earlier poll,[6] that they had achieved their ends was quickly altered as the political establishment rapidly lined up a solid voting bloc among the "unknowns." Nevertheless, public interest remained strong with discussion groups being organized all over the state. Committee hearings at the convention were heavily attended by citizens and received extensive coverage by the news media.

So shortly after the CONCON began, we ran our first Televote—the first experimentation of the Hawaii Televote model. We were particularly interested in the degree to which all our information and opinions on initiative and referendum, plus the sophisticated discussion on the differences between direct and indirect initiative, would actually educate our Televoters. Much to our surprise, the final results of our sample of over 400 Televoters were 86 percent in favor of initiative and 14 percent opposed. However, in our analysis of the survey results, we discovered a major flaw in the questionnaire design. We had not put in an "Undecided" or "Unsure" box. Thus we had forced the Televoters into an actual decision and not built in an indicator of indecision. Still, with all the direct and prolonged telephone contact we had with our Televoters, we were confident that the number of "undecideds" would have been negligible. We received no complaints about our oversight from any Televoter, but we realized that we lacked scientific confirmation of our hypothesis and knew we had to develop a better experimental design to test the actual impact of the Televote brochure in the future.

Even in this environment of widespread public interest, the most important question we sought to answer in our first two Televote polls was: Could the Hawaii Televote method be successful in getting a representative sample of the population to participate in the process? It is one thing to call someone and ask for a response "off the top of the head." It is quite another to use the Hawaii Televote method and ask people to give us their names and addresses, to read material on an issue, to talk about it with others, to think about it before responding, and to get them to respond.

We were quite concerned as we planned our first Televote experiment that we might not be able to get certain segments of the population in Hawaii to partake in such a complicated process on an issue that was, to most citizens, legalistic and remote. Would low-income, not-well-educated citizens who agreed to participate actually complete their Televotes? Would the Japanese American citizens, frequently underrepresented in conventional polls (without "weighting"), feel even less like signing up for such an exercise?

To add to our concern, almost halfway through the first Hawaii Televote, Professor Chadwick printed out the results on the first 150 Televotes. Much to our dismay, the sample was heavily skewed toward white males with high incomes and substantial educational levels—the worst possible scenario. What followed was a staff meeting where we decided to not panic. The sample of 150 was too small to draw any definitive conclusion, plus nearly half of the early respondents were the people who had actually called in their responses to our hotline—a "self-selected" sample of our random sample. We decided to continue to call back our sample—over and over—until we got at least 400 of the Televotes completed, and then see if we reached a fair level of representativeness.

After reaching our goal of 400 respondents, we examined our demographics again. They indicated a fairly representative sample of Hawaii's population and were as close to reflecting the citizenry as other traditional polls being conducted by political pollsters during the same period. (See Table 5.1 on Comparative Demographics.) It appeared that our first effort to bring a cross section of the public into a discussion of constitutional issues proved to offer great potential for representatives wishing to have better communication with a broad base of citizens, for those concerned with ways to educate the general public, and for those looking for means to increase citizen interest and participation in all segments of the community.

Having that major question answered, we were next struck by a serendipitous finding that would please participatory democratic theorists.

Table 5.1

Comparative Demographics: Official Statistics and Major 1978 Surveys

Background	Official Statistics						Major 1978 Hawaii Surveys			
	1	*2*		*3*	*4*		*5*	*6*	*7*	*8*
	Reg. Vot. Hi.	Potential Voters Hi.	Oahu	Gen. Pop. Oahu	Tuttle 2/78 Hi.	Oahu	SMS 9/78 Oahu	HT-1 7/78 Hi.	HT-2 8/78 Hi.	HT-3 11/78 Hi.
SEX										
Male	49.4	50.5	50.5	49.9	50.1	50.0	49.6	51.0	59.0	52.5
Female	50.6	49.5	49.5	50.1	49.9	50.0	50.4	49.0	41.0	46.6
AGE										
18-34	29.5	42.3	43.4	45.4	43.1	42.3	44.3	38.0	36.0	40.0
35-44	16.1	16.0	17.1	17.0	20.4	20.2	23.6	17.0	17.0	19.4
45-64	36.1	32.1	32.1	37.6	35.2	36.3	29.9	37.0	37.0	33.5
65 & Over	11.0	8.9	8.0					8.0	9.0	6.1
ETHNICITY										
Caucasian	36.6	25.7	25.0	33.0	31.5	32.4	37.7	35.0	38.0	34.6
Japanese	33.9	35.5	35.8	28.8	33.4	34.1	24.6	30.0	31.0	31.3
Haw'n/Pt. Haw	5.3	16.7	16.3	11.7	7.5	6.6	12.9	11.0	11.0	7.4
Filipino	9.0	7.8	7.0	10.1	11.9	10.7	4.4			3.6
Chinese	10.2*	5.1	6.3	6.6	6.1	6.7	5.6	10.0	4.0	6.1
Mixed	NA	6.7	6.6	4.1	NA	NA	6.8	NA	NA	NA
Other	5.0	2.5	2.9	4.1	6.8	6.7	5.6	15.0	15.0	8.9
PARTY										
Democrat	73.1	NA	NA	NA	60.9	60.1	NA	59.0	58.0	59.4
Republican	13.3	NA	NA	NA	19.2	19.0	NA	16.0	18.0	15.3
Independent	13.6	NA	NA	NA	NA	NA	NA	25.0	24.0	18.2
EDUCATION										
Less than H.S.	NA	NA	NA	11.9	12.1	11.2	5.3	10.0	6.0	5.6
H.S. Grad.	NA	NA	NA	47.1	24.3	22.5	32.8	21.0	18.0	21.0
Bus./Trade	NA	NA	NA	NA	32.3	32.5	NA	12.0	12.0	9.0
Some College	NA	NA	NA	30.5			44.8	35.0	25.0	22.8
College Grad.	NA	NA	NA		14.5	15.2			39.0	22.0
Post Grad.	NA	NA	NA	6.2	14.0	16.2	14.6			18.7

1 Registered Voters for the State of Hawaii according to Lt. Governor's Office of Independent Data Services (11/22/77).
2 Potential Voters according to the Hawaii Department of Planning and Economic Development based on 1976 data.
3 Federal data from the Office of Economic Opportunity based on 1975 data.
4 Dan Tuttle CONCON survey of General Population conducted for the First Hawaiian Bank. N=2,405.
5 SMS survey (determining community standards on pornography) of the General Population of Oahu. N=411.
6 Hawaii Televote-1 of the General Population of the State. N=400.
7 Hawaii Televote-2 of the General Population of the State. N=401.
8 Hawaii Televote-3 of Registered Voters of the State. N=395.
 * Includes Koreans.

What we noticed was that the response of the 86 percent of the Televoters who favored initiative and referendum indicated palpably responsible and sophisticated answers—not the sort of mindless massive support for "power to the people" with no restraints on majority rule and with no concern for the minority that many who fear greater democracy cite as problems with increased citizen involvement.

In the first place, the Televote poll on initiative and referendum provided citizens with considerably more information than they had received previously from survey researchers. Not only were they given basic definitions of initiative and referendum, but they were told of two different forms of initiative—direct and indirect. They were given data about states that used initiative and told of its use at the county levels in Hawaii. They also were supplied with several balanced arguments in favor of and opposed to initiative and referendum. Second, the respondents were given a wide range of alternatives from which to choose in deciding which form of initiative they would prefer if they favored initiative.

Although 86 percent of the sample favored initiative and referendum, the majority (56%) favored either indirect initiative or some combination of direct and indirect initiative. Seventy-four percent felt that getting initiatives on the ballot for the vote of all citizens "should not be made too easy," that is, they preferred a large number of citizens' names on the petition. (The Televote information had informed them that the usual range of required signatures was 5% to 15%, with the higher percentage being more difficult to obtain.) In addition, 74 percent felt that a certain percentage of citizens' names on the petition should come from all the islands so that the largest or larger islands could not force legislation on the smaller islands. This is significant because approximately 80 percent of the Televoters were from Oahu, the most populated island in Hawaii (with approximately 80% of the people of the state being located thereon). Therefore, given a range of choices from maintaining the system as it is (Expanded Representative State) to greatly expanded citizen lawmaking powers, most Hawaii Televoters chose increased participation with safeguards for minorities.

It is hard to comprehend how so many Televoters could construct such a refined political system without having used the information contained in the Televote. These responses are particularly interesting since the choices selected by the Televoters were not part of the public CONCON debate.

Another item of particular interest to us was to what degree the Televoters received any or some satisfaction from participating in this process. Our first inclination was to develop a "satisfaction scale" for them to answer after we had recorded their votes, for instance: "Were you very satisfied? Somewhat satisfied? Not quite satisfied? Very unsatisfied? Not sure?" We gave this kind of measuring device some thought, but felt it was biased toward eliciting a favorable response. After all, we found that our Televoters had gone to some trouble to participate, and many had been speaking over the telephone with our staff for weeks, so we felt it was unlikely that they would then tell us over the phone that they were dissatisfied—even if they were.

But we were truly interested in finding out if the Televoters were pleased and, in addition, if the process was satisfying enough that they would do it again. So our decision was to test this by being as direct as possible. Thus, at the end of the interview, when all their views were obtained, and all their demographic data was collected, we asked, "One final question: Would you be willing to participate in future Televotes?" They could respond "yes," "no," or "not sure." They knew we had their names, addresses, and telephone numbers. Many knew that if they did not call in their own responses, they would hear from us until they responded. But despite this, over 90 percent said they would participate again. This indicated to us an overwhelming participant approval of the Televote model. We had achieved a basic ingredient for sustainability.

Televote 2: Continuation of the CONCON Experiment

As we moved forward to conduct our second Televote, we were encouraged by our initial experiment that indicated the system worked. We had discovered through Televote 1 that: We got a fairly representative group of Televoters (very close to those obtained by commercial pollsters in Hawaii using conventional telephone and interview techniques); the results showed that citizens seemed to use the material and came up with reasonable and fair options; and the process seemed to satisfy the Televoters themselves, making the process sustainable.

We had previously decided that our second Televote would focus on the selection of judges, since this was a relatively high visibility issue in the pre-CONCON debate and was a major topic at the CONCON itself. But more important to us than the issue itself was the importance that Televote 2 would have in confirming what we found out in Televote 1 about the process. In other words, we had to replicate the experiment. We felt it was important to demonstrate that the first results were not a fluke.

As was the case with initiative and referendum, statewide public opinion had been obtained on this issue in the same polls conducted in January and April before the summer CONCON. In the first poll, election of judges was preferred by the largest group of respondents (37%) and selection of judges by an independent commission was the choice chosen by the smallest group of respondents (29%). Those preferring the "present system" (appointment by the governor with senate approval) were 30 percent of the respondents.[7] (Note that only 8% were undecided on this issue, compared to the 55% on the initiative issue.)

Only three months later, those favoring Hawaii's appointment system shrank from nearly one-third of the respondents to one-fifth. Election of judges decreased to 29 percent when respondents were also given a choice of selection by an independent commission subject to periodic voter approval (36%). The new results indicated growing dissatisfaction with Hawaii's judicial selection process and significant support for voters having some voice in making judicial appointments (nearly two-thirds of the citizens).[8]

Televote 2, on selection of judges, was conducted in July and August. It provided factual information and pro and con arguments for four methods of judicial selection: (1) appointment by the governor and approval by the senate; (2) election by the voters; (3) merit selection by an independent commission; and (4) merit selection by an independent commission with retention elections. Again, as in the previous two polls, the desire for some form of voter involvement in determining who sits on the bench was the preferred choice of the largest group of citizens. As in the April poll, the Televote results indicated that two-thirds of the respondents favored some method of selection of judges subject to democratic processes. This time, however, with information provided on the subject, only 17 percent preferred direct election of judges. Exactly half of the respondents favored the merit selection of judges by an independent commission with follow-up retention elections. Those preferring the appointment of judges decreased again to 16 percent from 20 percent in the previous poll. Again, as respondents were given more sophisticated options, allowing for a variety of ways to involve the citizenry in judicial selection, they were less likely to choose the extreme positions—in this case, total control of voters in the selection process (election of judges) or total exclusion of voters in the selection process (appointment of judges).

Confirmations

For Televote 2 we used our original design and operational procedures to register 550 Televoters. Once again, about 15 percent called back to our hotline on their own. And once again we had to make two or more phone calls to most of our participants to obtain their responses.

The results of Televote 2 confirmed what we had discovered in the first Televote. The demographical composition of the 401 Televoters was almost a duplicate of Televote 1. Again we see our group as being slightly higher in educational achievement and Caucasians being somewhat over-represented, but we had substantial participation from Japanese and Hawaiians, as well as from people with only elementary or secondary education. Most importantly, our demographics were again quite comparable with those of professional pollsters in Hawaii.

Another salient point confirmed by HT-2 was the high rate of satisfaction that the Televoters themselves had with the Hawaii Televote model. As in HT-1, over 90 percent said they'd be willing to be recruited for future Televotes. And this was despite the fact that there was no tangible evidence that their opinions had any visible impact on the CONCON itself.

The third result of HT-2, which we had also found in HT-1, was the use of information and the quality of the answers given in response to our more in-depth and sophisticated questions. Given more information and varied alternatives of the issues, the Televoters began to make subtle distinctions and to refine their choices.

Evaluation of Impact

Following the final tally of HT-2, we decided to conduct an evaluation of the nature and degree of the impact of the entire process connecting Televote to the CONCON itself. The major question we sought to answer was: Would Televote results have more impact on representatives when the opinions came from citizens who had information on the issues and time to discuss it with others and think about it before responding? We tried to answer this question two different ways: first, by polling the delegates to get their evaluation of the Televote, and, second, by examining the actions of the delegates in reacting to the Televote.

Immediately following the completion of the constitutional convention, we sent surveys to all the delegates asking them to evaluate Televote. Precisely half of the delegates (51) responded to our survey. Of those that responded, 85 percent said they felt the Televote had been either "very useful" or "somewhat useful" to them as delegates. More than three-fourths of the respondents said that Televote should be useful to state legislators. When asked how the Televote was useful to them, delegates most commonly replied that the results (1) reinforced opinions they already held; (2) were used in bargaining with other delegates; (3) were used in floor debates; and (4) were used by citizens' groups, like Common Cause, to help support their positions during their lobbying activities.

We had independently observed that the Televote poll results were used extensively in testimony at the constitutional convention. Even the president of the CONCON acknowledged privately to one of the Televote researchers that Televote 1, with its tremendous media exposure and use in testimony at the CONCON, had placed tremendous pressure on the delegates to pass initiative and referendum—although a majority of delegates opposed both.[9] In addition, the vice-president of academic affairs of the university, who had funded the project, called Becker into his office and notified him of "heat from downtown," in the form of some telephone calls from state officials, expressing their dissatisfaction with the university "getting involved in politics" by conducting polls that had been utilized to place pressure on representatives. He said he was going to have to discontinue the funding he had awarded for graduate assistants, and printing and mailing costs. However, he promised continued "moral support." Clearly, Televote proved it could have impact. It did not prove, however, that a majority of the political leaders were eager for more citizen input or participation, no matter how informed, deliberated, or sophisticated.

In determining the impact on public policy, if one were to look at the immediate results, it appears as if Televote, and public opinion in general, had little impact at the constitutional convention. As soon as the final election results were in, the well-organized, well-financed, antireform delegates with strong ties to Hawaii power holders began to mobilize support to include independents eager for key committee assignments. Before the first day of the convention, a solid majority of delegates united with minimal reform as their goal. The majority held secret meetings—one was publicized by the local CBS affiliate (KGMB), which showed delegates arriving at an unannounced meeting one Sunday afternoon and refusing to respond to reporters' questions—and vowed to decide issues according to their best judgment, unswayed by public pressure.

While the majority of the delegates viewed their role as a trustee, the public had a different view. The media, university, and community groups had been very successful in creating an awareness of the convention and constitutional issues and stimulating interest in its deliberations and outcome. A pervasive attitude was that it was a convention "of, by, and for the people." The most controversial issue at the convention became initiative and referendum—strongly supported by a majority of the people and strongly opposed by a majority of the delegates. Initiative and referendum failed to pass. The public was given no voice in the selection of judges, although selection was changed from appointment by the governor to appointment by a commission selected by the governor, legislators, and the supreme court chief justice.

In examining the impact of the Televotes, however, it is more insightful to view it as part of a continuing process of increasing public awareness and participation that has effect over time. It also does not operate within a vacuum but in conjunction with media and other democratic processes to promote an informed and active citizenry. For instance, ever since the 1978 constitutional convention, legislators and political leaders have been faced with the public placing initiative on the public agenda. In many legislative sessions after the CONCON, the state senate has passed bills creating statewide indirect initiative very similar to that favored by the Hawaii Televoters in 1978. The state house of representatives blocked similar bills, largely due to committee chairmen who refused to hold public hearings on the issue or even allow the committee to vote.

Over the years, two house judiciary committee chairmen who became embroiled in public controversy for killing pro-initiative bills were soundly defeated when they came up for reelection. The third chairman appointed to the committee who opposed initiative came from an outer island noted for its allegiance to the power establishment and labor unions (who also opposed initiative). Two staff members from his office told me privately that he informed his staff that he planned to follow the same strategy for killing initiative as his defeated predecessors and that he had to make sure that this one issue did not get "blown out of proportion" and lead to his defeat. Even if he ignores the majority of the public on this particular issue, it is believed his job is secure as long as he remains loyal to the powerful interests in his district. This example illustrates that there are designs within the system to insulate representatives from responding to the people. In other words, one lawmaker, representing only a small percentage of the population (one district), can kill legislation favored by a large majority of the population of the entire state. This is not an unusual tactic of politicians in the Expanded Representative State.

The resistance of the Hawaii political leaders to initiative and referendum at the state level also has led to the development of a pressure group devoted to this as a cause. They have become a very vocal and visible lobbying organization that keeps tabs on supporters and opponents of initiative and the development of initiatives across the United States and educates the public through conferences, brochures, ads, and so forth. This group still refers to the Televote results at CONCON in making their arguments in favor of initiative and referendum at the state level. One legislator, Sen. Mary Jane McMurdo, has become their spokesperson in the legislature and fights each session for initiative legislation.

Citizen activity also has increased dramatically at the county level, which has had initiative on the books for many years, largely unnoticed by the public. Since the convention, initiative at the county level has been used to make the Honolulu prosecutor elected instead of appointed, to rezone an area designated for high-rise condominiums to low-rise, and to rezone development land as preservation land.

The selection of judges, while not nearly as controversial or widely debated, also has surfaced again and again. While some reform took place in the method of selection, there is periodic demand for retention elections. Citizens seem to be willing to accept some form of appointment without much complaint, but regularly call for accountability to the citizens. The city prosecutor of Honolulu for eight years, Charles Marsland, fueled these feelings by accusing judges of bias and highlighting controversial decisions. There have been demonstrations at the courts when judges were perceived to disregard the public welfare in using judicial discretion to be lenient on criminals.

Therefore, in determining impact, one cannot look at the immediate results. In the same way that one would be foolish to judge the success of seed planting by returning the very next day to pick the fruit off a cherry tree, one must not restrict impact analysis to instant legislation. At the same time, one must be careful not to overemphasize the effect of planting the seed. Without good soil, water, fertilizer, and freedom from insects, fungus, and natural disasters, the tree will not bear fruit. Televote alone would have no impact. There must be citizen interest, activists willing to keep the interest alive, and citizens willing to struggle against the elements in society opposed to increased citizen participation. Televote may serve in different capacities at different times—seed, water, fertilizer—but the response of citizens seems to indicate very good soil for the growth of increased citizen involvement.

HAWAII TELEVOTES 3, 4, AND 5: INVOLVING CITIZENS IN SETTING THE AGENDA

One of the criticisms of Televotes 1 and 2 expressed by individuals wishing to increase citizen participation, as well as by other individuals who wished to dismiss the results, was that the university researchers "created" the agenda for public discussion. From the participatory democrat perspective, the public should be the ones determining agendas—not elites, whether professors or politicians. From the perspective of the supporters of the Limited or Expanded Representative State, professors should not be stirring up trouble, arousing the passions of the people by raising issues in areas in which the public had apparently been content or unconcerned.

We believed that this critique had some merit and it therefore influenced our design for our next series of Televotes. While an important function of "technics," the information providers and communication facilitators in the Telecommunitary Democracy model, is to help educate and to convey the latest research and knowledge to citizens and representatives, they also must be mindful to be good listeners in order to promote democratic agenda setting in the political process of policy making. The technics (Televote researchers) must not assume to know the public's interests or decide what should be the major public concerns. There may be times when the technics can initiate discussion in areas that the public has had little or no knowledge of in order to serve an important educational role. However, if the technics are always the decision makers about the topic for public debate, one of the most important aspects of a political system—setting the agenda—is removed from citizen control.

Therefore, in designing the next Televote projects, we felt that the first step should be to identify which issues the citizens considered most important for the state legislature to deal with in its impending session. Our third Televote poll, conducted during fall 1978, just prior to the 1979 legislative session, became known as our "Public Agenda Televote." Not only did we conduct it in order to provide information for the consideration of state legislators and the media, but also to guide us in picking the issues to be the subject of the Televotes during the legislative session.

In designing the Public Agenda Televote, we conducted research to choose issues that had been mentioned the previous year in a variety of arenas. We found a number of published public opinion surveys that had sought to locate and measure major areas of public concern. We analyzed a large number of campaign brochures of candidates to find out what they thought were the key issues. We read letters to the editors of the two major dailies in Honolulu. We asked university students. We researched positions taken by community groups and activists. In all, we identified 59 issues that seemed to arouse substantial interest or concern in the state. We placed them into eight different categories, such as transportation, education, crime, and land use, and asked our Televoters to check off all those they wanted the legislature to address during the 1979 legislative session. In addition, they were asked to list any issues of concern that we may not have included in the survey. In order to measure intensity of concern over each issue, we asked them to double-check those five they felt were most important for the legislature to handle.

As in HT-1 and HT-2, we used RDD and signed up 535 Televoters. Again, we stopped after we had obtained a predetermined number of responses (396). Again, we had a substantially representative sample. And again there was over a 90 percent rate of satisfaction. However, our results did hold one new surprise for us and taught us an important lesson.

The issue that the largest number of citizens (78%) wanted the legislature to deal with—"competency tests in reading and writing for high school"—had not been highly publicized or widely discussed. It was not an issue of primary interest to the Televote researchers or one frequently mentioned in campaign literature or speeches of political leaders. We had expected, however, that crime issues, which receive so much media attention, would be ranked high. Indeed, the next two issues in the ranking were "prohibit parole for career or habitual criminals" (73%) and "mandatory jail sentences for certain crimes" (72%). No issue relating to tax and money (many concerned with reducing various taxes), transportation, or governmental structure made the list of the top ten issues. The intensity scale offered very little change in the rankings.

Our astonishment at the number one ranking was shared by the news anchor at the CBS television station that broadcast our results. He insisted, with no proof to support his assertion, that he knew competency testing in schools was not the major issue on the minds of most citizens. Our view was that the results were instructive for us as well as the media or legislators. In this situation, we came to the realization that the concerns of the public may be quite different from the primary concerns of the technics (whether in the media, government, university, and so forth) and that we needed to be extra careful about making assumptions that we were responding to what the public wanted.

Another television station, the local ABC affiliate, took the top five Televote Public Agenda items and featured them in a week-long series on the "Public Agenda" during their evening newscasts. They not only presented the Televote results, but also provided information on each issue. The reporter who produced the series used a version of the Televote procedure by providing facts on the issues as well as pro and con arguments from various experts and community leaders in the state. This series provided a video preview of our legislative Televotes.

Letting public opinion be our guide, we conducted our legislative Televotes on issues ranked first, second, and third in the Public Agenda Televote. At the time that we began soliciting Televote participation, it did not occur to us to collect data to see if agendas set by the public increased public interest and participation. Our mission for Televotes 4 and 5 was to provide a public service through a communication forum for citizens and representatives on issues of high interest to the public. It was only after we began to conduct the Televotes that we discovered that enthusiasm was noticeably higher for responding to questions on these issues than it even was on HT-1 and HT-2. Completely unpredicted by us, our results showed that: (1) More Televoters called us with their answers rather than waiting for us to call them; (2) fewer call-backs had to be made to get responses; and (3) respondents frequently kept us on the phone to express additional views and add other comments on the issues. We seemed to have hit a responsive chord that made our process run smoother and quicker than previous Televotes.

We followed the same design procedures for these Televotes that we had used before: factual information, pro and con arguments, and discriminating options that provided more than yes/no responses. We also repeated the detailed process of review by multiple sources to check for bias and/or ambiguity. After the results were collected and analyzed, the information was hand-delivered by students, who had conducted the Televotes, to state legislators. News releases also were sent to the media and other public officials.

Again the news media was receptive to broadcasting and printing the results. The legislators, for the most part, however, were unreceptive. Students were surprised at the opinions expressed to them by many legislators that statewide public opinion polls are of no use to them. A variety of reasons were given: (1) The public does not know enough about or understand the issues; (2) our sample did not accurately reflect the views of the people in his or her district; (3) legislators are elected to use their good judgment and not bend to public pressure, which is emotional and irrational; and (4) polls are biased and inaccurate. A common view of many legislators was the stated belief that their role is to provide leadership, not be a rubber stamp of an ignorant public.

A specific critique of Hawaii Televote 4 was made by a staff member in the lieutenant governor's office. He raised two questions: (1) "Should public policy be determined by the results of a public opinion poll when those who are polled have been given little information on a complex subject?" and (2) "Can the results of a poll be relied upon, when the polling methodology indicates a high degree of accuracy, if facts have been distorted?" He concludes: (1) The public has been given too little information on the issue to truly understand the complexities; (2) the poll has distorted facts; and (3) distortion of facts has influenced the results of the poll.

Our response to the criticism was twofold. The first addressed the charge of relatively little information on complex issues. We realize that a two- to three-page information sheet cannot provide all the information relevant to deciding issues. We actually see Televote as only a part of a process of interaction between citizens and representatives. The Televote is useful for citizens as it gives them more information and a greater range of choices than they may have had before. It encourages their seeking further information on the issues, however, and asks them to discuss it with their family and friends. Televote can be useful to legislators in a representative society, not to bind the representative to a public demand, but to provide them with useful information on citizens' level of awareness, knowledge, and views on key issues. If legislators consider the views of citizens to be misguided, wrong, or inadequate, they can offer a service to citizens by supplying them with information that may enlighten them.

Even with its limitations, however, Televote provides a type of public opinion or public judgment that is more informed than the traditional polls, which are so extensively publicized, and the many secret and private polls used by many government officials in their campaigns when they are planning what to say to get elected. Finally, on almost every issue, there are experts and legislators on both (or many) sides. Few issues are decided on the basis of objective data. Legislators often decide how to vote on the basis of their own subjective value system and/or because of political pressure, inducement, or bargaining that has nothing to do with facts or expert opinion whatsoever. To say that the Televoters did not have enough data missed the point, then. The information in the Televote was simply a stimulant to think and discuss, much as it is used in the American legislative process.

Second, the charge that the Televote distorted the facts is the most serious from our perspectives of professional integrity and being independent telecommunitarian technics. We pointed out that the critic's own subjective reading of the information led him to infer that the Televote information "implied" something that is neither stated nor intended. In fact, as mentioned before, we ardently adhere to a rigorous process of questionnaire construction in which we have experts from a variety of political persuasions review the information to check for bias and distortion and then have a reputable polling organization review the final draft to see that their own professional standards are met. In addition, for the Televote he critiqued, we had consulted a law professor at the university to make sure that the information was clear and accurate from a legal perspective.

We learned, therefore, that no matter how conscientiously one strives to remove bias, and no matter how many individuals with different perspectives agree to the wording, the potential for misunderstanding or the reader's own subjectivity influencing his or her interpretation of the material is always present. This happens all the time when courts interpret laws of legislative bodies. The same problem exists with any form of communication, but is minimized when the communication becomes two-way instead of one-way. Individual perceptions influence how one defines reality. Rather than dismissing the critique of distortion of fact, however, we extended an invitation to the lieutenant governor to have her staff included in reviewing our future Televote drafts, prior to printing, in order to help us eliminate biases, distortions, or inaccuracies. We received no response to our invitation.

In conducting the two legislative Televotes based on the public agenda we discovered (1) greater enthusiasm from the public in participating than we expected; (2) general resistance and some hostility from (a) the media who felt the issues to be "unsexy" and (b) legislators who felt the Televotes were being used as a pressure device; and (3) cynicism from the lieutenant governor's office about the usefulness of Televote in policy making and no willingness to improve the method of educating citizens about issues through Televote or any other extensive educational project to involve citizens from all walks of life in thinking about issues. A pattern was beginning to develop in our research that reinforced the growing public perception found in National Election Studies (referred to in Chapter 3) that government is not responsive or attentive to citizens' preferences.

Only one legislative "representative" showed any interest in working with the Televote staff to improve communications between representatives and their constituents. But instead of a "public agenda," he was interested in a "hidden agenda." As we worked with him to develop other Televotes, we discovered that he wished to use Televote as a public relations vehicle in a district newsletter he was producing. He wanted to select the issues and the information to be included in the Televote. He let us know that he had already made up his mind on the issues and was quite certain the public already agreed with him. Therefore, he could appear to be soliciting public input, and following it, when in actuality he already had a position that he believed was popular. In other words, he wanted to use Televote to score some points with the voters.

Our commitment to serve as independent facilitators of two-way, interactive communication between the people and government prevented our involvement in such an enterprise. The suggestion of the legislator, however, further underscores the dilemma that telecommunitarian researchers face as they try to maintain their independence and professional integrity. If Televote, or any other civic education tool, is utilized in any form of decision making, safeguards (which Televote has built in the design through extensive review from outsiders of various political views) must be included to prevent the misuse and abuse of such a powerful technological device.

HAWAII TELEVOTE 6: A SYSTEMATIC TEST OF THE EFFECT OF INFORMATION AND DELIBERATION ON PUBLIC OPINION

After our constitutional and legislative Televotes, we decided to conduct a county poll on an issue that required local county and state cooperation—transportation. It was an issue of major concern and financial commitment to both county and state officials.

For quite some time the mayor of Honolulu (sometimes with city council approval and sometimes not) had been bickering with the state governor and state legislature over the best method for relieving

Honolulu's swiftly increasing traffic woes. The mayor favored a rapid transit system connecting several outlying areas with Honolulu's urban center. The governor favored building a four- or six-lane freeway across the island through the mountains that primarily would service commuters into and out of the urban core. Others were advocating an expanded city-run bus system, without involving the county or state in massive construction on the island.

Because federal funds were needed to support the projects, it was politically advantageous for the city and state to reach a compromise. The federal government, inundated with requests for transportation projects all across the nation, was reluctant to grant funds when Hawaii's political leaders were constantly squabbling. Due to a number of extraneous political factors involved in the infighting, neither side showed the slightest inclination toward compromise and both sides seemed determined to fight to the end, even if it meant losing all federal support in the process. Of course, each side chose to believe that the odds were on their side and that ultimately they would prevail. Therefore, no serious negotiation was necessary if they could eventually have things all their way.

We felt this issue was ideal for a Televote and for developing an experiment to test a major question left unanswered by our prior experiments. So we approached individuals in the mayor's office whom we had worked with on other citizen participation projects. Their proposal for HART, the fixed guideway, had failed to receive majority support from the public in several conventional public opinion surveys that had previously been conducted. We offered to conduct a conventional poll simultaneously with a Televote on the transportation issue asking the exact same questions. The traditional random telephone poll would provide no information or time to deliberate. The Televote would, of course, include information on the various alternatives (description, estimated costs, major beneficiaries, and so forth), as well as pro and con arguments, and give time to talk and think about the issue. We believed that the Televote would help take the personalities and inflammatory rhetoric out of the debate and thus produce new insights into what the public thought about the various proposals.

Planners in the mayor's office embraced the project and promised their cooperation. They were willing to give us access to their data concerning costs and benefits. We informed them that the state also would have to approve the factual information included in our questionnaire and that we would be soliciting input from them and others to provide alternatives and arguments against the city's position. Being convinced that their proposal was the most meritorious, the individuals working with us from the mayor's office did not quarrel with our research theory, methods, and standards. They believed that the Televote was a beneficial way of communicating alternatives to the public and that it would yield a public endorsement of their plan.

In the questionnaire design, rather than forcing respondents to choose between options, we sought instead to determine the level of support for various alternatives. We had two major hypotheses: (1) The traditional polling methodology, what we called Telepoll, would reveal more "undecideds" on the questions than the Televote, and (2) the level of support for the various alternatives was likely to differ in the group that had been given information (Televote) from the group with no information (Telepoll).

We concluded our polling in May 1980, having gained responses from over 800 Oahu residents (over 400 in each poll). But once again, our results contained some surprises (see Table 5.2). As we had anticipated, the "undecided" groups were three to four times larger in the Telepoll than the Televote. Yet, we also discovered that the support for the several alternatives varied only slightly when information and time to think and interact were provided. What appeared to occur is that the support for substantive choices remained fairly consistent while the "undecideds" lost ground to those who did not like any of the options being discussed by the politicians and the media.

Our analysis of the data led us to conclude that information provided to individuals who already have their minds made up is not likely to change their views significantly. In this case, the issue had been publicly debated extensively and heatedly argued for years. Public opinion polls had been conducted and publicized on the issue frequently. On the other hand, for those who are undecided, it appears likely, as our polls conducted during the constitutional convention indicated, that information provided in the Televote does influence and alter the outcome. In this case, the information

Table 5.2
Telepoll and Televote Comparative Data

City-sponsored options			State-sponsored options		
	Telepoll	Televote		Telepoll	Televote
Pro Bus	44%	48%	6-Lane Freeway	30%	38%
Pro Hart	30%	33%	4-Lane Freeway	29%	17%
Don't Know	19%	4%	Don't Know	22%	7%
Neither	7%	15%	Neither	19%	37%

provided on the proposed alternatives led to a reduction of the "un-decideds" but a substantive increase in those rejecting both the city-spon-sored and state-sponsored alternatives.

Clearly in Televote 6, the respondents were not manipulated into en-dorsing the plan of the mayor, who had been supportive of the poll from the beginning. The city, however, did not conduct the poll. It was con-ducted by independent researchers from the university who worked with both the city and the state in designing the questionnaire. As the Gamma Group researchers indicate in their discussion of Telecommunitarian Democracy, who controls communication in a society is as important as who controls the means of production.[10] Not only should the Televote poll be conducted by researchers who are not involved in policy making, but its design should always have input and be reviewed by a wide variety of competing individuals or groups in society to insure the fair treatment of the issue and the various options presented.

The mayor did not receive the results he had hoped, and believed, he would receive. That did not deter him, however. Neither did court decisions against the state proposals deter the governor or the state legislature. Instead, the issue remained a controversial one, with escalating costs and inconvenience to the citizens. Now, nearly ten years later neither proposal has been implemented and the state and the city are still quibbling over the issue. This appears to be an example of embracing public opinion if it supports your position and ignoring it when it does not, to the detriment of the general good.

Our results showed that even after years of discussion and debate, (a) no proposal had a clear majority, much less a consensus, and (b) the more the people who were undecided learned about the existing proposals, the less they liked them. What this data demonstrated was that the political leaders needed to go back to the drawing board to come up with new proposals and to involve the entire public in the process of thinking it through from the outset. These lessons were not learned and, nearly ten years later, traffic in Honolulu is nearing gridlock, with no real solution in sight. All that remains constant is that the political leaders haggle among themselves and refuse to adopt processes that involve the public in resolv-ing the issue.

NEW ZEALAND TELEVOTE: NATIONWIDE FUTURES PLANNING

In January 1981, Becker and I met with Dick Ryan, the director of New Zealand's Commission for the Future (CFF) to discuss Televote as a means of involving New Zealand citizens in futures planning. We were aware that in 1980 the CFF had commissioned Brian Murphy, director of the New Zealand National Research Bureau, to conduct nationwide surveys that would (1) measure public attitudes on living standards in New Zealand and (2) evaluate four different futures for New Zealand in terms of their respective impacts on the personal well-being of the New Zealand public.[11] The CFF was ready to move on to the next stage of their research—to help New Zealanders think through their own values and to select a preferred future for the nation. Through a process of thoughtful debate and delibera-tion, it was hoped that New Zealanders would blaze a democratically guided trail to the future for national policy planners.

After learning of the Hawaii Televote experiments, Ryan was convinced that Televote would serve as a useful tool for his small government agency to stimulate the average New Zealander into thinking seriously and crea-tively about the future. Utilizing his Televote experience, Becker became the organizer of a CFF research project with the following objectives: (1) to obtain a representative sample of New Zealand's population and to have them consider and evaluate the general ideas included in the CFF's four future scenarios; (2) to stimulate public interest in reading and using a series of CFF publications on these futures; and (3) to utilize the mass media (TV, radio, newspapers, magazines) in order to promote interaction between the CFF and the citizens on this subject.

With government funding and assistance from two major universities (Victoria and Auckland) and one teachers college (Christchurch), Becker crafted a network of three centers to draw a nationwide random sample of 900 to 1,000 New Zealanders. The many new participants helped validate and systematize Televote's rigid standards for achieving clarity and purging for bias. After Becker and other researchers at Victoria University worked with the CFF staff to construct and design the New Zealand Televote (NZT) instrument, it was sent to Alan McRobie in Christchurch and Murphy in Auckland for analysis and modification. All three research centers col-laborated on the evaluation and approval of all the information, ideas, and questions included in the New Zealand Televote.

To maximize public awareness, discussion, and participation, Becker weaved together a mass-media network including 11 of New Zealand's major newspapers and over 30 radio stations. Television stations (there are only two major networks in New Zealand, aptly named "One" and "Two") refused to join the Televote-related programming because they required a six- to nine-month preparation period. They did, however, report on the start of the actual Televoting and became embroiled in a controversy over its "New Zealandness" as the process unfolded.

The newspapers, however, were quick to publish the entire Televote questionnaire the day before the Televote centers started the "call-outs." This became a nationwide advertising campaign for NZT—front-page articles and full-page questionnaires—of the upcoming project and its content. But by also soliciting mail-in responses to the Televote from their readers, it was additionally a way to involve many more than the 1,000 New Zealanders the centers would induce to become the NZ Televote random sample. Although the responses to the newspaper survey were never intended to be considered adequate to determine what the general public might want or think about the future, it was seen as a means to stimulate much wider public thought about the CFF's alternative futures and to encourage general interest in participating in the poll if one was called and asked to become a New Zealand Televoter. It also presented us with some interesting comparisons between self-selected and random samples in terms of substantive results and demographics.

The radio stations also promoted a keen awareness and interest. They featured interviews, news items, commentaries, and talk-back programs about the New Zealand Televote prior to, during, and after the project.

The importance of the media participation project became clear as soon as the Televote interviewers began to recruit their randomly selected Televoters. Within the first few days of the call-outs, the interviewers detected considerable enthusiasm with a good deal of reference being made to the Televote survey published in the newspapers throughout the nation. In spite of dire predictions by many local "experts" that only Caucasian and educated citizens would participate, the New Zealand Televote was able to obtain participation from a scientifically predictable, highly representative sample of the entire adult population, including those from the lowest educational levels as well as Maoris, who normally resisted participation in New Zealand national telephone survey polls. One of the Televote staff members (who was of Maori ancestry) hypothesized that the Maoris chose to participate in the Televote poll because of the "personal method of recruitment" and the fact the Televote staff "encouraged discussion with family and friends before answering [which] fits well within the Maori social concepts."[12] The demographics of the New Zealand Televote show that the ability of the Televote method to obtain a fairly representative sample was not limited to the Hawaii population and, indeed, worked in a non-American society—and at a national level as well. (See Table 5.3.)

Although the New Zealand Televote had been tested twice to assure that its reading comprehension level was at the level of a 14-year-old, the task of reading, understanding, and filling out the Televote was time-consum-

Table 5.3
New Zealand Demographic Breakdown

Background	1976 Official Statistics	NRB Poll*	NZ Televote**
SEX			
Male	50%	49%	50.0%
Female	50%	51%	50.0%
AGE GROUPS			
15-24	25%	Weighted	17.2%
25-34	21%	to Official	25.1%
35-44	15%	Statistics	19.8%
45-54	14%		13.7%
55-64	12%		15.5%
65+	13%		8.7%
POLITICAL LEANINGS			
National	39.8%	35%	40.8%
Labour	40.4%	26%	22.9%
Social Credit	16.1%	9%	13.4%
Values	2.5%	2%	2.5%
Other	1.3%	1%	1.9%
None***		27%	18.5%
ETHNIC GROUP			
European	86.1%	95%	92.9%
Maori/Part	8.6%	3%	5.1%
Pacific Islander	1.8%	1%	.6%
Other	1.0%	1%	1.3%
HIGHEST EDUCATION			
Up to Sec. School	NA	44%	42.0%
Sec. School	NA	29%	24.9%
Tech. or Prof. St.	NA	7%	4.0%
Tech. or Prof. Qual.	NA	8%	13.9%
University Study	NA	5%	6.9%
University Qual.	NA	7%	8.3%

```
*    1980 National Research Bureau Nationwide Poll (N-2000)
**   1981 NZ Televote (N-964)
***  Includes the Don't Knows, Independents, and those who refused to
     state a "leaning."
```

ing and painstaking—much more so than our previous Televotes. Our most colorful, cartoon-laced Televote brochure provided descriptions of the philosophical values underlying the four different future scenarios that had been defined by the CFF through their prior research. Despite the effort required, all kinds of New Zealanders were attracted and completed the exercise with no complaints and in representative numbers. This was not true in the self-selected newspaper sample.

In responding to the questions, the Televoters were given three "games" to play. Game One was entitled "Pictures of the Future," which consisted of the likely status of five variables (employment, environment, world scene, economic development, and government) in the four New Zealand futures. These futures included themes of "big is beautiful," "privatization is best," "small is beautiful," and "modern technology is beneficial." For each variable Televoters had to indicate whether they liked, disliked, or were neutral about the status of that variable in each of the four future scenarios.

In Game Two the Televoters played "Your Turn to Predict." They were given 15 possible events of the future (such as full employment, larger cities, and greater participation by citizens in important decisions) and asked to indicate under which future scenario, guided by different philosophical points of view, the event was most likely to happen.

Finally, in Game Three, the Televoters were asked to choose their preferred future based on their own values. If they did not find one of the four futures outlined by the CFF as incorporating their range of values, they could create their own future with their own unique mixture of beliefs by choosing statements, or "building blocks," which were closest to their points of view, from the various future scenarios.

The researchers were amazed to find that the largest percentage of NZ Televoters (29%) chose to create their own future rather than select one of the four prepackaged futures described by the CFF! In spite of the complexity, and greater time demand required for one to read through a good bit of philosophical and policy information, the researchers concluded that a large proportion of New Zealanders demonstrated "a strong sense of individualism, a resistance to forced choices, and [willingness] to be innovative."[13] In addition, the researchers found that those taking the extra time to create their own futures were not necessarily those with the highest levels of education. In other words, the educational levels of the "innovative" group were highly representative of the educational levels of the rest of the Televote sample.

It appears that the intricacy of the New Zealand Televote had no impact on the rate or quality of participation (it may even have intrigued the Televoters). With the aid of advance advertisement in the newspapers and on the radio and fewer restrictions on participation (anyone over 15 years old in New Zealand could participate, compared to registered voters in Hawaii), the acceptance rate of those asked to participate in New Zealand surpassed that of any of the former Hawaii experiments (slightly over 70% in New Zealand compared to 50%–65% in Hawaii). In addition, 77 percent of those registered for Televote in New Zealand completed their questionnaire, compared to 68 percent to 74 percent in Hawaii. Thus, approximately 54 percent of all those contacted in New Zealand actually completed the Televote.

The researchers credit the media with a significant role in the high level of interest and cooperation demonstrated in this government-sponsored project of philosophical thinking and discussion of New Zealand's future. Over 4,000 individuals responded to the newspapers' requests for mail-ins of the published Televote survey. While these self-selected respondents were more likely to be highly educated, Caucasian males—not highly representative of the population—they were, nevertheless, indicative of a desire on the part of a large number of these citizens to be more involved in the complicated process of policy planning for the future of the nation.

In analyzing their data, the researchers concluded that: (1) New Zealand Televote (particularly with the help of the mass media from beginning to end) succeeded in making the public much more aware of the four development futures identified by the CFF; (2) the CFF obtained valuable public input in their work (participation by over 5,000 New Zealanders during a two-month time period); (3) the first nationwide anticipatory democracy exercise had been successfully completed; and (4) the New Zealand public is much more capable of grappling with very complex issues than many of the "experts" or conventional wisdom had predicted.

Finally, the results of the Televote indicated overwhelming majority rejection of radical new paths promoted by "growth enthusiasts" or "return-to-nature enthusiasts." The majority preferred futures that required a balancing of individualism and personal sacrifice for the common good. The researchers summed up their analysis with the following statement: "This study is a vivid demonstration that the New Zealand public is now ready, very willing, and eminently able to shoulder its responsibilities."[14]

The incumbent New Zealand political leaders at the time (the National Party), who had set out on a path of extensive growth and exploitation of natural resources, greater involvement in international affairs, and support of big business, were not inclined to agree that the public could or should be involved in planning New Zealand's future. Their own goals appeared to be radically different from those of a majority of the NZ Televote respondents. The year after the NZT, the government abolished the Commission for the Future and continued on its path to rapid growth and expansion. Three years later, however, the Labor Party wrested control of the government from the National Party and began to turn its policies more in the direction chosen by a majority of the New Zealand Televoters. Brian Murphy, one of the Televote researchers and dean of commerce at Auckland University, believes that the New Zealand government of the late 1980s, under new Labor Party leadership, was responding to and advancing the future path chosen by the bulk of New Zealand Televoters in 1981. He also believes that his polls and NZT had a definite impact on their thinking. As I noted earlier, Televote's impact on policy is not immediate, but is part of a general consciousness-raising experience (electronic town meetings and other activities), and its consequences take time to become apparent.

HAWAII TELEVOTE 7: THE HONOLULU ELECTRONIC TOWN MEETING (HETM) AND THE "PUBLIC BUDGET"—PLACING TELEVOTE INTO THE BIG PICTURE

Having received such widespread media support in developing a national dialogue on New Zealand's future, Becker returned to Honolulu with additional knowledge on ways to generate citizen participation in the age of electronic communication. From the beginning, we had envisioned Televote as a part of a much larger process of public discussion, consideration, and policy formation. Yet it had taken considerable energy, operating on a shoestring budget with no funding for staff, to develop the Televote design, research the issues, operate the surveying process, and analyze and distribute the data. It was a commitment we made to democratic research and intermediation, which required much personal sacrifice and dedication, with very little support or encouragement from established powers in society, until New Zealand—when some true democrats in government and the media lent willing and helpful hands.

While our experience in Hawaii had taught us that Televote's success and impact resulted in funding termination (much like the Alaskan LTNs), the New Zealand experience provided a new burst of energy and creativity for us in moving Televote into the next stage. We believed that even though we had run into great resistance and hostility from Hawaii government leaders and policy makers as we developed a means to increase public awareness and participation, we thought it possible to get the same support from the Hawaii media as had been obtained in New Zealand.

Hawaii professor Jim Dator, who was teaching courses on media and politics, as well as on designing more democratic futures, had previously worked extensively with the media in Canada and Hawaii. He agreed to join us in designing and conducting the 1982 Honolulu Electronic Town Meeting (HETM).[15] While Becker and Dator developed media support and programming, I pulled together a pool of volunteers and coordinated participation in the Televote aspect of the project from students at the University of Hawaii and Joseph Lipkind's classes at West Oahu College and Leeward Community College. The result was a very successful month-long multimedia event conducted by volunteers, who gave of their time and talents to promote a meaningful public dialogue. The response of the Honolulu media surprised us all. We received participation from both public and private television and radio stations as well as the two major newspapers. Time, equipment, and advertising all were donated in a media-coordinated event that reached vastly diverse audiences at different times of the day in a variety of ways.

The topic this time was another type of public agenda, a financial one. Ronald Reagan had been president for a little over a year and had made his economic plan, "Reaganomics," a hotly debated topic all over the country. With federal cutbacks in domestic spending, Reagan's policies had every state scrambling, trying to make their own budgetary decisions—raise taxes and/or cut programs.

We utilized the Televote format to bring the public into the discussion and gave them the means to establish a "Public Budget." In the Televote questionnaire, as well as in our media programming, we provided some factual information and conflicting arguments on Reaganomics. We also analyzed the state budget and presented information on how money was raised and spent in Hawaii. We included several alternatives for raising revenue in the state and detailed arguments for and against the various options. In soliciting public response, we asked their reactions to a number of alternatives to federal cutbacks, state spending in general, revenue-raising options, and major programs seeking public financial support in Hawaii. We also asked citizens to consider the information we furnished on the percentage of state funds going to different programs such as education, transportation, and health and asked them to respond by indicating whether they would spend less, more, or the same.

Methodology

Using the same methodology we had applied in our previous Televotes, the two colleges and one university cooperated (as in New Zealand) in collecting a representative sample of Honolulu's population to participate and to give us a scientific baseline of how Hawaii's total population—including all ethnic groups and educational levels—would respond to the Reaganomics questions after reading information, discussing the issues, and thinking about them. At the same time, other information on the "Public Budget" was widely available in the newspapers, on radio, and on television in order to expand and advertise the public debate and discussion. Our larger purpose was to get as many citizens as possible to think and talk about these important and complex issues. All Honolulu residents were encouraged to become informed and involved through the following coordinated activities.

Newspapers. The two major newspapers published the entire Televote (information and questions) for their readers in their joint Sunday edition at the start of the call-out (recruitment) and programming. Readers were advised to keep the newspaper questionnaire in their home as a guide to the ETM discussion and to respond to it after the conclusion of the month-long programming that would elaborate on the issues. The *Honolulu Advertiser* featured the Televote logo alongside a daily schedule of ETM programs and schedules.

Innovative Programs. An independent commercial television station (KIKU-TV, Channel 13) provided a studio and equipment for three half-hour shows, "Live Wires," produced by Dator and televised during prime time. The original plan for the shows was along the traditional lines of a televised panel discussion on Reaganomics with Dator in the role of moderator. When Dator discovered the extent to which the television station was willing to support the Honolulu ETM project, he felt the station and the public deserved something a bit more appealing. As Dator thought about his experiences working on the Futures Project for the Ontario Educational Communications Authority, he remembered an important lesson he had learned about an "information-rich environment." His media experiences had led him to conclude:

> it is necessary to compete for viewers' time and attention by presenting programmes in a form that they have demonstrated they prefer. Academics and other professionals mistakenly assume . . . that an important topic and a thorough discussion by important people is enough to attract an audience. In certain instances, that is enough. But generally the format of a programme is more important than the content.[16]

Or, in other words, the "medium is the message." And in this case the message was that we wanted citizens to participate in a comprehensive, in-depth exercise on a difficult and complicated process and we were committed to offering the material in ways that were media-competitive.

Dator also believes that if individuals in society are truly desirous of fostering citizen participation, then their schemes for reform should address a "popular dissatisfaction with governmental forms and procedures." His view is: "The obsolete, stuffy, pompous style of administrative, legislative, and especially judicial, processes is alienating in the extreme for most people—even if a few believe that to be boring and authoritarian is necessary for being taken seriously."[17]

Therefore, the unconventional Dator produced three educational television programs that featured a group of improvisational actors and actresses who adapted the Televote information and opinions into dramatic/satirical sketches that educated as well as entertained. The dramatic skits were presented in a clever, humorous format similar to that of the most popular national television comedy show at the time, "Saturday Night Live." In between the comic skits on the Televote issues (that included singing and dancing), Dator informed the audience that their input and opinions on the issues were needed. He provided telephone numbers to the viewers to call in their comments and responses to questions presented on the screen. The Televote staff, including Becker, myself, and students at the University of Hawaii, answered the telephone lines and recorded the responses.

Discussions. Traditional panel discussions also were provided. Oceanic Cablevision televised a series of programs on the Honolulu ETM issues on their community programming station. Becker moderated the panel discussion that featured local political and academic persons of widely diverse viewpoints.

Documentary. An information documentary was produced by Jonathan Peck, a graduate student, and repeated regularly for a month (twice a week) over Oceanic Cablevision's community programming channel. The documentary dealt with Reaganomics' impact on Hawaii and included interviews with the governor and other local political figures.

Radio. Becker worked with a popular deejay of a local music radio station (KKUA) and produced a series of interactive radio programs. The station's musical format was "Top 40s," so it interspersed its musical programming with interviews of experts during the day and call-in discussion during the evening. Becker and I collected taped opinions of people on the street on the Televote issue to be broadcast as well. Listeners could phone in their opinions by calling the station and talking on the air or calling the Televote office to respond in a less public way.

Call-ins. An hour-long call-in program on public television (KHET-TV) featuring Becker, Dator, and Lt. Gov. Jean King concluded the HETM after a month. The subject of the program was the Electronic Town Meeting itself. The three described and discussed the HETM project and responded to audience call-in comments and questions. Nearly 98 percent of all those who called in during the television program made favorable comments regarding the HETM.[18] The station manager said that the call-in rate was above average despite the fact that several of the phones in the phone bank were out of order.

Results

This experiment served as the most extensive ever employed in Hawaii to create a public awareness and involvement in a public debate on a complex set of issues. In all our media-sponsored material and programs, we sought public input beyond the scientific sampling we were conducting through the Televote questionnaire. The response from the public was an impressive willingness and eagerness to participate. In fact, during our call-in periods for the "Live Wires" television programs, we were deluged with phone calls. Having only four telephone lines, we were unable to accommodate all those desiring to participate and received an average of 125 calls during the 30-minute span of each show. We could have processed many more responses, but many call-ins kept us on the line expressing their views beyond the structured questions. Many enthusiastically congratulated us and thanked us for what we were doing. Dator estimates that only about 10 percent of those trying to reach us actually got through.[19]

The Honolulu ETM was remarkable in several ways: (1) The number of individuals willing to contribute significant time, talent, and resources to expand public awareness and interaction was surprising and impressive. Professors, students, actors, video experts, camera operators, newspaper editors, TV station managers, TV and radio program directors, deejays, artists, comedians, and others worked long and energetically in a communitarian fashion with no compensation at all other than a belief in the intrinsic value of participatory democracy. (2) The willingness of competitive media to cooperate in a nonprofit educational endeavor was encouraging. (3) The variety and range in the forms used to communicate with the public was, as far as our research indicated, unprecedented in electronic town meetings up to that time or since. The Honolulu ETM and Televote reached very diverse audiences and generated participation by a broad-based cross section of the population. (4) The response was keen and friendly with over 80 percent of those responding to the various methods expressing a willingness to join the HETM and Televote again in the future.

There was one example of someone in the media censoring our material. The program director at Oceanic Cablevision cut two segments from Peck's documentary. She removed the comments made by a state representative because she felt the representative was using the television station to promote her own achievements. She also spliced out a viewpoint of a Marxist, who stated that only a war would pull the United States out of its economic crisis, because she did not want the public to think Oceanic was endorsing his views (even though disclaimers were made at the start and end of the documentary). It is interesting to note that the program director's previous job had been with a politician from a political party different from the two whose views she censored.

Peck was indignant over the censorship and was quite vocal about the arbitrary manner in which the program director acted. He wrote a memo stating that such action calls for renaming the Oceanic "Community Programming Channel" the "*Oceanic* Programming Channel."

Certainly there is reason to be alarmed by the control exercised by one member of the media in this case. It highlights the necessity of building in safeguards so that freedom of the press does not apply only to those who own and/or run the presses.

There were also other problems, but not nearly as serious as the censorship issue. The Honolulu ETM faced difficulties (many due to financial limitations) and accumulated some critics objecting to the means and/or ends of the project. For example: (1) Many of the productions were not of the quality we would have preferred. This was due to poor equipment, time constraints, or lack of the volunteers' expertise necessary to perform the needed functions at a professional level. (2) We had to rely on what the media was willing to give us for free. We had many ideas about how to promote the programming or citizen participation but were constrained by our inability to pay for anything. Therefore, when we would have liked for the Televote to have been published in the newspapers at the end of the HETM as well as at the beginning, we had to settle for the one-time printing that the newspapers gave us at no cost. (3) We needed far more telephone lines than we had available to accommodate those trying to get through to us for some of our call-in shows. A computer-tallying system would have helped a lot, but was unavailable in Hawaii at the time. Other components used in Washington and Alaska to expand participation were beyond the realm of possibilities for the Honolulu experiment since there was no government or financial support for the project.

The criticisms of the HETM, which will be discussed more generally later on, were similar to those made of Televote. It was argued that issues are too complex to be dealt with in a four-page brochure, half-hour or hour-long radio or television programs, or hour-long documentaries. A few critics were outraged by the satirical style of "Live Wires" and argued that serious issues of public policy cannot be dealt with in such a flippant, ostensibly superficial style. They felt that even though facts were given, as well as pro and con arguments, the manner in which Reaganomics was presented made it appear to be the subject of ridicule rather than a subject presented objectively for "serious" public discussion.

Taking into account the limitations and criticisms of Televote and the Honolulu ETM, we concluded, however, that we had found evidence for the beneficial use of media in heightening citizens' awareness and knowledge and inducing their participation. As with every previous Televote, we learned things we had not anticipated, we discovered ways to improve our efforts, and we met new questions that challenged us. Our desire to create new designs and to continue our research was spurred once again, however, with the public's warm welcome of our work.

LOS ANGELES TELEVOTE: GOVERNMENT AND MEDIA
PROMOTING PUBLIC EDUCATION AND INTERACTION
ON REGIONAL ISSUES AND STATE INITIATIVES

A graduate student of Dator's observed the Honolulu ETM and transplanted the concept to his home state, California, by persuading the Southern California Association of Governments (SCAG) to utilize it in their planning. SCAG is a voluntary association of local governments in Southern California that work together in developing comprehensive plans ordinarily dealing with air and water quality, transportation, housing, regional growth, and economic development. Based on the low cost and success of the Honolulu ETM, SCAG embraced the idea. SCAG executive director Mark Pisano felt Televote and related programming were ideal for SCAG's use. He described Televote as "the best public participation tool I've seen in a long time. It puts SCAG issues before the public in an entirely new way, in a concentrated and concerted manner."[20] Dator and Becker served as advisors for the Los Angeles Televote conducted in October and November 1982.

The goals of the Los Angeles Televote, which covered six regional issues and four initiatives from the 1982 California ballot, were the same as for the Honolulu ETM: (1) increase public access to the Televote process (by having newspapers publish the Televote); (2) increase the number and types of players; and (3) utilize other modern communication technologies to educate and involve the citizens. An additional goal of the LA Televote, however, which makes it different from the Honolulu ETM, was to promote government and planning interfaces with Televote, ensuring that Televote was linked to policy-making processes rather than separated from them. While we had no objections to such a goal in Hawaii, our previous Hawaii experiences taught us to expect resistance, evasiveness, and/or skepticism from Hawaii policy makers. While the LA Televote was sponsored and funded by government for the purposes of using public "input" for planning, we previously had experienced university funding being abruptly curtailed when Hawaii officials complained about public "pressure" created by the Televotes.

Even with government funding, however, the LA Televote was a very inexpensive civic program ($23,000) because the organizers were able to obtain a similar level of cooperation and voluntary contribution from the local media. In addition, some media and communication companies contributed cash for the rental of sophisticated phone-answering and call-counting equipment and to pay for telephone services.[21]

The LA Televote sought to duplicate Honolulu's variety of program formats that placed major emphasis on two-way communication. Every form of media communication had a built-in feedback mechanism designed to obtain and measure citizen input. The California phone company's donation of technologically advanced answering and call-counting systems allowed greater participation than the rudimentary, "bare bones" budget volunteer phone-answering system utilized in Hawaii. During the ten-day programming cycle, the LA Televote received over 35,000 replies. The automatic, high-volume telephone system was used for almost all this programming in addition to a few programs that allowed for on-the-air comments and questions.

Programming and media coverage that coincided with the random sample Televote polling, which provided informative pamphlets to Televoters, included: (1) ten three- to five-minute segments on a television evening newscast; (2) a 30-minute wrap-up television special at the end of the Televote week; (3) ten segments on a morning radio news show with ten live on-the-air opinion polls conducted; (4) ten segments on two different Spanish-speaking radio news programs; (5) a 30-minute radio talk show with call-ins from listeners; (6) daily newspaper listing of all the Televote programming; and (7) information articles on the Televote issues published in the newspapers.

The LA Televote added two components not utilized in the Honolulu ETM: (1) an interactive computer network and (2) a high school Televote center. The LA Televote ballot was entered into The Source computer data base. The Source is a computer network established and run by the Source Telecomputing Corporation, which offers over 750 programs and services to subscribers including electronic mail, news, government and politics, education, and shopping. The Televote ballot became an interactive file on The Source that provided the Televote information to users and allowed them to receive the Televote questions and offer comments and suggestions. Subscribers to the service were able to read comments of others and develop a computer dialogue on the issues.

The designers of the LA Televote felt that its educational potential is also useful in helping the educational system to train students to become politically aware and active citizens and to develop planning skills. They chose a Los Angeles high school to serve as a demonstration project for developing problem-solving skills, which they considered relevant to responsible participation in the political system. "Project Citizen," involving 40 high school students, lasted for four weeks and revolved around the "Televote Game," which was a simulation designed to explore the different perspectives surrounding each of the Televote issues. For each issue, three or four students were given different roles representing different points of view on the issue, which they then discussed and debated with the other students. Not only did they discuss these issues in the class, but each student was also responsible for distributing, collecting, and tabulating ten Televote ballots in his or her community. Their class assignments included watching the Televote programming on television, including one segment that featured their actual classroom debates. Students also were assigned to take their discussion out of the classroom and get their family and friends involved in the Televote activities. The organizers of LA Televote stated, "the students were actually functioning to stimulate political activity in their community and at home."[22]

However, the most remarkable new discovery of the Televote process in Los Angeles was how closely the results of the random sample on the four state initiative issues matched the actual voter results in the election held immediately following the Televote. As in Hawaii and New Zealand, the LA Televote sample was highly representative of the overall population, but prior to Los Angeles there had never been another indicator available to see how closely the sample actually matched the views of the larger population from which it was drawn. On all four issues, the Televote results were within plus or minus four percentage points of the actual vote in the area on the issues and accurately predicted the results of the election on each issue. By contrast, the TV poll, which did not employ scientific random sampling, but was a self-selected group, only predicted the outcome on half the issues. Table 5.4 demonstrates how the scientific random sampling compared to the election results and the results of the television poll.[23]

Although the types of audiences reached in Los Angeles may not have been as diverse in some ways as in Honolulu, since most of its programming took place on news programs or talk shows, and since entertainment formats were not a part of the government-sponsored Los Angeles project, the raw number of citizens participating in a ten-day project was still very impressive. The Los Angeles Televote continued and expanded the development of Televote, and also demonstrated that the greater the cooperation between media, policy planners, and educators, the greater the potential for the success of Televote to achieve its participatory democratic goals.

HAWAII HEALTH DECISIONS 1, 2, AND 3: USING TELEVOTE TO BRING THE PUBLIC INTO HEALTH POLICY PLANNING

Finally, after several years of conducting Televote polls in Hawaii, we were contacted by Donald Toews and Dr. Henry Ichiho of the Hawaii

Table 5.4
Comparative Results: General Election, Random Sample Televote*, and TV Poll

Issue		General Election	LA Televote	TV Poll
Beverage Containers	yes	43.5%	45.2%	49.6%
	no	56.5%	54.8%	50.3%
Nuclear Weapons	yes	62.0%	66.3%	47.4%
Freeze	no	38.0%	33.7%	52.6%
Water Conservation	yes	46.5%	49.4%	59.2%
	no	53.5%	50.6%	40.8%
Handgun Ban	yes	48.5%	48.9%	34.1%
	no	51.5%	51.1%	65.9%

* Televote random sample of 408 residents of Los Angeles, 18 years or older.

Department of Health about the possibilities of using Televote to help them get more and better public input into health policy planning. Conventional public opinion polling had been part of the health department's policy-making process for many years, but Toews and Ichiho felt the necessity for something better—and they had heard about the Hawaii Televote model and thought it would enrich the administrative decision-making process. They believed that their role as administrators was to respond to public needs and to maintain a high-quality feedback system that allowed for effective public evaluation of their efforts.

The Hawaii Health Decisions Televotes, sponsored by the Hawaii Health Department, broke new ground again in Televote experimenting. It was the first time we had been approached by actual, practicing policy makers, who were familiar with our work and who determined on their own that Televote was a very useful tool for their work. Also, it was the first time the Hawaii Televote model was fully funded for researchers and staff and did not have to rely on volunteers or university classes to conduct the poll. And finally, it was the first time in Hawaii that policy makers had expressed a genuine desire to be directed in their planning by the desires of the public, whom they sought to educate on the issues to be resolved.

In fall 1983, I served as consultant for the first Hawaii Health Decisions poll (HHD-1) utilizing Televote methodology. The Family Health Services Division, through the Maternal and Child Health Branch of the Department of Health, had received a federal grant to develop policies and programs for dealing with teen pregnancies, unmarried mothers, adoption, and health problems of infants born to teenagers. The broad guidelines of the grant mandated the health department to (1) look into societal causes for the growing number of births to unwed teenage mothers; (2) identify the major reasons that adoption was an option so seldom used; (3) establish innovative, comprehensive, and integrated approaches to the delivery of care services for pregnant adolescents, particularly unwed mothers; and (4) assist families of adolescents to understand and resolve the societal causes that are associated with teenage pregnancy.

The HHD-1 Televote included facts on adolescent health problems in general as well as on teenage pregnancy and adoption in particular. It also contained a variety of ways to cope with adolescent problems, along with arguments for and against each. Questions were posed to discover (1) the extent to which the respondents felt that the health problems specified were problems facing Hawaii's teenagers; (2) their views on adoption; (3) the advice they would offer to unwed pregnant teenagers; and (4) their level of support for an array of methods to convey health services to Hawaii's youth. Relatively unconventional concepts, like community health organizations (CHOs), were on the menu.

The Televote results indicated majority accord on the causes, but no clear majority on any conventional solution. However, for new ideas, such as CHOs, there appeared to be strong community support (69%), although a significant minority (23%) did not know how they felt about them. We interpreted the large "not sure" group to the fact that CHOs were an unfamiliar notion in Hawaii and a number of citizens felt they needed more information before forming a definite opinion.

Toews is currently analyzing how these findings impacted the decision making in the Department of Health and whether and to what extent they influenced actual public policy. The initial reaction of the policy makers in the health department, however, was satisfaction. They were pleased and impressed that the representativeness of the sample was comparable to the more conventional polling they had done. And they viewed Televote as an efficient and effective approach to educating a representative sample of Hawaii's population about original thinking on health care delivery.

Increasing Participation in Televote: Unexpected Results of HHD-2 and HHD-3

Two years later, the health department utilized Televote again, this time conducting two polls simultaneously on wholly different issues involving entirely different populations. HHD-2, sponsored by the Crippled Children's Branch, addressed a primarily philosophical issue: children's rights and parents' rights (more specifically, who should provide and fund medical services for children when parents are unable or unwilling to do so). HHD-3, sponsored by Maternal and Child Health, dealt with a specific community health program: the future of the Waimanalo Health Clinic, which dispensed prenatal care, maternity services, and pediatric care.

The sample for HHD-2 was randomly drawn from all adult residents on Oahu, whereas the sample for HHD-3 was randomly selected from the much smaller Waimanalo community on Oahu. Whereas the residents of the island of Oahu are extremely diverse in ethnicity, level of income, and level of education, the Waimanalo residents included a greater percentage of lower-income families with less education than the average population of the state. We were quite sure from past experience that we would get a highly representative sample of all Oahuans for HHD-2, but we were worried that the complexity and difficulties inherent in the Televote method might pose some problems for obtaining a representative sample of the citizens of Waimanalo.

As had happened so often in our previous experiments, what actually transpired caught us off guard. Not only did we receive a representative sample of the population involved in both surveys, but our Waimanalo Televote demographics on ethnicity and income levels were a closer representation of the Waimanalo population than were the demographics of the Oahu Televote for Oahu's population on the same variables!

One demographic that was significantly skewed in the Waimanalo Televote was sex—36 percent male respondents and 64 percent female respondents. The actual population is about evenly divided. Our analysis of this tremendous discrepancy, which is not at all apparent in the Oahu Televote, is that this project focused on a health clinic that specialized in services for women and children, and thus it was of more interest to women, overwhelmingly the principal patrons of the clinic. Also in HHD-3, unlike our procedures in many other Televotes, we did not ask to speak to the head of the household (to help compensate for the fact that in Hawaii women are more likely to answer the phone than men). Finally, the sponsors of the survey believed that women would be more likely to know about the services of the clinic and be better able to evaluate its merits. Therefore, an overrepresentation of women in the survey was not a negative factor to them.

Actually, we began to suspect that our fears of not obtaining a representative sample in Waimanalo were groundless after we did our recruiting for HHD-3. In HHD-2 we were able to recruit 58 percent of those we asked to participate—well within our range of 50 percent to 65 percent in previous Hawaii Televotes. In HHD-3, however, we were astounded to receive our highest participation rate out of all Televotes we had ever conducted—nearly 75 percent of those we asked to participate agreed to do so.

In analyzing how we could have been so far off base in our predictions about the participation of the residents of Waimanalo, we were led to the following conclusion: HHD-3 hit a sensitive nerve. It touched something direct, real, and of tangible relevance to the people of the community—its health clinic. By contrast, HHD-2 was of a more philosophical and abstract interest to the citizenry. Thus, we believe that this experiment (serendipitously) demonstrated that when a public opinion survey or citizen participation project concerns an issue or issues that people think are vitally important to them, and they are convinced that their opinion is needed and can make a difference, this overcomes the sociopolitical tendencies to abstain from civic participation so deeply rooted in contemporary American society.

Furthermore, since we chose the same size sample from the small community of Waimanalo as we did from the much larger area of Oahu, we discovered that as we did our recruiting, many of those we contacted already had heard of the Televote from their neighbors and relatives, whom we had contacted earlier. They already had begun a discussion on the subject even before they agreed to receive our Televote in the mail. Several expressed gratification that they were now to be a part of the project. It was our first experience in recruitment where a substantial number of potential Televoters already had heard of our project from Televoters we had signed up to participate. It certainly made our survey efforts easier and more enjoyable. It also showed that if Televote is widely distributed in an area (about 20% of the households were involved), it can generate an intensive, interactive dynamic in that community.

Measuring the Extent to Which Televoters Read and Discuss the Contents

In all our previous Televotes, we were not so naive to believe that all our Televoters read all our information and all Televoters discussed the Televote with someone else. Indeed, we had assumed that some undetermined number of Televoters read all, most, some, or none of the material presented in the Televote brochures. Our first two Televotes on initiative and on selection of judges had indicated sophisticated responses very different from the responses of conventional polls conducted during a reasonably close time period. Also in the New Zealand Televote, the results indicated that a large percentage of the respondents chose the more complicated and difficult choice of creating their own future from the information provided rather than choosing one of the prepackaged futures (which did not require integrating any other data from the questionnaire). We also believed that some other undetermined number of Televoters discussed the material with others. We had been satisfied with the belief that whatever number read the material and discussed it with others, it was more than any conventional public opinion poll, since none encourages or allows for discussion and deliberation in the systematic way as does Televote.

In HHD-2 and HHD-3 we decided to try to gain some insight into how many respondents read how much of the material and discussed it with others. Also since the two Televotes were conducted concurrently, and were targeting dissimilar samples, we were able to gain a clearer notion about the extent to which this number might vary from survey to survey and population to population.

Thus, after our Televote interviewers had obtained the responses to the substantive and demographic questions on each Televote, they asked each Televoter: (1) "Other than the questions, how much of the Televote did you read?" (2) "Did you discuss the Televote with anyone else?" (3) If yes, "With whom?"

The general level of those who reported they read all the Televote was quite high (see Table 5.5). Nearly four out of five (77.3%) of the Oahu Televoters said they read all, while nearly two out of three (65.2%) of Waimanalo Televoters said they read all the material. We interpreted the 12 percent disparity to be due in part to the generally lower level of education in the Waimanalo sample (there were twice as many college graduates and people with some postgraduate education in the HHD-2 sample) and in part to the firsthand knowledge many of the Waimanalo Televoters had about the subject of HHD-3. The number of those who said they read no material other than the questions was uniformly low (less than 10% in both Televotes).

More than half of the Televoters in both surveys reported they discussed the Televote with someone else (see Table 5.6). Still, the reported level of discussion was substantially less than the reported level of reading all, most, or some of the Televote. Factors that we believe helped explain the different percentages of those who read the Televote in the

Table 5.5
Amount of Televote Read by Televoters

Response	HHD-2	HHD-3
All	77.3%	65.2%
Most	11.2%	16.7%
Some	6.0%	9.8%
None	5.5%	8.3%

two samples (lower level of education and more direct knowledge of the issue) had no significant effect on the reported amount of discussion the Televote generated.

By far, Televoters in both surveys preferred to discuss the Televote with their spouses (see Table 5.7). The Waimanalo Televoters (disproportionately female) had a slightly lesser tendency than the Oahu Televoters to do so. Instead, they had a slightly greater inclination to discuss the brochure material and issue with their children. This is understandable, since the clinic served women and their children.

We would expect that there would be a certain inflationary factor in Televoters' responses to these questions (akin to the inflationary factor that most pollsters expect in response to questions about income and education level). Some people are embarrassed by their low income or low educational level, and we believe that some Televoters were reluctant to admit that they did not read or discuss the Televote.

We believe, however, that there are factors in the results that indicate a minimal degree of inflation. For example, the substantial difference in the

Table 5.6
Discussion of Televote

RESPONSE	HHD-2	HHD-3
Yes	51.9%	50.4%
No	48.0%	49.5%

Table 5.7
With Whom Televoters Discussed Televote*

	HHD-2	HHD-3
Spouse	41.1%	33.4%
Kids	4.6%	12.3%
Parents	5.9%	9.6%
Friend	15.1%	10.3%
Other**	32.4%	34.4%

  * Some Televoters spoke with more than one person.
 ** Includes Relatives, Neighbors, Co-workers

percentage of Televoters who said they read all, most, or some of the Televote (90%–95%) and those who said they discussed the Televote (50%–52%) shows that approximately 40 percent of the Televoters who claimed to have read at least some of the Televote were not hesitant to tell our interviewers that they did not follow our instructions to also discuss the issue with others.

Then, there are a number of internal consistencies to indicate that most Televoters in both surveys were being frank. For example, lesser-educated Televoters were less likely to say they had read all the Televote.

Even discounting for some inaccuracy in the responses, we believe our data indicates a moderately high level of reading and discussion of the Televote and its contents. We believe not only that this adds a certain quality of thought and deliberation to the opinion data gathered, but that the Televote method increased the level of public education in the community quite unlike conventional methods of public opinion polling.

SUMMARY

This chapter has detailed the Televote odyssey from its early beginnings in a school district of California to its final experiment in a small Hawaiian community. Televote has been tested in California, Hawaii, and New Zealand on a variety of issues and for a variety of purposes. With each Televote we advanced our knowledge, improved our techniques, and asked new questions. And from the first design of the Hawaii Televote model to the last experiment we are convinced that the basic approach weaved together the quantum qualities of randomness and interactivity in a way to increase citizen involvement in government—whether representative or participatory democracy. We also came to understand that Televote's efficiency was especially enhanced when made a part of a wider, more complex democratic process like the Electronic Town Meetings.

The final chapter will look closely at critiques that have been made by others of Televote and corresponding Electronic Town Meetings. It also will present a concluding analysis of how Televote can be best institution-alized in the future so as to maximize its effectiveness in helping develop a more Participatory Representative State or the more radical Repre-sentative Participatory State—the polity most compatible with the prin-ciples of quantum politics.

NOTES

1. Earl R. Babbie, *Survey Research Methods* (Belmont, Calif.: Wadsworth, 1973), pp. 165–166. Babbie states that a response rate of 50% for mail questionnaires is *adequate* for analysis, 60% is *good*, and 70% is *very good*. He also notes that in computing response rates, the "accepted practice" is to omit all those that could not be delivered for various reasons. Although he acknowledges this does not produce a pure random sample of the total population, it is common practice. Also he states the researchers must be careful to compare their results with other data such as demographics to examine how closely their sample reflects the population at large.

2. The texts that we used for our methodology training were: Kenneth Webb and Harry P. Hatry, *Obtaining Citizen Feedback: The Application of Citizen Surveys to Local Governments* (Washington, D.C.: Urban Institute, 1973); Charles H. Backstrom and Gerald Hursh-Cesar, *Survey Research* (Evanston, Ill.: Northwestern University Press, 1963); and Babbie.

3. Gerry Keir, "Con Con Poll," *Honolulu Advertiser*, 19 February 1978, p. A1.

4. Gerry Keir, "Laws for Action by Public Favored," *Honolulu Advertiser*, 25 February 1978, p. A1.

5. Gerry Keir, "Most Favor Initiative, Referendum," *Honolulu Advertiser*, 10 May 1978, p. A1.

6. Theodore L. Becker and Richard Chadwick, "Problem-Solving CONCON Desired, Says University Poll," *Honolulu Advertiser*, 17 May 1978, p. A1.

7. Gerry Keir, "Change in Judge Selection Favored," *Honolulu Advertiser*, 25 February 1978, p. A1.

8. Keir, "Most Favor Initiative, Referendum," p. A1.

9. Statement of William Paty, 1978 Hawaii Constitutional Convention President, made to Ted Becker, professor in charge of the Televote project.

10. P. J. Arnopoulos and K. Valaskakis, *Telecommunitary Democracy: Utopian Vision or Probable Future* (Montreal: UNESCO, 1982), p. 46.

11. Details on the New Zealand Televote are found in Theodore L. Becker, Alvin Clement, Alan McRobie, and Brian Murphy, *Report on New Zealand Televote* (Wel-lington: Commission for the Future, 1981).

12. Ibid., p. 11.

13. Ibid., pp. 13–14.

14. Ibid., p. 33.

15. For Jim Dator's description of the project, see Jim Dator, "The 1982 Honolulu Electronic Town Meeting," in *The Future of Politics*, edited by William Page (London: Frances Pinter, 1983), pp. 211–217.

16. Ibid., p. 214.

17. Ibid., pp. 214–215.

18. Ibid., p. 216.

19. Ibid., p. 215.

20. California, Southern California Association of Governments, *Report on the Los Angeles Televote* (Los Angeles: SCAG, 1983).

21. Ibid., p. 4.

22. Ibid., p. 9.

23. A similar comparative data chart appears in Theodore L. Becker and Richard Scarce, "Teledemocracy Emergent: State of the American Art and Science," in *Progress in Communication Sciences*, edited by Brenda Derwin and Melvin J. Voight (Norwood, N.J.: Ablex, 1986), p. 281.

6

Evaluating Televote: Responding to Criticism and Setting Future Agendas

C hapter 5 was devoted to the contributions in data and theory of a dozen Televote experiments. As I noted, the Televote researchers, throughout the series, were open to serious and thoughtful critiques from others—as well as themselves—in a continuing attempt to assess and improve the process. I am well aware that the system is still not perfect, and never will be. Indeed, many important questions remain to be tested—and answered.

I realize, too, that it has taken a long time to compile, evaluate, and present a comprehensive explication of the Televote experiments—the philosophy and theory behind them, the discussion of all the data, and a detailed interpretation. Up to this point, there have been three published articles by various members of the Televote research staff (Becker and Slaton, 1981; Becker, 1981; Becker and Scarce, 1986). They have discussed various aspects of Televote and have presented some of the data and some analysis of the Televote findings. However, Chapter 5 is the first comprehensive presentation of Televote up to this time.

The early reports of Televote, however, have attracted some attention, as I mentioned in the previous chapter. The Gamma Group, at McGill University in Montreal, was favorably impressed and considered Televote to be the closest approximation to their ideal model of telecommunitarian democracy.[1] Their positive reaction was encouraging. On the other hand, they presented no critique and, thus, did not stimulate us to reexamine our design.

Benjamin Barber also presents Televote as a positive example of the democratic experimentation being conducted across the country in his book *Strong Democracy*. Again, no specific critique is presented of Televote.

There has been an intensive, itemized evaluation of Televote in a comparative study of teledemocracy projects. This critique emanates from a small group of analysts led by F. Christopher Arterton—formerly a political science professor at Yale, a research fellow at the Roosevelt Center in Washington, D.C., and currently the dean of the Graduate School of Political Management (of the state of New York) in New York City.

Unfortunately, despite spending numerous pages and sections of chapters in two recent books (Arterton, 1987; Abramson, Arteron, and Orren, 1988) evaluating Televote, they set forth data that is so inaccurate that the assessment offers very little insight into ways to redesign Televote. As I will demonstrate, Arterton is a devoted adherent to the Expanded Representative State. In his attempts to justify the current political system, he misrepresents Televote to those who read his work and finesses the major issues of system change that the Televote experiments treat seriously.

The first part of this final chapter will address these specific critiques of Televote and highlight the myriad distortions of the Televote process and goals. Arterton has established quite a professional reputation, lately, as a thorough evaluator of teledemocracy projects. His charges against Televote are numerous and severe. But they are, at heart, ideologically driven. He and his colleagues make this clear and I will portray this, I hope, with equal clarity.

The second part of this chapter will discuss some real shortcomings in the Televote experience to date. There are truly important things to know that we have yet to address, that we have yet to study, that need to be known so that we can better comprehend how to develop better systems for citizen participation in planning, problem solving, policy making, and implementation in a future system of more effective democratic governance.

The last part of this chapter will be my conclusion, my summing up, my integration of all that has gone before in this work. I believe there is a unity here—one that I have tried to elucidate throughout.

We live in a new age—one characterized by rapid technological developments; great expansions in our knowledge of physical and human behavior; potential manmade cataclysms of unprecedented magnitude; numerous democratic revolutions of one kind or another. This study has made the point—over and over again—that the Televote experiments (as well as other participatory democratic theories and projects) are an amalgamation of key aspects of these technological, theoretical, scientific, and political changes of the twentieth century.

The concluding part of this final chapter will make my final statement as to how these changes merge and, therefore, lend even greater credibility to the potential for a new form of participatory democracy, in other words, the Representative Participatory State.

RESPONDING TO THE CRITICS

F. Christopher Arterton has spent a good portion of two books critiquing Televote. His evaluation and analysis is based on a visit to Hawaii in 1985 where he interviewed Becker and Dator (but not Chadwick or Slaton) as well as the articles that have been published on or about the Hawaii model of Televote.

Arterton commences his study by defining "teledemocracy" as "the use of communications technology to facilitate the transmission of political information and opinion between citizens and their public leaders."[2] He says unequivocally at the outset that he does not view teledemocracy as "a politics that would undercut our established representative machinery."[3]

In selecting Televote for study, Arterton found that it fit his prerequisite that it be in a category of "policy-neutral projects" designed by disinterested democrats. As he describes the role of the organizers: "They merely provide greater opportunities for citizens to exert influence, while they try to avoid influencing the outcomes of the process they set in motion."[4]

Unfortunately, though, for purposes of effective and useful independent evaluation, Arterton's information on Televote was incomplete and much of what he adduces is either incorrect or misrepresented. In addition, there are two major defects in Arterton's research design that weaken its capabilities to identify and assay Televote's merits and demerits. First, I will address the problems with his methodology and then I will look at the specific critiques made about the Hawaii Televote model to consider their value and their potential for the upgrading and sustainability of Televote for the future.

Methodological Problems in the Arterton Televote Studies

In his 1987 book, *Teledemocracy: Can Technology Protect Democracy?* Arterton exposes his personal bias in favor of the presently constituted American representative system. His own definition of teledemocracy indicates a lack of interest in, or concern about, any reforms that may fundamentally affect the existing structural relationship between citizens and representatives—for example, to make representatives more strictly accountable to the democratic controls of the citizenry. Placing his definition of teledemocracy within the confines of my own typology, Arterton's

Table 6.1

Arterton's Criteria for Evaluating the Effectiveness of Teledemocracy Projects*

---

1) Access--the range of citizens able to participate in a teledemocracy project.

(2) Reach--the percentage of those citizens able to participate who actually do become involved.

(3) Effectiveness--whether or not citizen participation can have a direct influence upon public policy.

(4) Agenda setting--the level of control citizens are able to exercise over the issues to be decided , the alternatives to be considered, the timing of and order of participation, and so forth.

(5) Diversity of access paths--the number of ways through which citizens can learn about and participate in a project.

(6) Duration--the length of time and number of iterations over which an institution for citizen participation lasts.

(7) Individual or group based--whether citizens can participate as individuals or as members of organized interest groups.

(8) Initiative--the degree to which citizens must discover and generate for themselves opportunities to become involved and the information upon which that involvement is based.

(9) Costs--the burdens, financial and otherwise, imposed on citizens in connection with their participation.

(10) Educative value--the degree to which participants learn about the subject matter or policy area under consideration.

(11) Political competence--through their participation in a teledemocracy project, the skills and confidence to become more generally politically active.

---

* F. Christopher Arterton, Teledemocracy: Can Technology Protect Democracy? (Newbury Park, Ca.: Sage Publications, 1987) 63.

criteria for evaluation are to determine if teledemocracy projects (like Televote) strengthen the representative function in the Expanded Representative State—in other words, he asks to what extent do the teledemocracy projects facilitate communication between citizens and public officials through the use of modern technology.

Inappropriate Application of Criteria. The first major methodological problem arises with his list of 11 criteria (see Table 6.1) created to evaluate the projects.

As actually applied by Arterton, however, these criteria are primarily relevant to a Full Participation State since he uses them to measure the extent to which all citizens are fully involved in decision making that has a "direct influence upon policy."[5] Arterton evaluates 13 projects, including Televote, frequently using the terms "direct democracy," "plebiscite," and "universal participation" as standards by which to evaluate the success of the projects—despite the fact that none of these (particularly Televote) state this to be their goal. Thus his criteria for evaluation, as applied, are (1) inconsistent with his own definition of teledemocracy and (2) inapplicable to the goals of all the project organizers of the projects he evaluates. It is hardly surprising, then, that Arterton finds none of the projects to succeed on all the dimensions by which he measures citizen participation. Indeed, the conclusion of his 1987 book that "teledemocracy offers us improvements in democracy, not a major transformation nor a final fulfillment,"[6] should be seen as success in terms of his own definition (and the criteria of the project organizers) even though he seems to be saying, by his inappropriate applications, that they have been unsuccessful.

In dealing with Hawaii Televote specifically, Arterton credits the model with responding to two major problems of modern survey research by (a) allowing respondents time to think about the issue and (b) encouraging them to talk about it with others. He states that requesting respondents to reflect on the issues with others in a social context is an "achievement [that] is a major virtue of Televote."[7] He further points out that Becker has written that Televote is "one step along the path toward teledemocracy."[8] Therefore, Arterton acknowledges some Televote success and realizes that the Televote designers do not claim it to be the ultimate form of, or the path toward, a full participatory democracy in America.

On the other hand, when we address certain of Arterton's specific criticisms of Televote, we will see how this methodological flaw of utilizing criteria that do not match the goals of the projects affects his conclusions of success or failure. It also will provide insight into how and why Arterton and two coauthors of a 1988 book, *The Electronic Commonwealth*, pronounce a harsher verdict on Televote and conclude that rather than enhancing democracy, Televote "shortchanges the democratic process."[9]

Improper Application of Classification System. The 1988 study of Televote includes another serious methodological shortcoming, in other words, misclassifying the project under analysis. Referring to "the shallowness of polling as a form of democratic participation,"[10] Arterton determines that Televote is a "foe of democracy,"[11] "trivial,"[12] and "superficial."[13] Yet he and his collaborators arrive at such a harsh judgment only because they fail to make pivotal distinctions in their own classification scheme. Worse yet, they present incomplete, as well as erroneous, information that makes their classification scheme appear to be appropriate.

Televote Is Not Instantaneous. A particularly glaring illustration of improper classification is how they lump Televote together with Warner Communications' QUBE system and AT&T's "900" system. In the QUBE system, viewers vote instantly on their own initiative, using an interactive voting device attached to their television set, during or after programming on a local cable television station that the viewers pay to receive.[14]

The AT&T "900" system is a computer tally system used by many in the media to receive instantaneous telephone responses by citizens to questions posed by a television or radio show. Once again, citizens must pay to give their opinions.

Under the section titled "Participation by Electronic Plebiscite: The Case of Hawaii Televote,"[15] Arterton and his colleagues devote five pages out of ten presenting the problems with QUBE, various users of the "900" voting, and other "instant" pollings of citizens in their homes. At one point, they refer to interactive cable television programming as presenting a "*televote* ballot."[16] (Emphasis mine.) In a footnote they acknowledge that Televote differs from these forms of polling in "one important respect—speed"[17] (Televote allows time for deliberation). In the body of the section critiquing Hawaii Televote, they emphasize swift response as well as other problems with instant voting that are all irrelevant to a discussion of Televote.

While acknowledging the speed factor as a difference between Televote and the media-designed methods of obtaining public opinion, albeit in a footnote with little elaboration, Arterton chooses to ignore the difference completely in his conclusion. Televote makes a major point of giving respondents a few to many days to think and talk about the issue, whereas the other forms of electronic vote tallying usually require immediate responses or responses within one day. The Televote evaluators go into a lengthy description of the ABC network's use of the "900" number to determine who won the debate between Reagan and Carter and decry the lack of public deliberation. This long description of the ABC poll is within the same paragraph beginning with a two-sentence statement about Televote allowing time for deliberation, but pointing out that Televote allows only "token" time and can fall victim to "automated politics."[18]

The lumping of Televote in this discussion with the "900" polling on candidates is like mentioning the limitations of an information pamphlet designed by neutral technics, but making the case against it by describing a slick campaign brochure produced by a public relations consultant. To question the amount of time for deliberation given in the Televote process is legitimate (but it should be acknowledged that the deliberation is far greater than what conventional polls offer, which is none). But to lump the Televote practice of deliberation time on complex substantive issues, which is an essential feature of the design, with instant polling to determine a winner in a televised political debate with all its hype, slogans, and personality differences, is to take two diametrically opposed goals and call them the same. Even worse, the evaluators refer to AT&T and Warner Communications' instant pollings as Televote's "progeny."[19] Instant self-initiated polling is not a progeny of Televote. They are both the children of modern technology, to be sure. But as frequently is the case with siblings, they have travelled in two different directions—Televote seeking to integrate the lessons of life into a mature and wise development and the other to indulge in quick and instant gratification. Televote is still immature and has many important lessons to learn. But it is nevertheless unfair to compare it to those who do not aspire to similar aims.

Televote Is Not a Self-Selected Sample. As I emphasized in Chapter 5, one of the most significant changes we made in adapting Campbell's version of Televote to the Hawaii model was to switch from a self-selected to a random sampling of the population. We learned from Campbell's experiment that reliance on a self-motivated and/or self-selected sample has a significantly skewed bias in favor of well-educated Caucasian males (similar to, but less than, that which exists in the U.S. Congress). We wanted to broaden the diversity and have a much more representative image of the entire population. Results of other activities conducted coincident with many of the Televotes, which relied on self-appointed participants, indicated a similar slant to that found in the Campbell experiment.

As discussed earlier, when we conducted our first Hawaii Televote, we found that those who called back their responses without our prompting (approximately 15% of the sample) were weighted heavily in favor of well-educated Caucasian males. These results resurfaced in New Zealand. Comparing respondents who filled in New Zealand newspaper ballots (N = 4,018) with the scientifically chosen group (N = 964), we found that the Televoters closely resembled the composition of the New Zealand population (see Table 5.3 in the previous chapter), while the newspaper set were 69 percent male, 98 percent Caucasian, and 42 percent college-educated (15% in NZ Televote). The Los Angeles Televote project also revealed similar warpage in the self-initiators. What is more, the results of the actual election indicated that the randomly selected Televote respondents provided an accurate picture of the election outcome, being within the scientifically determined 5 percent margin of error range on every issue (ranging from .4% to 4.3% variation from the true vote), whereas the unrepresentative newspaper sample predicted the actual vote in only half the cases. Even on those issues in which the final outcome was forecasted by the newspaper sample, the responses were still 6 percent to 15 percent off the mark in reflecting the levels of support for and opposition against the issues. These results of the Los Angeles Televote also offer a challenge to Arterton's rhetorical query: "One can question, however, whether a group that is demographically representative of the general population is indeed politically representative."[20]

The designers of the Hawaii model of Televote, as well as other earnest pollsters utilizing scientific methodology, understandably bristle when distinctions are not made between scientific sampling and the self-selected voting done with increasing frequency in the American commercial news media. It is particularly disturbing to have the media acknowledge that their polling is not scientific, yet introduce their stories (and often present them as lead stories) with phrases such as "The Public Favors" or "The Public Opposes." The Televote experimentation has demonstrated time and again that "the public" is not represented in these self-selected samples, but a very biased result is evident in every self-selected sample we obtained.[21] It does a grave disservice to Televote, and makes doubtful the credibility and integrity of an evaluation of Televote, to fail to make such important distinctions, ones we have been making since our first experiment.

Arterton also ignores the initial preparations we made for assuring a representative sample. In one of his evaluations, he points out that only 15 percent of the Televoters responded within the allotted time and states that "the televote managers then departed from their own design and, like conventional pollsters, called participants and solicited an on-the-spot response from them."[22] We understood, however, from our own familiarity with the literature on mail surveys that a very small percentage of individuals actually respond to mail surveys without subsequent rewards, reminders, and/or prompting. We always had planned a system of call-backs for a majority of our Televoters. Also, it was never a part of our methodology to obtain "on-the-spot responses." If Televoters did not have their questionnaires already filled out when we called (as many did), we set up an appointment, usually two to three days hence, to call them again. We also reemphasized our desire to have them discuss the Televote with others.

Our design to obtain a representative sample of the population stands in contrast to the Televote evaluators' faith that "democracy thrives on self-initiated participation rooted in civic concern and civic education."[23] On the contrary, it appears from our empirical research that elitism thrives on self-initiated participation. The data consistently indicates radical demographic skews in self-initiated participants, while there is no evidence to witness self-initiators as greater promoters of democracy for others, as possessing a greater public conscience or more civic concern, or as being less self-interested in their participation.

While clearly some self-motivated actors are more politically alert and are knowledgeable on particular issues, one of the purposes of Televote is to elevate individual levels of awareness and information. Having a superior data base does not necessarily make one less subjective and more objective, particularly on issues grounded in value judgments. Yet Televote can play a part in heightening civic education and broadening the political discourse well beyond that taught in public schools. For instance, no civics courses were taught at the public school I attended in South Carolina, very few high schools in Hawaii offer any government or civics courses, and education majors in both states can graduate from universities and colleges without having taken a single course in U.S. government. The general paucity of civic education opportunities in America makes it clear that for many to learn how to effectively participate in the system, they have to be self-initiators, making them a part of a select group. That we take such great pains to avoid this mistake makes it particularly disturbing to be cavalierly and carelessly lumped together with projects that rely on self-selection (because it is cheap and easy).

Specific Criticisms of Televote

Recognizing the methodological problems in Arterton, Abramson, and Orren Televote studies, there are many Televote-specific criticisms that also need to be addressed and evaluated. These judgments fall under two general categories. The first attempts an objective analysis that concludes: Televote does not live up to its own ideals and fails to elicit significant changes and impact in citizen participation. The second unveils the subjective perspective underlying the former analysis—in other words, even if Televote increases participation, that participation is not beneficial to the present American representative system of government. As will be clear in the explication of the "objective" critique, Arterton and his colleagues' study of Televote is overshadowed by the underlying prejudice against one of Televote's goals—to lend aid and assistance to the development of a representative system that is truly representative of the economic, ethnic, and political diversity present in the American citizenry, that is, the Representative Participatory State, a representative system in tune with the technology and knowledge of the twentieth century, informed by the quantum perspective.

Restricts Access. One of Televote's major failings (according to Arterton's 11 standards for evaluation) is the way by which it restricted those who can participate: by using only random samples. The Televote experiments were not developed, however, with the goal of reaching the Full Participation State. Instead, we sought to obtain in-depth, thoughtful opinion from a more informed representative sample of the population that could serve as a useful guide for representatives who are inundated with pressures from well-organized, wealthy, and/or powerful special interests. Televote was seen as a useful means to communicate the views of the citizenry (by way of scientific random sampling) to the representatives and to provide a clearer view of the entire range of citizen opinion than they receive from a small, but vocal and organized, minority or from random samples using conventional polling techniques that elected representatives routinely discount as being superficial and thoughtless.

While that remained our target throughout all our experiments, we felt that Televote's educational potential could germinate much broader public consciousness of and discussion on issues, particularly if the material were disseminated widely. In later Televotes, therefore, we expanded our distribution system (having to rely on the media's donation of time and space due to a lack of funding), but we always maintained our randomly selected group, which we felt offered a valuable scientific baseline of the views of a "silent majority." Clearly our ideal scenario would be universal distribution of the Televote material to aid in universal public debate. But we know that would be extremely expensive and virtually impossible to accomplish, given our meager resources.

Low Participation Rate. Participation also fell short in Arterton's eyes because, according to him, only 50 percent of those contacted agreed to participate. Actually, data available to Arterton shows the rate ranged from 50 percent to 65 percent in our early Televotes but improved in our later Televotes—for example, over 70 percent in New Zealand and 75 percent in Waimanalo agreed to participate. He continues the discussion of low participation rates by noting that only 72 percent of those who agreed to participate eventually did so. In fact, the completion rate ranged from 70 percent to 83 percent. Multiplying the percentage of those who agreed to participate by the percentage of those who completed their Televote, Arterton announces that this participation rate is lower than presidential elections and about the same as congressional elections.[24] To bolster his brief, Arterton used our lowest figures to claim that only 36 percent of those contacted finally participated, when actually those who agreed to and did participate were sometimes as high as 54 percent—greater than the voter turnout in the 1988 presidential election and much superior to the percentage of eligible voters who cast ballots for congresspersons.

We would agree that we have not demonstrated an overwhelming demand from citizens eager to participate. In fact, we expected resistance, particularly from the poor, uneducated, and ethnic minorities, so we designed our recruiting system to coax participation from those we contacted who often lamented, "The politicians don't care what I think" or "My opinion doesn't count for anything." From surveys conducted of citizens' views on government leaders' responsiveness to public opinion (see Chapter 3), we realized that there was significant citizen cynicism about the value of using their time to express their views. Rather than falsely assure the skeptics that politicians really cared about their views, we stressed that we needed their participation in order to lend validity to our claim that the Televote responses represented the views of a representative sample. Although cynicism was the most common resistance we found, others expressed inadequacy and lack of knowledge. We particularly encouraged them at this point to discuss the issue with family, friends, and co-workers and to take their time to think about the issue. We also emphasized that their opinions were extremely important—to us. Very few citizens were rude or uncooperative. Of course, there were those who simply were suspicious that Televote was another gimmick used by telephone hucksters and charlatans.

While not satisfied ourselves with the participation rates, and while we continue to look for ways to spur greater participation, we were pleased that from the outset we were able to obtain a representative sample of the population or at least as good a representative sample as conventional polls, which require much less time and commitment from their participants. In terms of increasing the participation rates, we are hindered by the larger problem inherent in the American political system itself: meager civic education in public schools; representatives who show and/or express disdain for public opinion; and processes designed to allow wealthy and powerful minorities greater and more effective access to policy makers. Our Televotes were conducted in an environment that is less than hospitable to citizen participation in policy making.

Nevertheless, we found, through experimentation, ways to increase participation: (1) combine Televoting with Electronic Town Meetings over an extended period of time; (2) let the public determine the issues to be included in the Televotes; (3) select issues in which the Televoters have firsthand knowledge; (4) publicize the Televote process; (5) conduct Televotes in smaller areas where there is greater opportunity for participants to interact with each other. We plan to continue to explore this issue and to analyze participation rates, but we believe that our relatively low participation rate is more of an indictment of the American representative system and its resistance to enlightening and engaging an informed citizenry.

No Proof of "Political" Representativeness in Televote Sample. Arterton argues that the demographics of the Televote participants, although close to the demographics of the full population (with the exception of educational levels), are no proof that Televoters are politically representative of the total population. He speculates that Televoters are more likely to be joiners and already active and therefore their opinions may differ from the nonparticipants who resemble them in other ways. To support this view he points out that the educational level of Televoters tends to run ten points higher for Hawaii Televoters.[25]

Indeed the educational levels of Hawaii Televoters were higher than those of the general population, as is the case in most conventional polls and in all other American teledemocracy projects that have recorded demographic data on their participants. I do not claim to know the views of the nonparticipants, nor can I claim unequivocally that the Televote results are the same results that would be achieved if every single citizen voted on the issues.

Our goal with Televote, however, as Arterton himself acknowledged, is to broaden the opportunity for citizens we called upon to participate. We made great efforts to ease the burdens of those not normally accustomed to participation through our information presentation, packaged in a "user-friendly" format and through our initiating a low-key, friendly, sympathetic contact. Considering that we obtained a close approximation of the public, and certainly a greater diversity than found in any of our elected representative bodies, I would have to concur with Lester Milbrath and M. L. Goel's belief that in a representative democracy citizens should have the right not to participate if they so choose.[26]

This attitude is not to dismiss criticisms that Televote may not sufficiently involve the traditional nonparticipant. On the contrary, we have demonstrated success with obtaining demographically representative samples, some progress with achieving greater involvement of those with low educational levels (New Zealand and Waimanalo), and a desire to learn more about nonparticipants who may want to be heard but have inadequate means for being heard. We recognize that some citizens have different values, goals, and agendas that do not include political participation. Arterton's utopian criticism on this point that Televote's " 'representative participation' constitutes a major retreat from the plebiscitory, direct democracy principle of universal involvement"[27] is totally irrelevant to the Televote goal.

Televote Is an Unrealistic Design of Politics without Advocacy, Strong Self-Interest, or Leadership. Arterton also describes our even-handed, telecommunitarian approach of presenting issues in our Hawaii Televote model, demonstrating no intent to " 'stack the deck' on one side of an issue,"[28] as being unrealistic and, despite our best intentions, as tending to limit political information to our Televoters. He points to the lessons learned from American broadcast law, which tries to mandate fairness but which has had limited success in such an endeavor. To Arterton's way of thinking, trying to be neutral and provide balance in information may tend to limit political information.

As I noted in my discussion of the results of the Televote projects, what we found was a more informed and sophisticated public opinion after Televote information was supplied. Arterton has no data to support a view that supplying balanced arguments limited, rather than increased, political facts and opinion readily available to Televoters.

While clearly there will be problems with maximizing the "policy-neutral" stance of Televote organizers, it is not an impossible task. Arterton himself has identified 12 recent experiments across the United States in addition to Televote that he maintains reach such a high standard. Institutionalizing such a system is much more difficult, and will be discussed in greater depth in the discussion of Televote's future later in this chapter.

Failure to Allow Participants to Establish the Televote Agenda and Frame the Debate. In both of his studies, Arterton faults Televote for not allowing the Televote participants to participate in setting the agenda for discussion. In 1988, three years after the last Televote experiment, he and his collaborators wrote: "Even more damning is that televoters played no role in deciding which issues ought to be the subject of the plebiscite, which issues ought to be placed on the public's agenda for constitutional action."[29]

In truth, the subject of the first two Televotes was determined by the Hawaii Televote organizers, primarily due to the time constraints of funding that started approximately the same time as the constitutional convention, thereby allowing no time for advance planning. However, it is incredible that Arterton and his colleagues fail to acknowledge what was in much of the information provided to them in 1984—in other words, that we recognized the problem ourselves and remedied it. In fact, as detailed in the last chapter, we developed the "Public Agenda" Televote as our third experiment—one that determined the issues for our legislative Televotes. Furthermore, the public also was allowed to establish its financial agenda and priorities in our seventh Televote—"The Public Budget." Every other Televote was done in cooperation with official policy makers who said they wanted to use Televote as an aid to getting public input for specific problems they had to resolve. All of this data was available to Arterton in a published article that he cites, one in which we explain the public agenda and our rationale for developing it. Arterton excluded acknowledgment of it in both studies.

He continues to lambaste the Televote planners because they did not allow the Televoters the "opportunity to frame the 'pro' and 'con' arguments about the issues under discussion; once more this was the exclusive province of the televote staff."[30] While the Televoters did not contribute to the "pro" and "con" arguments in the brochure, they were certainly encouraged to think about the issue and to discuss it with others, thereby extending the debate.

Also, whenever compatible interactive programming was taking place coinstantaneous with the Televote, such as in the Honolulu Electronic Town Meeting, we notified the Televoters and encouraged them to watch and to call in their questions, ideas, and views, which included the opportunity to enlarge the scope of the debate. In addition, Arterton ignores the painstaking process we went through (detailed again in the very articles he cites) to obtain the "pro" and "con" arguments from those most vocal or active in making them. We did not create the arguments in ivory tower isolation. Not only did we seek input for the arguments, but we returned to the various individuals or groups for their review of our presentation of their arguments. That entire process hardly makes the development of the arguments the "exclusive province" of the Televote staff.

Televote Information Is Inadequate for Deciding the Issues. Televote never was intended to provide comprehensive, exhaustive information on issues. Instead, the idea was for it to be a means to convey some useful factual data and to serve as a catalyst for further interaction. Nevertheless, Arterton judges that the Televote information is "inferior in fact to current press coverage of issue politics,"[31] and that it provides more "caricature than the curriculum of a civic education."[32] To make his point, he presents the entire Televote argumentation on election of judges produced in the brochure on judicial selection. He acknowledges the information is "accurate, impartial, and objective," but says it "trivializes the nature of democratic deliberation" and ignores the classic arguments against the election of judges found in *The Federalist Papers.*[33]

What Arterton totally fails to grasp, however, is that the Televote questionnaire actually expanded the scope of the debate on selection of judges that had been the subject of public discussion and polls for months, that is, from a simple dichotomy between election or appointment to offering four alternatives for selection of judges. In addition, after receiving the Televote material, the sentiment of Hawaii respondents changed from favoring outright election of judges to a preference for merit selection with subsequent retention elections. On this issue, as well as all the other issues,

Televote disseminated details and alternatives not covered by the press and obtained responses that indicated the new information aided in the development of opinions that displayed more refined intellectual distinctions than those gathered by the conventional polls conducted during the same time period. (See the detailed description of the Televote on initiative and referendum in the previous chapter where indirect initiative became the preferred choice of Televoters.) How, then, could this be said to "trivialize . . . democratic deliberation"? And in what curriculum of "civic education" available to most citizens are there discussions of indirect initiative and four choices of judicial selection?

The other example used to demonstrate the alleged mundane presentation of information in the Televotes is the New Zealand Televote that allowed respondents to choose their own future based on their values and policies consistent with those values. Arterton selectively quotes from the information provided from one scenario and deprecates it as follows:

> It is difficult to see how anyone could dissent from such a future, worded as it is, though of course in real life the politics of free enterprise are a source of intense controversy. The text for education here is so short, conclusory, and leading in tone that it could educate New Zealanders only in the crudest of ways. Once again, it was no advance over the education delivered by the organized press.[34]

What Arterton fails to mention is that only 12 percent of the Televoters chose the future (he states hardly anyone could resist) after reading all the materials related to that scenario. Furthermore, the Televote had been criticized by New Zealand media and methodology pundits stating the material was too complex for a public opinion poll and that New Zealanders would not complete it. Of course, that Televote proved to be among the most successful in participation rates and representativeness of the sample.

Actually, these criticisms were the indirect result of Arterton's misapplication of his own criteria—the extent to which Televote achieves full direct democratic participation. Even if he did not omit and distort the information on Televote he still would have said that Televote failed to live up to his criteria. Instead, Televote has been very successful in attaining the goals of the teledemocratic definition offered by Arterton himself—use of communication technology to facilitate the transmission of political information and opinion between citizens and their public leaders—and offers the potential for even more service in a Representative Participatory State.

This latter point really presents the greatest problem for Arterton: To what extent do the teledemocracy projects (particularly Televote, seen by

Gamma as being the closest proximity to a telecommunitarian system) seek to change the existing political system? He makes it clear he wishes to see no major change in the established representative system and argues throughout his books against direct democracy. When he then judges the projects by direct democratic standards, he sets up a fail-safe, shifty way to condemn the projects for either their failure or their success in achieving their goals.

Arterton's misunderstanding and/or falsification of the Televote design and practices, and his own partisanship in favor of the established system, lead him to be particularly critical of Televote's relationship with elected representatives and leaders. His oversimplification and/or mislabelling of Televote as a plebiscite produces another set of criticisms that he has with the Televote efforts to increase public input in decision making. Arterton, like Michael Malbin, who expressed his opposition to teledemocracy in an article entitled "Teledemocracy and Its Discontents," is opposed to changes in the United States to give ordinary citizens more control of the political process. Adopting the Madisonian perspective, Arterton correctly labels the teledemocracy projects as following in the divergent Jeffersonian tradition.[35] The following section will bring the Madison-Jefferson differences into the twentieth century as I discuss Arterton's and Malbin's fundamentalist objections to Televote goals and practices.

Public Officials Not Involved in the Televote Process. Arterton acknowledges in neither of his studies the persistent efforts we made to get political leaders involved in the Televote process. He states that in interviews he conducted, "Becker and Dator were somewhat disdainful of politicians and the current political processes."[36] He adds that if a mayor or governor staged a Televote, participation rates might be higher because there would be legitimacy added to the process.

Arterton makes no attempt to explain or explore why two political science professors might exhibit disdain for politicians since his personal observations and impression of teledemocracy projects that included politicians led him to conclude that "the public officials involved were genuinely open to citizen participation."[37] Of course, he barely touches upon the strong resistance and pronounced hostility of numerous politicians in the Washington, Pennsylvania, and Alaska projects he studied (which are discussed in Chapter 4) or notes that their eventual support for the projects was a result of tremendous citizen pressure, not any original eagerness and openness on the part of most politicians, although there were a few notable exceptions.

Again ignoring information readily available to him, Arterton misinterprets the Televote procedure and agenda. From the outset we tried to work cooperatively with political leaders. We saw Televote as a useful means of communication between government officials and citizens. We felt politicians could (1) provide information to educate citizens on issues through the Televote and (2) be enlightened by the better-informed public opinion conveyed directly to them at no cost to them.

At the orientation for Hawaii CONCON delegates, Becker introduced the Televote program and offered to assist in trying to obtain a more informed public opinion for the delegates' consideration. We were granted an office at the convention site, which was staffed by someone from Hawaii Televote, in order to increase the contact with and usefulness to the delegates. Many delegates used our Televote results in the ensuing public debates. We polled the entire delegation after the convention to obtain their evaluation and feedback and to solicit their views on Televote's future usefulness for state legislators. As noted in Chapter 5, only half the delegates responded to our questionnaire, but over three-fourths of those indicated that Televote was useful to them and would be useful for state legislators as well.

When we conducted our "Public Agenda" Televote, we also sent the questionnaire to all state legislators to identify issues that topped their list, as well as the public's, for legislative action. The response from the legislators was so insignificant (two replied) that it made any effort to mediate between them and the public impossible. Nevertheless, we dispatched the results of all our Televotes to them and other political leaders and tried to enlist their input in developing the information and arguments in the Televote brochure.

As discussed in the previous chapter, we were open to advice on the design of Televotes from politicians who expressed problems with the information provided. After a critique of a Televote, we invited the lieutenant governor and her staff's advice on our Televote design, to no avail. A couple of years later, however, after the termination of the widely heralded Honolulu Electronic Town Meeting and its associated Televote, the same lieutenant governor appeared on a PBS program with Becker and Dator and lauded both projects. She was running for governor at the time.

When Arterton makes the argument that if a mayor or governor sponsored the Televote, participation might be higher, he again overlooks the Televote we managed in cooperation with the mayor of Honolulu (HT-6 on transportation). The notable feature of those Televote results is that the mayor was displeased that the results did not endorse his plan and chose to ignore the Televote results as quickly as he got them.

Also disregarded is the fact that the New Zealand and Los Angeles Televotes were both sponsored by governmental bodies with the official sanction of political leaders. In addition, the last three Televotes were underwritten by the Hawaii Department of Health.

Arterton's implication is that no effort was made to work with political leaders. There is extensive evidence to the contrary. What did occur is that we often ran into stone walls in the person of political leaders who did not want to be involved with, or subjected to, greater involvement of the public. Their reasons usually were cloaked in the usual Madisonian and Burkean lingo that representatives are better informed and more capable of necessary compromise and that the public is incapable of the wise judgments made by erudite and altruistic representatives. On a couple of occasions, observed in the last chapter, we happened upon some political leaders raring to work with the Televote staff, but not in earnest to create a genuine dialogue with the people. We were disillusioned to learn that they simply wanted to identify with Televote for public relations purposes.

Also we discovered the heavy price to be paid when politicians feel the heat of public pressure via democratic technics. Our funding was unceremoniously cut at the University of Hawaii when "downtown" complained to the university administration about the intense public pressure exerted on them from the first two Televotes.

As already noted, our record on working with government leaders was not a complete zero, but we had enough experience with their turning their backs on our results or dragging their feet to conclude that our representative system is sorely lacking in means by which unorganized individuals without significant resources (time, money, political connections, etc.) can impact policies or planning. Our experiments repeatedly reinforced the notion held by a majority of citizens that has been repeatedly expressed in public opinion polls: Politicians don't really care what they think. Arterton admits his observations of political leaders may be naive and that maybe they really express interest in participatory democracy in order to co-opt or manipulate the process. He quickly dismisses the probabilities, however, and challenges those who make such assertions to "specify concretely the mechanisms of collusion and suppression and to document empirically their strength."[38] There is significant documentation in the history of Televote, as well as other projects, to underscore Arterton's naivete. More serious, however, than his self-proclaimed innocence is his highly selective and fallacious presentation of the Televote design and practice—he concludes that Televote is a foe of democracy while he ignores the numerous examples of political leaders' animosity to increased citizen participation and lauds their professed concern for increasing citizen participation.

Televote Had No Impact on Public Policy. Arterton also argues that Dator and Becker were not interested in Televote or the Honolulu Electronic

Town Meetings having direct impact upon policy.[39] Instead, he says they justify "their project in terms of psychological rather than political benefits."[40] This attitude, he maintains, trivializes participation because participation is not coupled with action. What occurs, according to Arterton, is that citizens are reduced to the humble status of appealing to the representatives to "consider" their views and are not empowered to have any more effect on public policy than if they had not participated.

Again, Arterton twists the true purpose of Televote. It is not that we had no desire for Televote having direct repercussions on policy. We were not that naive to expect that it would. What we do argue, however, is that to judge the success of the project only by the degree to which it leads automatically to specific legislation is to perform a superficial analysis of impact. To study Televote's effects at CONCON, Arterton simply asked the Hawaii governor's "chief political aide" (unnamed) and his press secretary if they had heard of the results from any of the Televotes or the Electronic Town Meetings. They said, "No." Therefore, Arterton concluded that impact on public policy was "almost nonexistent."[41]

In his 1988 study, Arterton and his fellow researchers added additional proof of "no impact" by using HT-1 as an example. They state that the first Televote found "a whopping 86 percent of televoters favored the adoption of some sort of referendum process in Hawaii, but the convention made no proposal for one."[42] As previously discussed, while Televote (and many other kinds of public and political pressure) did not influence enough delegates to vote for initiative, it was the first indication that the public was overwhelmingly in favor of initiative. Each state legislative session since that Televote has had to contend with strong and growing support for initiative that has taken the form of a unified lobbying organization in the state. Two key House committee chairs, as previously noted, have been defeated after refusing to hold public hearings on initiative. Even today, the Televote results (HT-1) are featured in a videotape shown around Hawaii to educate others on initiative and its near consensual public support.

Televote alone cannot guarantee political impact. It itself is not a plebiscite. It is, however, an effective device to increase political cognizance in its participants and to discover the depth and breadth of thoughtful public sentiment. Citizen activism on issues is stimulated by the knowledge gained that public opinion can be mobilized so solidly on an issue. Representatives can pay attention or shunt it aside. They are wise to pay attention, to respond, to interact, and to continue to educate and inform where they feel the public is uninformed or misinformed. To turn their heads away or to show contempt for widely shared and deeply felt public opinion may be their own undoing as indicated by the defeated legislators in Hawaii and the defeated political party in New Zealand.

Televote Should Not Have Direct Policy Impact: The Modern Version of the Madisonian versus Jeffersonian Debate. This is the point where we get to the heart of Arterton's dissatisfaction with Televote. Arterton sees Televote as a foe of "democracy" because he views it as an attempt to replace the democratic process with pure majoritarianism, seeking to make representatives slaves to public opinion. In his view, this is antithetical to the extensive and complex deliberation process that our representative system was designed to employ. "Such a tyranny of the majority," he argues, "cannot encompass the whole of democratic participation."[43]

To this he adds that democracy is not necessarily harmed because the CONCON delegates ignored the Televote indicating 86 percent of the population favored initiative. "If the delegates are not to deliberate but only to record majority opinion," he argues, "then there is no need to convene political assemblies or constitutional conventions at all."[44]

How is it that Arterton presumes that representative bodies deliberate, but that the public does not? Does he assume that citizens form their opinions in a vacuum with no give-and-take from others? Why in dismissing public opinion for its lack of deliberation (which, by the way, has not been proven) does he completely overlook the many ways in which American representative bodies are woefully lacking in utilizing deliberation in their decision making? For instance, committee chairs are allowed to kill bills with no consultation with others simply by refusing to hold public hearings or refusing to hold votes on certain bills. Furthermore, representatives often make decisions on the basis of trade-offs for votes on other issues ("logrolling"); because their party leaders tell them to vote in a certain way (party discipline); because some major campaign contributor applies pressures (the increasing power of money in campaigns and in lobbying); and because they are ignorant of riders that have been placed on bills to sneak through legislation that would not stand up under public scrutiny. All of these practices, as well as many others, are not uncommon features in the American legislative process at all levels. They refute the assumption or ideal that representatives' opinions and votes are mainly based on unbiased data, unanimous expert opinion, and the give-and-take of public debate.

The point is that Arterton's methodology, research, analysis, and interpretations are all clouded by his ideological bias, a prejudice contrary to that of the Televote organizers. The fact that they both are guided by ideological leanings is not necessarily bad—as Chapter 4 points out. The problem arises when the bias taints research and evaluation that are cloaked in the pretext of "scientific objectivity." Quantum theory makes us more aware of such pitfalls.

Arterton's political bias is purely Newtonian—a philosophical worldview at the heart of the design and development of the American political system. Madison's famous propaganda in favor of such a system, written over 200 years ago, argues that the American republican system was intended to place representatives in power who are more likely to be patriots and lovers of justice using their wisdom to determine the true interest of their country and to guard against majority passion and faction.[45]

Michael Malbin offers additional arguments against teledemocracy that fit comfortably into the Madisonian and Newtonian mold. He states emphatically, as though it were fact, that, "There is no conceivable way the public could 'refine and enlarge' its own views in a manner that would be conducive to sound legislation. The public is, and necessarily will remain, poorly informed on most issues."[46]

Calling legislators who read issue polls "with jaundiced eyes" as possibly a "democratic republic's best friends,"[47] Malbin makes the following case against a greater role for citizens in America. First, the system was wisely designed for the following reasons and goals. (1) To the framers, "democracy was less basic to them than liberty."[48] (2) Personal rights granted in democracies are endangered by majority tyranny. (3) Majority tyranny is most likely to occur if the people get swept up by a common, single special interest or passion. (4) Representatives from the vast, complex republic are more likely to represent different interests and therefore make compromises through give-and-take. Malbin states the process was designed "to force legislators to deliberate and to think of the needs of others."[49]

Second, the mechanisms designed to give citizens more power—initiatives, polls, and direct democratic activities—have the following defects. (1) Too much power is placed in the hands of those who frame the issues. (2) Citizens providing responses in the isolation of their own homes are not contributing to the very important deliberative process. "Opinions only become refined through the give and take of discussion with people whose backgrounds and opinions differ from one's own."[50] (3) Citizens are unable to participate effectively in the types of discussions that representatives engage in because they are ill-informed or uninformed on most issues.

While Malbin accurately conveys the arguments of the framers of the Constitution, he fails to address the perspective of Jefferson, the author of the Declaration of Independence, whom Malbin credits as listing the inalienable rights the Constitution was most concerned with protecting.

Jefferson argues that the "mass of the citizens is the safest depository of their own rights and especially, that the evils following from the duperies of the people, are less injurious than those from the egoism of their agents."[51] He also maintained that the framers designed a system that was not sufficiently republican and accountable to the people. He did not fear majority tyranny nearly as much as elite abuse. In fact, he believed that "the good sense of the people will always be found to be the best army. They may be led astray for a moment, but will soon correct themselves. The people are the only censors of their governors."[52]

Jefferson offers an excellent argument that can be used to support Televote when he states: "Cherish therefore the spirit of our people, and keep alive their attention. Do not be too severe upon their errors, but reclaim them by enlightening them. If once they become inattentive to public affairs, you and I, and Congress and Assemblies, judges and governors shall all become wolves."[53]

Clearly, there is a fundamental tension between the teledemocracy projects, Televote included, that share Jefferson's sanguine and positive views of the citizenry and the Madison–Arterton–Malbin perspective that fears and loathes it. At least, the modern-day Madisonians should acknowledge where their ideal fails in many ways to be attained. To continue the extremist diatribe against the masses while ignoring the palpable inadequacies and failures in the American representative system weakens their own arguments.

For instance, Malbin argues against public opinion polls because they do not add to the deliberative process—in other words, "the give and take of discussion with people whose backgrounds and opinions differ from one's own." In a Congress overwhelmingly consisting of wealthy or upper-middle class, white, Anglo-Saxon, Protestant males over age 50, the occupational mode of which is lawyers, exactly where is the discussion taking place between people whose backgrounds differ? In arguing against paying attention to public opinion polls of an uninformed public, are we to accept that our representatives, bombarded with money and pressure from powerful lobbyists and political action committees, really have a balance of information that produces policies that are best for society as a whole?

Malbin patronizes public opinion in the United States when he considers its role in making law. He acknowledges that referenda may be useful "in small countries, or on statewide constitutional issues, or in local areas in which citizens may know almost as much as their representatives about the issues. But on complicated legislative matters, referendums merely give special interest groups an opportunity to use demagogic advertising appeals to frustrate the legislative will."[54] How can Malbin denigrate citizen decision making because of its vulnerability to the manipulators of special interests, but applaud the representatives, who are at least as vulnerable (if not more so) to the wiles and direct power of special interests?

In designing Televote, we shared the Jeffersonian view that all powers in the United States derive from the people and should remain there—by and large. We did not start with an idealized notion of representatives whose knowledge, deliberation, and wisdom lead to the best decisions for the good of the total citizenry. Instead, we sought ways (1) for both the people and the representatives to become more enlightened and to work together and (2) to help develop ways for an educated and deliberative public to play a more direct role in planning and policy making so as to increase its role in a future, more democratic polity. As democratic designers, we do not want our fear of technology to paralyze and victimize us. We want to learn to adapt it so as to help attain our participatory democratic goals. The next section will take a look at areas that Televote needs to explore in moving toward that end and will place Televote in the bigger picture of democratic trends in the Quantum Age.

AREAS FOR FUTURE TELEVOTE TESTING AND DEVELOPMENT

Sustainability

Arterton correctly notes that each Televote has been a "one-shot endeavor, lacking the cumulative presence or follow-through that would be necessary to document the continued attractiveness of this form of participation or to experiment fully with their consensus-building conception of participation."[55] From the outset we had seen the value of studying the extent to which participation in Televote would change if Televoters were asked to participate in a series of Televotes. One of the ideas behind asking Televoters if they would be willing to participate again was to develop a Televote advisory group along the lines proposed by Robert Dahl.

We envisioned a comprehensive study to test the following: (1) Could interest in Televote be sustained over time? (2) Would responses continue to indicate a more sophisticated and comprehensive understanding of the issues? (3) Could consensus building effectively take place over time through a Delphi adaptation of Televote? (4) Would legislators show as little interest in an ongoing project as in a one-time presentation of public opinion? (5) How would continued participation affect the degree to which (a) Televoters discussed the issues with others, (b) deliberated before responding, and (c) sought additional information to enrich the deliberative process? It is a study that needs to be done, but will require greater resources than we have had available in running our previous experiments.

Lessening the Potential for Privatizing the Citizenry

Jean Beth Elshtain has written a critique of the QUBE system in which she argues that QUBE's tactics of gathering instant opinion are merely "a compilation of opinions [that] does not make a civic culture; such a culture demands a deliberative process in which people engage one another as citizens."[56] She adds that QUBE "has nothing to do with promoting civic culture or rousing social conscience."[57]

Arterton applies Elshtain's critique to Televote even though there are fundamental differences, as discussed earlier, between QUBE and Televote. In fact, Elshtain's critique is not about public opinion polling, but is about interactive television "polls" that dupe citizens into believing they are participating in the political system. Her argument is that "interactive television embraces a view of human nature and the human condition that is opposed to the view that people are social beings who require certain conditions for the development of their capacities."[58]

While Televote is clearly distinct from QUBE, and while I believe Elshtain's critique of all interactive television based on a QUBE analysis is unfair and inaccurately portrays the intent and method of many forms of interactive television, Elshtain's argument against interactive television might be applied to Televote. It could be argued that Televote privatizes citizens since they act in their individual homes rather than in a public arena with the other Televoters (individuals unrelated to themselves), which may help citizens determine their own collective identity and collective good that Elshtain feels is necessary in a "real democracy."[59]

I am sympathetic to Elshtain's concern. Before I accept that face-to-face assemblies are superior to other forms of communication, however, I believe such needs to be studied. While we have been surprised at the extent to which Televotes have obtained responses that indicate concerns for the larger community, not mere self- or narrow interests, it is possible that those opinions could become even more refined with a view toward the common good with face-to-face interaction with other Televoters.

This is an area we also have wanted to explore since our first Televotes, but lacked the necessary resources to subsidize the experiment. Our design was to conduct the Televote in the usual way and then to bring the Televoters, or a random sample of them, together in a face-to-face assembly. We intended to allow public testimony and additional expert opinion to be a part of the Televote assembly. Not only would we compare the difference in the Televote opinions obtained through each process, but we would conduct a follow-up study to allow Televoters to contrast and evaluate the two methods of participation from their own perspectives.

In developing an in-person assembly project, it is very useful to keep in mind Jane Mansbridge's study of town meetings in a small town in Vermont. Mansbridge found that the face-to-face, one-person/one-vote style of the town meetings gave an inaccurate impression that a democracy of equal opportunity existed. As she conducted her interviews after her observations, she had citizens confide their reasons for either not attending the meetings or failing to speak up. Included in their reasons are: (1) feeling inarticulate and lacking the verbal and legal skills of others; (2) fearing ridicule if they make a mistake; (3) being bullied by those with more power (for example, a lawyer telling a farmer to shut up or he would have a lawsuit filed against him); (4) feeling the real decisions are made in private caucuses outside the assembly; (5) fearing personal criticism if disagreement is expressed; (6) fearing that enemies would be made; (7) experiencing headaches and other physical symptoms due to the stress of participation; (8) disliking the constant arguing; and (9) being ignored if they bring up matters others do not want to discuss (for example, a woman asked a question about the budget four times before she was finally answered). Mansbridge found a great deal of empirical evidence to support all these reasons for such anxiety and the reluctance of some to participate.[60]

In fact, Mansbridge discovered that those traditionally lacking in power in the American political system—uneducated, poor, inarticulate—did not fare any better in the town meetings. In addition, the personal sacrifices were greater when public ridicule and attack coincided with lack of power. While the townspeople were very kind toward those in the inner circle, being careful to save face for them despite palpable incompetence and/or corruption, they were not empathetic to the powerless, whom they perceived to be outspoken and thick-skinned, not needing the same emotional protection granted to the inner circle. Yet great empathy was extended to the members of the established powers in town, which led to many relevant issues being shielded from public discussion. Instead, the issues were swept aside when raised by someone excluded from the informal decision-making process. Mansbridge's conclusion is that the democracy in the town meetings—"the mechanism of one-citizen/one-vote, majority rule in an open assembly . . . consistently overrepresents certain interests. This pattern persists even when overt conflict erupts."[61]

While Mansbridge has no quarrel with the articulate, educated, and/or established individuals being the spokespersons or decision makers when all those affected by the decisions have common interests, she is correct in pointing out that the interests of the inarticulate, uneducated, poor, and/or newcomers are not always in line with those of the people exercising power. It is important, she argues, not to pretend common interests exist when they do not and that mechanisms must be designed to represent the interests of those traditionally alienated from power.[62]

Therefore, I believe that Elshtain makes too much of face-to-face assemblies and ignores their dangers. It is possible that Televote's design helps alleviate some of the problems, by allowing for anonymity in interaction, deliberation, and judgment. When part of an Electronic Town Meeting, the Televoter can view face-to-face discussions—and even participate via call-ins with no fear of ridicule, reprisals, and so forth. Obviously, though, there needs to be substantial comparative study of the dynamics and results of face-to-face assemblies and the relative anonymous systems of Televote and Electronic Town Meetings. This, too, will require significant financial backing to accomplish.

Institutionalizing Televote Neutrality

I believe the Televote university-based model contains many safeguards to reduce manipulation and control by those wishing to obtain certain results. Our method of review from diverse individuals and inspection from professional survey firms helps uncover most biases that may influence the results of the Televote. In addition, the work of academics is subject to a high level of professional critical scrutiny, and the tenure system will help insulate any "tenured" technics against outside or topside pressures. This does not guarantee that bias may not creep in or that the politics within the university may not lend themselves toward manipulative practices. The necessity, then, is that academics, critics, and outside observers must keep a keen eye on projects designed to educate and involve the public and hold them to a high level of objectivity and impartiality.

While I believe that the university-based model of Televote, with its standards of open inspection, offers the least likely chance for abuse, I am troubled by the eagerness of others—using other models—to turn Televote and Electronic Town Meeting–style formats into public relations and/or profit-motivated enterprises. An example is a Hawaii multimillionaire and former congressman who used his money to produce a series of electronic town meetings as a major part of his 1986 campaign for governor of Hawaii.

Several individuals who worked in his "town meetings" were disturbed when the candidate seemed to follow the same agenda and pattern for each meeting, showing no effort to incorporate the citizen concerns and views expressed if they were contrary to his preestablished positions. While significantly outspending his opponent in the gubernatorial race, he lost and left Hawaii to establish a new business: Quick Tally. The new venture, in collaboration with his campaign media consultant (the person who had produced the Alaska Television Town Meeting), endeavors to sell the "electronic town meeting" expertise to other candidates to utilize in their campaigns for various offices. Very sophisticated tabulating devices are utilized in the Quick Tally "town meetings" that obtain instant citizen opinion on issues dealt with in the candidate's "meet-the-public" forum. It offers a novel gimmick that draws citizens into alleged "interaction" with candidates.

Unfortunately, those seeking to profit financially from the sincere effort of those wishing to design more and better ways to involve the public in decision making seem to be making great strides while the genuine advocates of a more participatory democracy scrounge for resources and have to contend with ideological antagonists of participatory democracy. For instance, a group called "Choosing Our Future" in San Francisco has modeled itself after the Honolulu Electronic Town Meeting. After many years of research and coalition building with community groups, Choosing Our Future produced an interactive television program on ABC that was called "The Electronic Town Meeting." While negotiating with an NBC affiliate in San Francisco to produce another ETM on the future of the Bay Area (but within a new, community-based organizational structure called "Bay Voice"), they were notified by Quick Tally's lawyers that since Quick Tally has legally protected the term, Bay Voice could no longer use the term "Electronic Town Meeting." It would seem that the term "electronic town meeting" is generic, and this was an attempt to trademark something like "electric waffle iron." Besides, the term "electronic town meeting" was used by others before Quick Tally entered the picture.[63]

Even though Quick Tally may have had questionable legal standing, their financial reserves were much richer than those of Bay Voice—primarily a volunteer, low-budget organization. In addition, Quick Tally had a contract with the national NBC organization to televise a national electronic town meeting in fall 1989, which may have intimidated the local affiliate who did not want to get embroiled in such a controversy.

This example is indicative of the manifold dangers facing Televote if it is not institutionalized in some fashion that separates the honest effort to involve citizens from attempts to profit from citizen involvement or to use it simply as a ploy to bolster the existing representative system—one that cares little to nothing about increasing citizen participation. As cynics criticize without offering constructive adjustments, profiteers barge ahead and deform the intent and purpose of participatory democratic designs. That does not mean that the future of Televote is bleak. In fact, the contrary is just as likely to be true. A short review of the nature of Televote's superstructure will explain why this is so.

ASSESSING TELEVOTE'S FUTURE IN TERMS OF ITS SUPERSTRUCTURE

This study has focused on Televote as a form of citizen participation designed to utilize modern communications technologies to facilitate citizen involvement in present and future representative systems. The discussion of Televote was preceded by a presentation of the theoretical and historical superstructure, which places Televote in the context of a continually evolving American representative system. As I believe I have made clear, radical changes have occurred in the world since the creation of the American representative system, all of which are favorable to the future development of Televote—and the Representative Participatory Polity.

First, our understanding of the physical world is extremely different. Whereas the Newtonian worldview was perceived as an objective means to reveal certainty, predictability, and absolutes, our quantum world teaches us the limitations of such thought when applied to the study of all phenomena, whether in the natural or social sciences, or in personal or social life. Barber showed how a Newtonian scientific approach to studying social phenomena provided the theoretical guide for American liberal democracy. Whether formal students of Newton or not, American political practitioners, theorists, and researchers usually have operated on the basis of scientific laws handed over to us during the Enlightenment.

Sixty-two years ago, however, in his presidential address before the American Political Science Association (APSA), Prof. William Bennett Munro of Harvard University called to political scientists to move beyond their "bondage to the Eighteenth-Century"[64] and look to the new discoveries of quantum theory for new ways to think about politics, political theory, and political institutions. He stated:

> The general acceptance of the quantum theory has wrought a revolution in all the exact sciences. . . . All things in the physical universe are relative to all things else.
>
> It has been said that no metaphysical implications are necessarily involved in the quantum theory or in the doctrine of relativity, but it

is difficult to believe that this can be the case. A revolution so amazing in our ideas concerning the physical world must inevitably carry its echoes into other fields of human knowledge. New truths cannot be quarantined. No branch of knowledge advances by itself. In its progress it draws others along. By no jugglery of words can we keep Mind and Matter and Motion in watertight compartments; hence it is inconceivable that a greatly changed point of view, or a series of far-reaching discoveries, in any one science can be wholly without influence upon the others, even upon those which are not closely allied.[65]

The twentieth-century revolution in scientific thinking, quantum theory, presents natural and social scientists with evidence that the path of objectivity leading to fundamental truths that we have been following for over 300 years may not be leading us to the most realistic and useful understanding of our reality. In fact, there may be no "reality" as we have previously defined it. Subjectivity, and the impossibility of complete objectivity, must be accounted for in our research and analysis and in our institutions. Probabilities not predictability; interdependence not independence; and interconnection not separation must become meaningful components of our theory, study, and practice of life in all its complexities.

While it can be (and frequently is) argued that natural and social phenomena are different and to seek a theory that adequately explains both is misguided, it can also be argued that there is good reason for political theorists and scientists to recognize the way they approach their work is similar to that of natural scientists. When a revolution in scientific thinking occurs in either field, it is useful to reexamine the assumptions of the theory and methodology. In doing so in this thesis, I have concluded that the quantum revolution offers useful guides for the development of a participatory democratic theory, which is the theoretical base for Televote design and development. As discussed in Chapter 1, the use of quantum theory can lead to significant changes in one's view of human nature as well as political processes and systems. Quantum perspectives open up political institutional possibilities not available through a Newtonian perspective. Televote is a form of democratic participation that is a product of revolutionary changes in the scientific knowledge of the eighteenth century. It utilizes probability theory to randomly select participants. This method of selection produces a highly representative sample of the relevant population. The rationale for Televote fits within the quantum worldview: The perspective that our subjectivity influences our objectivity and the two cannot be separated. Therefore, all policy discussions involve a complex intermingling of the values, attitudes, and perceptions of all those decision makers. Thus, decisions in a democratic representative system should incorporate the opinions of the full range of the diversity of the citizenry, not merely the views of a select, like-minded elite whose views of justice and the good of society are colored by their similar life circumstances and the realities of their world, which are substantially different from the daily realities of those they claim to represent.

Quantum theory also has enriched our understanding of one of Televote's essential ingredients—the emphasis on and importance of interdependence and interaction. When we first designed the Hawaii Televote model, we felt the interactivity we encouraged would aid in our recruitment of those who felt inadequate. If they were told they could talk about the issue with others, maybe they would not feel so intimidated by the Televote process. As I began to learn more about quantum theory and to see its parallels with my developing participatory democratic theory, I obtained a greater appreciation for the intrinsic value of the interactive component of Televote. Rather than focusing primarily on our initial concerns of obtaining informed and deliberated opinion from a representative sample (our first Televote), we began to build in more interactive components (various forms of interactive media). We also began to appreciate the importance of moving away from views of democracy that focus on individual rights and opportunities to participate and move toward a view of democracy that develops greater understanding, consideration, and ways to stimulate and encourage the essential interconnectedness of individuals in a society (our last Televote).

The scientific knowledge of the eighteenth century could not, and did not, lead to democratic theories that centered on probability and randomness. In fact, it sought to reduce subjectivity from decision making and to promote objectivity rather than seeing the two as practicably inseparable. It focused on separating units and observing their behaviors, rather than understanding the inadequacy of that mode of analysis. Televote, therefore, is more a product of twentieth-century thought than a descendant of eighteenth-century thought. While it remains connected in many ways to ideas of the past, its full development and its uniqueness are attributed to the radical new scientific knowledge of the present.

Second, dramatic changes in American democratic history have created a favorable climate for the present and future development of Televote. Women, blacks, 18-year-olds, and the propertyless have obtained full citizenship rights since the U.S. Constitution was created. The diversity of the citizenry, including the explosive increase in the population of those of Asian, Hispanic, and Jewish ancestry, has revolutionized the concept of

American representation. As long as propertied, Caucasian males were just about the only citizens, those attributes in representatives did not distinguish them so dramatically from those they were to represent. Although the diversity in U.S. citizens has changed significantly in the last 200 years, there is little diversity among the "representatives."

The democratic spirit cherished by the eighteenth-century revolutionaries also is treasured by the twentieth-century advocates for more democracy. The irony is that the revolutionaries of yesterday became the perpetuators and ancestors of the status quo and that the democrats of today often represent values and goals that status quo defenders of the American representative system abhor. It seems to be an inevitable tension in a democratic system designed by a small elite for a small elite that has withstood 200 years of change because it was able to open up, to expand, and to grow. Its survival, therefore, has been predicated on its ability to modify itself.

Televote is a natural outgrowth of these historical changes in American society. It aids the unrepresented in their quest to be heard. It broadens the political discourse to include their views. It is a proven way to contribute to the growth of a more participatory democracy. If the American system of democracy is to continue to change itself in order to accommodate greater diversity, it is difficult to see how the Televote and Electronic Town Meeting structures are not viable future options.

Third, technological revolutions since the late eighteenth century have fundamentally altered the number of citizens who have the ability to be well informed and directly involved. Satellites, computers, airplanes, telephones, television, and automobiles are inventions since the U.S. Constitution was written that have radically transformed our world. We no longer need days or weeks away from our homes to meet with others, leaving our affairs untended or tended by slaves or hired hands. Participation in public affairs and public discussions no longer need be reserved to those who have the economic means to travel great distances and be away for long periods of time. Information is also available to us instantly through "live" broadcasts, computer mail, and telephones.

For all of its pitfalls and the anxieties expressed by so many about the "Big Brother" potential of modern technology, it remains a part of our lives, used by its advocates and critics alike. Very few critics refuse to use the modern technologies as they continue to revolutionize their own personal and political lives. It is my belief that for all its problems, modern technology helps, more than it hinders, the promotion of democratic values and possibilities. Right now, its power is mostly directly controlled by those who own the large communication industries and is in service to the maintenance and hegemony of the Expanded Representative State and its dominance by that small, wealthy elite and those beholden to them.

However, Televote, itself, is a product of the same technological revolution in many respects. Its democratic goals do not derive from technological advances, but the means to achieve those goals are better advanced through this very same technology. Televote and town meetings on a national (or state) scale were not possible prior to this century. Now they are. When the time is right, they will be ready to be put to their more democratic utilization.

Televote in the Expanded Representative State

The 12 Televote experiments detailed in the last chapter indicate Televote's capabilities for integration into the current American representative system. It can obtain representative samples of public opinion. It can obtain informed and deliberated opinion. It works most effectively with other uses of modern communications technology that contribute to the education and interaction of citizens.

Televote's cost for statewide samples ranged from $20,000 to $30,000— when volunteers were not utilized. With volunteers, it was much less ($5,000–$10,000). Thus, it is not too costly to implement if governmental priorities shift from promotion of capitalism to promotion of democracy. This last year we have seen the U.S. government deciding to spend a minimum of at least $50 billion to bail out a corrupt and incompetent U.S. savings and loan industry; spend $6 billion to develop the prototype for the stealth bomber (anticipated cost of future bombers is $500 million for each), whose use is now questionable; and on and on. With these examples of astronomic waste or misuse of taxpayers' money, quibbling over the very low costs of promoting democracy, educating the public, and being more responsive to the total citizenry seems absurd indeed.

Advocates of more democracy in our representative system from Jefferson through Dewey to the current time have wondered how to enlighten the public, to educate them, to involve them in responsible decision making. Televote is only one of many democratic tools designed to increase the participation of an informed public. It is not a question of whether it is possible; it is simply a question of priority.

Televote in the Representative Participatory State

While Televote has been designed for, and utilized in, the Expanded Representative State, we see Televote's potential as even greater—an instrument to be used in a radically new type of representative system, where representatives are chosen randomly from the citizenry at various levels of government. The idea is not novel, although it has been slow in moving into the current discussion of representative systems. Our Televote experiments spur our visions of truly representative bodies, not obtained through multimillion-dollar electoral campaigns, PAC control, restrictive election procedures, incumbent advantages, and glittery public relations. We see the possibilities of civic-minded citizens acting responsibly in a multitude of legislative activities to gain control of their destiny.

Since 1984 in Minneapolis, Minnesota, an institute called the Jefferson Center (with Robert Dahl on its advisory council) has conducted experiments with "policy juries" to advise representatives on public policy.[66] The policy jury is composed of 12 individuals of diverse viewpoints chosen from a randomly selected group of 100. Based on the concept of the jury system, the policy jurors attend public hearings, discuss the issues at hand, and make policy recommendations. Depending on the size of the area covered, the representatives may be sent from a policy jury at the local level to serve on a county or statewide policy jury with representatives from other local areas.

The "policy juries" of the Jefferson Center have been utilized in conjunction with the Minnesota Senate and the League of Women Voters has demonstrated interest in cosponsoring policy juries in some of their activities.

As radical as the concept of randomly selected legislative assemblies appears in contrast to the adulated and venerated American electoral representative system, the scientific theory, the historical developments, the modern technologies, and the massive experimentation with democracy in so many aspects of our modern lives—through co-ops and workplace democracy and through increased representation in policy development arenas once left exclusively to a narrowly defined elite—are all helping the political superstructure for radical democratic structural change in our political institutions to emerge rapidly.

How and when the next dramatic surge for more democracy will take place in the United States is unclear. Neither the most knowledgeable sources and observers in the Philippines, the Soviet Union, and China— nor America's vaunted Central Intelligence Agency or National Security Council—could predict the circumstances or the timing of the political changes in the direction of massive public demand for more democracy in those countries. The random occurrence of catastrophes and crises in our universe could spur the next great democratic revolution in the world. Whether it is environmental, political, social, or economic disaster that strikes next, or some combination of them, there are alternatives available to advance democracy as a solution that have been studied long and hard by many desiring to bring the American political system in line with changes in the twentieth and twenty-first centuries.

In discussing the Chinese students' and workers' massive demonstrations and demands for more democracy in Tiananmen Square and other areas of China, political observers like Cyrus Vance, Henry Kissinger, and John Chancellor used the metaphors "the genie is out of the bottle" and "the toothpaste is out of the tube" to describe the impossibility of the Communist system placing a cap on democracy. The spirit is out. The passion remains. Repression demolished the "Goddess of Democracy" in the bloody end to the pro-democracy demonstrations in China in June of 1989, but it only strengthened the desire for more of what the "Goddess of Democracy" stood for.

The 1989 Chinese demands for democracy also demonstrated that modern technology through telephones, facsimile machines, video, radio, and "live" telecasts can be essential ingredients for democratic struggle. Technology magnified the brutality of Chinese leaders and united the oppressed people. It unified the world community in moral support for the struggle for democracy.

My point is that for all the present-day unlikelihood of change from an Expanded Representative State to a Representative Participatory State, recent political turmoil throughout the world should caution those in favor of the status quo from thinking that the unthinkable does not happen. In fact, expecting the unexpected seems to be a more accurate predictor of trends. Whenever the time for real democratic change in the United States arrives, there are the theorists, researchers, and practitioners I have discussed in this treatise who have devoted their lives to answering the question that baffled the Chinese students: "What would your democracy look like?"

Televote is a citizen participation tool designed in this Quantum Age to expand and promote a more representative democracy. It is a result of the fundamental changes in America and in the world that have led to radical new ideas, tools, and designs. It is born of the American democratic spirit and belongs to the American inventive tradition.

Over a half century ago, APSA president Munro bemoaned the lack of advancement made in our political system when he stated: "If the Fathers of the Republic were to return to life, after their long sleep of a century, they would be equally appalled by the stupendous progress of the American people in all material things and by the relative lack of it in the art of government."[67] The endeavor of this thesis is to contribute to the progress of the American people in the development of their democratic system and to advance greater and more meaningful citizen participation in the Quantum Age.

NOTES

1. P. J. Arnopoulos and K. Valaskakis, *Telecommunitary Democracy: Utopian Vision or Probable Future?* (Montreal: UNESCO, 1982), p. 56.

2. F. Christopher Arterton, *Teledemocracy: Can Technology Protect Democracy?* (Newbury Park, Calif.: Sage, 1987), p. 14.

3. Ibid.

4. Ibid., p. 44.

5. Ibid., p. 63.

6. Ibid., p. 204.

7. Ibid., p. 77.

8. Ibid.

9. Jeffrey B. Abramson, F. Christopher Arterton, and Gary R. Orren, *The Electronic Commonwealth: The Impact of New Media Technologies on Democratic Politics* (New York: Basic Books, 1988), p. 177.

10. Ibid., p. 165.

11. Ibid., p. 22.

12. Ibid., pp. 170, 172, and 174.

13. Ibid., p. 173.

14. Ibid., pp. 164–177. Also see a detailed explanation of QUBE in Theodore L. Becker and Richard Scarce, "Teledemocracy Emergent: State of the American Art and Science," in *Progress in Communication Sciences*, edited by Brenda Dervin and Melvin Voight (Norwood, N.J.: Ablex, 1986), pp. 274–275.

15. Abramson, Arterton, and Orren, p. 166.

16. Ibid., p. 168.

17. Ibid.

18. Ibid., p. 175.

19. Ibid., p. 170.

20. Arterton, p. 162.

21. While self-selected groups tended to produce samples heavily weighted with well-educated males, we found examples in other experiments we conducted with the ABC television affiliate in Honolulu that indicated for issues that dealt primarily with Hawaiians or some other segment of the population, there was usually an overrepresentation of that segment in our sample. For instance, on the issue of reparations for Hawaiians, Hawaiians felt passionately about the issue and participated in much greater percentages than in any other poll or for any other segment of the population.

22. Abramson, Arterton, and Orren, p. 169.

23. Ibid., p. 170.

24. Ibid., p. 169.

25. Arterton, p. 79.

26. Lester W. Milbrath and M. L. Goel, *Political Participation: How and Why Do People Get Involved in Politics?* (Chicago: Rand McNally, 1977), pp. 144–155.

27. Arterton, p. 80.

28. Ibid., p. 81.

29. Abramson, Arterton, and Orren, p. 174.

30. Ibid.

31. Ibid., p. 173.

32. Ibid.

33. Ibid., p. 174.

34. Ibid.

35. Arterton, p. 195.

36. Ibid., p. 82.

37. Ibid., p. 199.

38. Ibid., p. 200.

39. Ibid., p. 82.

40. Abramson, Arterton, and Orren, p. 172.

41. Arterton, p. 91.

42. Abramson, Arterton, and Orren, p. 171.

43. Ibid., p. 165.

44. Ibid., p. 171.

45. James Madison, "Federalist Paper #10," in Alexander Hamilton, James Madison, and John Jay, *The Federalist Papers* (New York: New American Library, 1961), pp. 77–84.

46. Michael Malbin, "Teledemocracy and Its Discontents," *Public Opinion* (June/July 1982): 59.

47. Ibid.

48. Ibid., p. 58.

49. Ibid., p. 59.

50. Ibid.

51. Thomas Jefferson, "Letter to John Taylor," 28 May 1816, in *Social and Political Philosophy*, edited by John Somerville and Ronald E. Santoni (Garden City, N.Y.: Doubleday, 1963), pp. 251–254.

52. Thomas Jefferson, "Letter to Edward Carrington," 16 January 1787, in *Jefferson Writings* (New York: Literary Classics of the United States, 1984), pp. 879–881.

53. Jefferson, "Letter to Edward Carrington," pp. 879–881.

54. Malbin, p. 59.

55. Arterton, p. 82.

56. Jean Beth Elshtain, "Democracy and the Qube Tube," *Nation* (7–14 July 1982): 109.

57. Ibid., p. 109.

58. Ibid., p. 110.

59. Ibid., p. 108.

60. Jane J. Mansbridge, *Beyond Adversary Democracy* (Chicago: University of Chicago Press, 1983), pp. 59–76.

61. Ibid., p. 76.

62. Ibid., pp. 60–61.

63. Personal correspondence with Duane Elgin of Bay Voice; and *On the QT* 1.1 (1989).

64. William Bennett Munro, "Physics and Politics—An Old Analogy Revised," *American Political Science Review* 22.1 (1928): 3.

65. Ibid., p. 2.

66. Information on the Jefferson Center obtained from Minnesota, Health and Human Services Committee, Senate, *Final Report: Policy Jury on School-Based Clinics* (St. Paul: Minnesota Senate, 1988); and "The Missing Voice in Presidential Contests," *Star Tribune*, Minneapolis, 4 January 1989.

67. Munro, p. 10.

Bibliography

Abramson, Jeffrey B., F. Christopher Arterton, and Gary R. Orren. *The Electronic Commonwealth: The Impact of New Media Technologies on Democratic Politics.* New York: Basic Books, 1988.

"Agrippa." Address, Massachusetts Convention, 20 January 1788. In *The Antifederalists,* edited by Cecelia M. Kenyon, 131–160. Indianapolis: Bobbs-Merrill, 1966.

Alaska. Office of the Governor. *Report on Alaska Television Town Meeting of the Alaska Public Forum.* Juneau: Office of the Governor, 1980.

Alaska. State Legislature. Division of Public Services. *Providing a Participatory Legislative Environment.* Juneau: Alaska State Legislature, 1982.

Allen, W. B., and Gordon Lloyd. *The Essential Antifederalist.* Lanham, Md.: University Press of America, 1985.

Almond, Gabriel. "Separate Tables: Schools and Sects in Political Science." *Political Science* (Fall 1988): 828–842.

Arnopoulos, P. J., and K. Valaskakis. *Telecommunitary Democracy: Utopian Vision or Probable Future.* Montreal: UNESCO, 1982.

Aronson, Sidney H. "Jackson's Political Appointments." In *New Perspectives on Jacksonian Parties and Politics,* edited by Edward Pressen, 233–254. Boston: Allyn & Bacon, 1969.

Arterton, F. Christopher. *Teledemocracy: Can Technology Protect Democracy?* Newbury Park, Calif.: Sage, 1987.

Auerbach, Jerold S. *Unequal Justice.* London: Oxford University Press, 1976.

Babbie, Earl R. *Survey Research Methods.* Belmont, Calif.: Wadsworth, 1973.

Bachrach, Peter. "Interest, Participation, and Democratic Theory." In *Participation in Politics,* edited by J. Roland Pennock and John W. Chapman, 39–55. New York: Lieber-Atherton, 1975.

———. *The Theory of Democratic Elitism: A Critique.* Lanham, Md.: University Press of America, 1980.

Backstrom, Charles H., and Gerald Hursh-Cesar. *Survey Research.* Evanston, Ill.: Northwestern University Press, 1963.

Barber, Benjamin. *Strong Democracy: Participatory Politics for a New Age.* Berkeley: University of California Press, 1984.

Barrow, Deborah J., and Thomas G. Walker. *A Court Divided.* New Haven, Conn.: Yale University Press, 1988.

Beard, Charles. *An Economic Interpretation of the Constitution.* New York: Macmillan, 1931.

Becker, Theodore L. *American Government: Past, Present, Future.* Boston: Allyn & Bacon, 1976.

———. "The Constitutional Network: An Evolution in American Democracy." In *Anticipatory Democracy,* edited by Clement Bezold, 289–302. New York: Random House, 1978.

———. Review of *Teledemocracy: Can Technology Protect Democracy?* by F. Christopher Arterton. *American Political Science Review* (1988): 1376–1377.

———. *Unvote for a New America.* Boston: Allyn & Bacon, 1976.

———, ed. *The Impact of Supreme Court Decisions.* New York: Oxford University Press, 1969.

Becker, Theodore L., and Richard Chadwick. "Problem-Solving CONCON Desired, Says University Poll." *Honolulu Advertiser,* 17 May 1978, p. A1.

Becker, Theodore L., Alvin Clement, Alan McRobie, and Brian Murphy. *Report on New Zealand Televote.* Wellington, New Zealand: Commission for the Future, 1981.

Becker, Theodore L., and Richard Scarce. "Teledemocracy Emergent: State of the American Art and Science." In *Progress in Communication Sciences,* edited by Brenda Dervin and Melvin Voight, 263–287. Norwood, N.J.: Ablex, 1986.

Benson, Lee. *The Concept of Jacksonian Democracy.* Princeton, N.J.: Princeton University Press, 1961.

Bezold, Clement, ed. *Anticipatory Democracy: People in the Politics of the Future.* New York: Random House, 1978.

Black, Hugo. *A Constitutional Faith.* New York: Alfred A. Knopf, 1968.

Blau, Joseph L., ed. *Social Theories of Jacksonian Democracy.* Indianapolis: Bobbs-Merrill, 1954.

California. Southern California Association of Governments. *Report on the Los Angeles Televote.* Los Angeles: SCAG, 1983.

Callenbach, Ernest, and Michael Phillips. *A Citizen Legislature.* Berkeley, Calif.: Banyan Tree Books, 1985.

Campbell, Angus, Philip E. Converse, Warren E. Miller, and Donald Stokes. *The American Voter.* New York: John Wiley & Sons, 1968.

Campbell, Vincent N. *The Televote System for Civic Communication: First Demonstration and Evaluation.* Palo Alto, Calif.: American Institute for Research, 1974.

Capra, Fritjof. *The Turning Point: Science, Society, and the Rising Culture.* New York: Simon & Schuster, 1982.

Clark, Leroy. *The Grand Jury: The Use and Abuse of Political Power*. New York: Quadrangle/New York Times Book Co., 1975.

Clinton, George. "Letter to the Citizens of the State of New York," 22 November 1787. In *The Antifederalists*, edited by Cecelia M. Kenyon, 307–312. Indianapolis: Bobbs-Merrill, 1966.

Cohen, Felix. "Americanizing the White Man." *American Scholar* 21.2 (1952): 48–52.

Congressional Quarterly. 21 January 1989.

Conway, Margaret. *Political Participation in the United States*. Washington, D.C.: Congressional Quarterly Press, 1985.

Crozier, Michael, Samuel Huntington, and Joji Watanuki. *The Crisis of Democracy*. New York: New York University Press, 1975.

Dahl, Robert A. *After the Revolution?* New Haven, Conn.: Yale University Press, 1970.

———. *Polyarchy: Participation and Opposition*. New Haven, Conn.: Yale University Press, 1971.

Dator, James A. "Futuristics and the Exercise of Anticipatory Democracy in Hawaii." In *Political Science and the Study of the Future*, edited by Albert Somit, 187–203. Hinsdale, Ill.: Dryden Press, 1974.

———. "The 1982 Honolulu Electronic Town Meeting." In *The Future of Politics*, edited by William Page, 211–220. London: Frances Pinter, 1983.

———. "Quantum Theory and Political Design." Paper presented at the G. Duttweiller Institut Conference, January 1984.

———. "Reforming American Government: Within-System Tinkerings." Unpublished manuscript, 1972.

———. "Rethinking Honolulu City Governance." City and County Charter Commission Retreat, Honolulu, 19 August 1981.

Dewey, John. *Reconstruction in Philosophy*. Boston: Beacon Press, 1957.

Dewey, John, and James H. Tufts. *Ethics*. New York: Henry Holt, 1932.

DeWitt, John. "Letter to the Free Citizens of the Commonwealth of Massachusetts," 27 October 1787. In *The Antifederalists*, edited by Cecelia M. Kenyon, 96–102. Indianapolis: Bobbs-Merrill, 1966.

Dolbeare, Kenneth M. *American Political Thought*. Monterey, Calif.: Duxbury Press, 1981.

Downs, Anthony. *An Economic Theory of Democracy*. New York: Harper & Row, 1957.

Dry, Murry. "The Constitutional Thought of the Antifederalists." *This Constitution: A Bicentennial Chronicle* 6 (1987): 10–14.

Duncan-Clark, S. J. *The Progressive Movement*. Boston: Small, Maynard, 1972.

Dye, Thomas R., and L. Harmon Zeigler. *The Irony of Democracy*. Monterey, Calif.: Brooks/Cole, 1984.

Elliot, Jonathan. *The Debates in the Several State Conventions on the Adoption of the Federal Constitution as Recommended by the General Convention at Philadelphia, in 1787*. 2nd ed. 5 vols. Philadelphia: J. B. Lippincott, 1896.

Elshtain, Jean Beth. "Democracy and the Qube Tube." *Nation* (7–14 July 1982): 108–110.

Feigert, B. Frank, and Margaret Conway. *Parties and Politics in America.* Boston: Allyn & Bacon, 1976.

Ferguson, James E. "What Were the Sources of the Constitutional Convention." In *The Confederation and the Constitution,* edited by Gordon S. Wood, 1–14. Lanham, Md.: University Press of America, 1976.

Freud, Sigmund. *Civilization and Its Discontents.* London: Hogarth Press, 1930.

Friedrich, Carl. *The New Belief in the Common Man.* Boston: Little, Brown & Co., 1943.

Fromm, Erich. *The Sane Society.* New York: Rinehart, 1955.

Fuller, R. Buckminster. *No More Secondhand God.* Garden City, N.Y.: Doubleday, 1971.

Gatell, Frank Otto, and John M. McFauk, eds. *Jacksonian America 1815–1840.* Englewood Cliffs, N.J.: Prentice-Hall, 1970.

Ginsberg, Benjamin. *The Consequences of Consent: Elections, Citizen Control and Popular Acquiescence.* Reading, Mass.: Addison-Wesley, 1982.

Glenn, Jerome C. "Social Technologies of Freedom." In *Anticipatory Democracy,* edited by Clement Bezold, 251–275. New York: Random House, 1978.

Gosnell, Harold Foote. *Getting Out the Vote.* Chicago: University of Chicago Press, 1927.

Greenberg, Edward S. *The American Political System: A Radical Approach.* Cambridge, Mass.: Winthrop, 1977.

Gregory, R. L. *Eye and Brain: The Psychology of Seeing.* New York: McGraw-Hill, 1973.

Hamilton, Alexander, James Madison, and John Jay. *The Federalist Papers.* New York: New American Library, 1961.

Hamilton, Charles V. *The Bench and the Ballot.* New York: Oxford University Press, 1973.

Harris, Fred R. *America's Democracy: The Ideal and the Reality.* Glenview, Ill.: Scott, Foresman, 1980.

Hays, Samuel P. *Conservation and the Gospel of Efficiency.* Chicago: University of Chicago Press, 1957.

Hobbes, Thomas. *The Leviathan.* Middlesex, England: Penguin Books, 1968.

Hume, David. *Philosophical Works,* edited by Thomas H. Green and Thomas H. Grose. 1882 reprint. London: Scientia Verlag Aalen, 1964.

Jackson, Andrew. "Jackson Defends the Spoils System." In *Jacksonian America 1815–1840,* edited by Frank Otto Gatell and John M. McFauk, 118–129. Englewood Cliffs, N.J.: Prentice-Hall, 1970.

Jefferson, Thomas. *Jefferson Writings.* New York: Literary Classics of the United States, 1984.

Jefferson, Thomas. "Letter to John Taylor," 28 May 1816. In *Social and Political Philosophy,* edited by John Somerville and Ronald E. Santoni, 251–254. Garden City, N.Y.: Doubleday, 1963.

Johansen, Bruce E. *Forgotten Founders: How the American Indian Helped Shape Democracy.* Boston: Harvard Common Press, 1982.

Kariel, Henry S. *Beyond Liberalism, Where Relations Grow.* San Francisco: Chandler and Sharp, 1977.

Keir, Gerry. "Change in Judge Selection Favored." *Honolulu Advertiser,* 25 February 1978, p. A1.

——. "Con Con Poll." *Honolulu Advertiser,* 19 February 1978, p. A1.

——. "Laws for Action by Public Favored." *Honolulu Advertiser,* 25 February 1978, p. A1.

——. "Most Favor Initiative, Referendum." *Honolulu Advertiser,* 10 May 1978, p. A1.

Kennedy, David M., ed. *Progressivism: The Critical Issues.* Boston: Little, Brown & Co., 1971.

Kenyon, Cecelia M., ed. *The Antifederalists.* Indianapolis: Bobbs-Merrill, 1966.

King, Martin Luther, Jr. "Letter from Birmingham Jail." In *Freedom Now,* edited by Alan F. Westin, 12–19. New York: Basic Books, 1964.

Kolko, Gabriel. *The Triumph of Conservatism.* New York: Free Press, 1963.

Ladd, Everett Carl. *The American Polity: The People and Their Government.* New York: W. W. Norton, 1987.

Landau, Martin. "On the Use of Metaphor in Political Science." *Social Research* 28 (1961): 331–353.

Lee, Richard Henry. "Letter," 10 October 1787. In *The Antifederalists,* edited by Cecelia M. Kenyon, 215–233. Indianapolis: Bobbs-Merrill, 1966.

Lincoln, James. "Address to South Carolina Legislature." In *The Antifederalists,* edited by Cecelia M. Kenyon, 183–186. Indianapolis: Bobbs-Merrill, 1966.

Locke, John. *Second Treatise of Civil Government.* Cambridge: Cambridge University Press, 1967.

Lowndes, Rawlins. "Address to South Carolina Legislature." In *The Antifederalists,* edited by Cecelia M. Kenyon, 178–183. Indianapolis: Bobbs-Merrill, 1966.

McDonald, Forrest. *Novus Ordo Seclorum: The Intellectual Origins of the Constitution.* Lawrence: University of Kansas Press, 1985.

Macpherson, C. B. *The Political Theory of Possessive Individualism.* New York: Oxford University Press, 1964.

Malbin, Michael. "Teledemocracy and Its Discontents." *Public Opinion* (June/July 1982): 58–59.

Manicas, Peter. *The Death of the State.* New York: G. P. Putnam's Sons, 1974.

Manley, John F., and Kenneth M. Dolbeare, eds. *The Case Against the Constitution.* Armonk, N.Y.: M. E. Sharpe, 1987.

Mansbridge, Jane J. *Beyond Adversary Democracy.* Chicago: University of Chicago Press, 1983.

Margenau, Henry. *The Nature of Physical Reality: A Philosophy of Modern Physics.* New York: McGraw-Hill, 1950.

Matthews, Richard K. *The Radical Politics of Thomas Jefferson.* Lawrence: University of Kansas Press, 1986.

Mazor, Lester J. Letter. *New York Times*, 23 October 1980.

Milbrath, Lester, and M. L. Goel. *Political Participation: How and Why Do People Get Involved in Politics?* Chicago: Rand McNally, 1977.

Mill, John Stuart, and Jeremy Bentham. *Utilitarianism and Other Essays*, edited by Alan Ryan. New York: Penguin Books, 1987.

Milner, Neal A. *The Court and Local Law Enforcement: The Impact of Miranda*. Beverly Hills, Calif.: Sage, 1971.

Minnesota. Health and Human Services Committee. Senate. *Final Report: Policy Jury on School-Based Clinics*. St. Paul: Minnesota Senate, August 1988.

"The Missing Voice in Presidential Contests." *Star Tribune*, Minneapolis, 4 January 1989.

Mueller, Dennis C., Robert D. Tollison, and Thomas D. Willett. "Representative Democracy Via Random Selection." *Public Choice* 7 (Spring 1972): 60–61.

Munro, William Bennett. "Physics and Politics—An Old Analogy Revised." *American Political Science Review* 22.1 (1928): 1–11.

Nisbet, Robert. *Community and Power*. New York: Oxford University Press, 1982.

Nozick, Robert. *Anarchy, State, and Utopia*. New York: Basic Books, 1974.

On the QT 1.1 (1989).

Orton, B. M. "Media-based Issue Balloting for Regional Planning." Dissertation, Rutgers University, 1980.

Parenti, Michael. *Democracy for the Few*. New York: St. Martin's Press, 1983.

Pateman, Carole. *The Problem of Political Obligation: A Critique of Liberal Theory*. Berkeley: University of California Press, 1985.

Peltason, J. W. *Fifty-Eight Lonely Men*. New York: Harcourt, Brace & World, 1961.

Philadelphiensis. "Letter to *Independent Gazetter*," 21 February 1788. In *The Antifederalists*, edited by Cecelia M. Kenyon, 76–80. Indianapolis: Bobbs-Merrill, 1966.

Pinchot, Amos R. E. *History of the Progressive Party 1912–1916*. New York: New York University Press, 1958.

Piven, Frances Fox, and Richard A. Cloward. *Why Americans Don't Vote*. New York: Pantheon Books, 1988.

Pressen, Edward, ed. *New Perspectives on Jacksonian Parties and Politics*. Boston: Allyn & Bacon, 1969.

Rand, Ayn. *The Fountainhead*. New York: New American Library, 1943.

Rawls, John. *A Theory of Justice*. Cambridge, Mass.: Harvard University Press, 1971.

Roosevelt, Theodore. "Introduction." In S. J. Duncan-Clark, *The Progressive Movement*, ix–xvii. Boston: Small, Maynard, 1972.

Rousseau, Jean Jacques. *The Essential Rousseau*. New York: New American Library, 1974.

———. *The Social Contract*. New York: New American Library, 1974.

Saltis, Janas F. *Seeing, Knowing and Believing*. Reading, Mass.: Addison-Wesley, 1966.

Schubert, Glendon. "The Evolution of Political Science Paradigms of Physics, Biology, and Politics." *Politics and the Life Sciences* 1.2 (1983): 97–124.

Schultz, Charles. *The Use of Private Interest.* Washington, D.C.: American Enterprise Institute, 1977.

Schuman, David. *A Preface to Politics.* Lexington, Mass.: D. C. Heath, 1977.

Segall, Marshall H., Donald T. Campbell, and Melville J. Herkovits. *Influence of Culture on Visual Perception.* Indianapolis: Bobbs-Merrill, 1966.

Slater, Philip E. *The Pursuit of Loneliness.* Boston: Beacon Press, 1971.

Smith, Adam. *The Theory of Moral Sentiments.* Indianapolis: Liberty Fund, 1976.

———. *The Wealth of Nations.* New York: P. F. Collins & Sons, 1959.

Smith, Steve. "Alaska Communications, Development and Democracy." In Majid Tehranian, "Electronic Democracy," report given to UNESCO, Honolulu, 1985, 139–172.

Steiner, Max. *The Ego and His Own.* New York: Libertarian Book Club, 1967.

Stilger, Robert L. "Alternatives for Washington." In *Anticipatory Democracy,* edited by Clement Bezold, 88–99. New York: Random House, 1978.

Storing, Herbert J. *What the Anti-Federalists Were For.* Chicago: University of Chicago Press, 1981.

Tehranian, Majid. "Development Theory and Communications Policy: The Changing Paradigms." *Progress in Communications Sciences* 1 (1979): 120–166.

———. "Electronic Democracy: Information Technologies and Democratic Prospects." UNESCO Report, Honolulu, 1985.

Theobald, Robert. "The Deeper Implications of Citizen Participation." In *Anticipatory Democracy,* edited by Clement Bezold, 303–314. New York: Random House, 1978.

Tocqueville, Alexis de. *Democracy in America.* Vol. 1. New York: Alfred A. Knopf, 1945.

Toffler, Alvin. *The Third Wave.* London: William Collins Sons, 1980.

Truman, David B. *The Governmental Process.* New York: Alfred A. Knopf, 1951.

Underhill, Ruth M. *Red Man's Continent: A History of the Indians in the United States.* Chicago: University of Chicago Press, 1953.

Van Deusen, Glyndon G. "Major Party Thought and Theory." In *New Perspectives on Jacksonian Parties and Politics,* edited by Edward Pressen, 138–158. Boston: Allyn & Bacon, 1969.

Verba, Sidney, and Norman H. Nie. *Participation in America: Political Democracy and Social Equality.* New York: Harper & Row, 1972.

Webb, Kenneth, and Harry P. Hatry. *Obtaining Citizen Feedback: The Application of Citizen Surveys to Local Governments.* Washington, D.C.: Urban Institute, 1973.

Webe, Robert H. *The Search for Order, 1877–1920.* New York: Hill and Wang, 1967.

Westin, Alan F., ed. *Freedom Now.* New York: Basic Books, 1964.

White, William Allen. "Changes in Democratic Government." In *Progressivism*, edited by David M. Kennedy, 19–30. Boston: Little, Brown & Co., 1971.

Wills, Gary. *Explaining America: The Federalists.* New York: Doubleday, 1981.

Wolf, Richard. " 'Incumbent Party' Keys House Seats." *USA Today*, 27 October 1988, p. A1.

Wood, Gordon S. *The Creation of the American Republic, 1776–1787.* Chapel Hill: University of North Carolina Press, 1969.

Younger, Richard D. *The People's Panel: The Grand Jury in the United States, 1634–1941.* Providence, R.I.: Brown University Press, 1963.

Index

ABOUT THE AUTHOR

CHRISTA DARYL SLATON is Assistant Professor of Political Science at Georgia Southern University. During her graduate school career, she co-designed, tested, and analyzed a new method of public-opinion polling/citizen participation that she and her coworkers call Televote. She has published articles in *Political Science* and *Mediation Quarterly*.